Cambridge Studies in Historical

POVERTY, ETHNICITY, AND THE AMERICAN
CITY, 1840–1925

Cambridge Studies in Historical Geography

Series editors:

ALAN R. H. BAKER   J. B. HARLEY   DAVID WARD

Cambridge Studies in Historical Geography encourages exploration of the philosophies, methodologies, and techniques of historical geography and publishes the results of new research within all branches of the subject. It endeavors to secure the marriage of traditional scholarship with innovative approaches to problems and to sources, aiming in this way to provide a focus for the discipline and to contribute toward its development. The series is an international forum for publication in historical geography that also promotes contact with workers in cognate disciplines.

POVERTY, ETHNICITY, AND THE AMERICAN CITY, 1840–1925

Changing conceptions of the slum and the ghetto

DAVID WARD

University of Wisconsin–Madison

WITHDRAWN

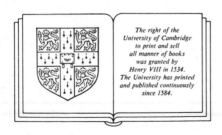

The right of the University of Cambridge to print and sell all manner of books was granted by Henry VIII in 1534. The University has printed and published continuously since 1584.

CAMBRIDGE UNIVERSITY PRESS

CAMBRIDGE

NEW YORK   NEW ROCHELLE   MELBOURNE   SYDNEY

Published by the Press Syndicate of the University of Cambridge
The Pitt Building, Trumpington Street, Cambridge CB2 1RP
32 East 57th Street, New York, NY 10022, USA
10 Stamford Road, Oakleigh, Melbourne 3166, Australia

© Cambridge University Press 1989

First published 1989

Printed in the United States of America

Library of Congress Cataloging-in-Publication Data
Ward, David, 1938–

Poverty, ethnicity, and the American city, 1840–1925: changing
conceptions of the slum and the ghetto/David Ward.

p. cm.—(Cambridge studies in historical geography; 13)
Bibliography: p.
Includes index.
ISBN 0 521 25783 2.   ISBN 0 521 27711 6 (pbk.)
1. Urban poor—United States—History—19th century.
2. Immigrants—United States—History—19th century.   3. Minorities—
United States—History—19th century.   4. Slums—United States—
History—19th century.   5. Central business districts—United
States—History—19th century.   6. United States—Social
conditions—1865–1918.   I. Title.   II. Series.
HV4044.W37 1989
362.5′0973—dc 19   88-28250
                                                                   CIP
British Library Cataloging-in-Publication applied for.

WITHDRAWN

MILSTEIN
HV
4044
.W37
1989

Contents

Part II: The relationships reformulated

Illustrations

Preface

For almost two centuries periodic preoccupation with the problems of poverty has emphasized the relationships between the poor and their immediate environment. This essentially geographic formulation of poverty is usually expressed as the relationships between the adverse environments of the inner city and the presumed pathological social conditions among its impoverished residents. These conditions are often directly attributed to the adverse environment of the inner city, but whenever they seem to be unresponsive to environmental improvements, they are judged to be part of a deviant subculture or the result of personal deviance. Assumptions about high levels of personal deviance among the poor and within the inner city have, therefore, encouraged a strong emphasis on clinical and therapeutic approaches at the individual or familial level. Nevertheless, the overrepresentation of ethnic minorities among the poor has tended to reinforce arguments about the distinctive social world of the poor. Although poverty is confined neither to ethnic minorities nor to the inner city, several presumed indicators of pathological social behavior have for long been attributed to those minorities that are concentrated in the inner city. The validity of these associations remain questionable, but they are entrenched in much of the current debate about poverty.

This debate has taken the form of evaluations of public policies initiated in the late 1960s and designed to respond to changing interpretations of poverty. In retrospect critics of policies that necessitated an enlarged commitment to public expenditures have argued that these efforts have exacerbated the problems they were intended to resolve. These unintended consequences of reform were attributed to the inability of the poor to respond to policies that failed to consider the implications of the deviant or pathological way of life within the inner city. In particular, a range of social problems were directly linked to the fragility of the nuclear family and the looseness of household arrangements among the poor.

Other critics, with more confidence in the benefits of intervention, have attributed the persistence of poverty to an unnecessarily narrow view of poverty. This narrow perspective resulted in a misguided emphasis on those obstacles to advancement that are associated with the inner-city environment. The environmental and institutional limitations of the inner city are themselves consequences of the uneven development of a capitalist political economy. Under these circumstances the adverse environment of the poor in both the inner city and elsewhere results from the economic insecurity of low wages and unemployment. Under conditions of inadequate social insurance the apparently deviant household arrangements of the poor are viewed as a means of coping with their economic predicament.

Current debates about the relationships among poverty, minorities, and the inner city are rooted in evaluations of policies initiated about two decades ago, but the issues of this debate have a much longer ancestry. In many respects the underlying arguments of this debate were formulated during the second quarter of the nineteenth century, when the first wave of mass immigration from Europe exacerbated anxieties about the social order of the rapidly growing seaports of the northeastern United States. Interpretations of poverty became part of a set of assumptions about the immigrant slums and the presumed deviance of their residents. At different times these assumptions implied varying degrees of environmental or cultural determinism, as well as complex reciprocal interactions between environment and culture. Despite this range of interpretations of poverty, most policies recognized that inadequate sanitation, overcrowded housing, and the impoverished public environment of the inner city exacerbated the problem of poverty, but efforts to diminish these visible consequences of industrialization were more effective than those that confronted economic insecurity more directly. Primarily because improvements in urban living conditions coincided with periods of suburbanization, the precise environmental obstacles of the poor were often linked to their immediate residential circumstances rather than to their access to expanding employment opportunities.

Moreover, the majority of the past residents of the inner city eventually overcame their adverse environment and made their way at different rates into the mainstream of suburban America. Some interpretations of this selective mobility have concluded that the damaging impact of the inner city was contingent upon the cultural resources of different ethnic groups. The definitions of these resources are often imprecise and vary from adaptations of their ancestral culture to the rapid adoption of social arrangements that approximated those of middle-class America. Under these circumstances the inner city could be their temporary rather than their permanent abode. This genetic conception of inner-city poverty was also part of a broader interpretation of assimilation. Ethnic resources were not only instrumental in coping with the adverse environment of the inner city, but they were often redefined in successive generations so that ethnic identities continued to influence the patterns of life in suburban America.

These conclusions are, however, based upon retrospective evaluations of groups over several generations; many of those groups were, in fact, judged to be deviant at the time of their initial settlement in the inner city. Moreover, discrimination complicated the degree to which ethnic resources made advancement possible. Not only have judgments about the same group changed over the course of several generations, but the degree to which the inner-city environment provided opportunities for advancement has fluctuated during the course of industrialization. These shifts in the degree to which various kinds of employment were concentrated in the central business district and in the complexity and fluidity of the internal stratification of the urban labor force radically altered the inner-city environment confronted by successive migrant groups.

The current debate about the problems of poverty retains many elements of these earlier dialogues. Some observers stress the cultural differences between the current and prior residents of the inner city while others emphasize changes in the location and kind of employment within and between cities. In the period of mass immigration, there was also a tendency to stress the moral and cultural limitations of the most recent immigrant arrivals during periods when shifts in the political economy exercised profound changes in the location and kinds of urban employment. Although there were clearly variations in the ways in which different ethnic groups coped with the inner city, for some groups and blacks in particular, discrimination in the labor market and shifts in the organization of the labor market presented obstacles that were beyond the capacities of the most flexible of ethnic resources. This book examines the changing conceptions of these relationships between migrants and the inner city from an explicitly geographic perspective during the period of mass immigration to the United States from about 1840 until the introduction of immigration restriction in 1923–4.

The evidence about these relationships is disproportionately drawn from the testimonies of both hostile and sympathetic outsiders. Moreover, in the formulation of public policies, these outsiders often created objects of reform that were closer to their interpretations of poverty than to the conditions of life among the poor. From time to time, outsiders did provide a rich ethnographic record of the poor and during these periods the interpretations of sensitive outsiders coincided more closely with the fragmentary records that the poor left about themselves. The bulk of these fragmentary records have, however, only become part of the interpretation of poverty retrospectively and for these reasons, this book comprises firstly an examination of the changes in the formulation of the relationships between the migrant poor and the inner-city environment from 1840 to 1925 and secondly, a re-examination of those relationships on the basis of retrospective reinterpretations of ethnicity and poverty proposed during the past half century.

My debts are numerous and here I acknowledge only those in my immediate environment. The book was completed during my term as an Associate Dean of the Graduate School at the University of Wisconsin-Madison. I thank Dean Robert M. Bock for providing the kind of flexibility in my administrative obligations that made it possible for me to keep my research in motion. The Department of Geography is a stimulating milieu for research and at various times, Martin Cadwallader, Robert Ostergren, Robert Sack, Yi Fu Tuan, as well as Paul Boyer of the Department of History, provided me with critical reactions to my efforts. I would also like to thank the Department of Geography at University College London for their support of a Visiting Professorship during which the final revisions were made.

POVERTY, ETHNICITY, AND THE AMERICAN
CITY, 1840–1925

1

The slum, the ghetto, and the inner city

Changes in the social geography of cities are among the most definitive indicators of the industrialization of Western urban life over the past two centuries. During the initial phase of this transformation, the concentration of industrialized production in cities exacerbated environmental pollution and housing congestion at a time when the increasing dependence of production on the wage labor of migrants strained traditional responses to social problems. The earliest use of the term *slum* expressed anxieties about these negative consequences of industrialization. Neither unsanitary and congested living conditions nor residential segregation appeared abruptly with the industrialization of urban employment; however, industrialization changed the scale of these developments and provoked anxieties about the management of larger and more highly differentiated urban communities.

While many migrants came from the immediate hinterlands of industrializing cities, substantial numbers were also drawn from afar. In the United States industrialization was inextricably linked with foreign immigration, and by the late nineteenth century foreign-born immigrants and their native-born children constituted a majority of the populations of most northeastern and midwestern cities. For a long time migration and urbanization were associated with the diminution of ethnic loyalties and affective ties and the development of new social groupings based upon class interests or occupational status. This social transformation has proved to be both prolonged and varied. In the United States the complex migrations of Native Americans, Europeans, Africans, Asians, and Latin Americans have created a population with a striking level of ethnic diversity. This diversity has itself changed both in relation to the varying chronologies of migration from different source areas and in relation to the rate and kind of assimilation amongst those who became immigrants. Migrants have been viewed as temporary sojourners and immigrants as permanent settlers, but many immigrants arrived as migrants and con-

1

sequently the term *migrants* will be used broadly to include the migrant generation of immigrant groups.

From the broad perspective of generalizations about the social transformation of modern society, the persistence of both migrant ethnicity and minority status over several generations has been regarded as an exceptional or residual phenomenon. Some groups have maintained their ethnic identities by a process of redefinition, but the degree to which they are culturally distinct from American society at large or from each other remains a matter of debate. Other groups have encountered temporary, prolonged, or permanent obstacles to their economic advancement, and their predicament has been linked to their minority status.

The term *ghetto* has become a popular and evocative expression of the negative consequences of the residential segregation of ethnically defined migrants in the inner-city slums. Throughout the second half of the nineteenth century, the poor were identified with the slums, and although there were speculations about the cultural and hereditary limitations of the foreign-born poor, these deficiencies were broadly applied to the poor in general. With the shift in the predominant sources of foreign migration from northwestern to southern, central, and eastern Europe towards the turn of the nineteenth century, the desirability of assimilating these "new" immigrants complicated anxieties about poverty. Applied initially to the residential quarters of East European Jews who arrived in American cities towards the turn of the nineteenth century, the term *ghetto* gradually acquired a more general meaning to describe the residential segregation of any minority group in the slums of the inner city. In its initial American usage the ghetto was regarded as a slum where the presence of newly arrived immigrants exacerbated social problems related to adverse living conditions and residential segregation. Today the term usually refers to the extensive concentrations of blacks and other deprived minorities in the inner sections of American cities.

The slum and the ghetto were more than definitional terms, for they also implied strong causal connections between the poverty and social problems of the migrant poor and their segregation in the adverse environment of the inner city. During the second half of the twentieth century this negative image of the ghetto has become integral to interpretations of the current residents of the inner city. In contrast, during the same period the validity of this image to describe the experiences of those East European migrants to whom it was first applied has been questioned.[1] Reevaluations of the migrant experience have explored a more complex set of connections among poverty, ethnicity, and the urban environment. For some groups concentration in the inner city was a source of local political power, a basis of economic advancement, and the ghetto was a symbol of ethnic identity. From this perspective the original view of the migrant experience formulated during the nineteenth and early twentieth centuries exaggerated the pathological social consequences of residential segregation in the adverse environment of the inner city.

These retrospective reinterpretations of the migrant experience in American cities during the era of mass immigration have revealed the degree to which the cultural resources of ethnic groups alleviated many of the immediate problems of the urban environment, but the degree to which the changing structural environment of American capitalism also obstructed or facilitated the material advancement of these groups is less fully documented. In contrast, the original negative definition of the immigrant slum apparently had a prophetic validity as a description of the predicament of the deprived minorities who dominate the inner cities today. This prophetic validity is itself a matter of debate, and recent discussions of the slum and the ghetto have become part of a broader dialogue described as the "urban question." This question confronts the degree to which the environmental constraints and social problems of the inner city are integral parts of the structural inqualities of the capitalist political economy.[2] Both cultural and structural approaches to migration have questioned the relationships between the migrant poor and the inner-city environment, but these relationships were also a matter of dispute during the course of the experience of the mass immigration between about 1840 and 1925. Specifically, the precise definitions of the residents and their urban environment and the directions and the amplitudes of the connections between them were debated in relation to three different responses to the social problems of the city. Each of these responses claimed a validity based upon a "scientific" approach. Their different perspectives were, however, rooted not only in the rapidly accumulating body of observations on social problems but also in changing conceptions of poverty and the social order of the city. These changing conceptions were grounded in essentially geographic considerations of relationships between the migrant poor and their urban environment.

The relationships formulated

These responses form the subjects of the three chapters of Part I of this book. The first response is derived from those antebellum reform movements that proposed moral diagnoses of poverty. The slums were places where the most extreme manifestations of poverty and pathological living conditions were concentrated. Since the virulence of contagious diseases was linked to moral as well as environmental deficiencies, these highly publicized slums were the focus of most attention. Old assumptions about the endemic nature of poverty were abandoned, but confident assumptions about the "reformability" of the poor were initially based upon concepts of moral influence. The mission and the asylum were the means by which immoral influences were removed. Their presumed effects were based upon the same concepts of contagion as those upon which fears of epidemic diseases were based. As the affluent had moved into their own exclusive residential areas, so had the poor been left to the contagious influences of the most depraved amongst them. The slums were the sources of this immoral contagion. The mission was a bridge-head of personal influences within the slums, and the asylum was a refuge to which those in need of more deliberate institutional influences could be removed.

Unsanitary conditions, however, extended far beyond the limits of these notorious slums and included most poorly drained sections of the city. Room overcrowding and lot congestion compounded the effects of poor sites, although it was only later in the nineteenth century that housing reform became the dominant focus of environmental improvement. As fears about congestion replaced those about contagion, a greater proportion of the blame for slum conditions was attributed to environmental defects and a lesser proportion to the moral defects of the poor. Massive investments in the improvement of the sanitary environment did diminish the impact of site conditions on living conditions, but the vast expansion of inadequate and often overcrowded housing created a more extensive and contiguous area of slums increasingly identified as the "social abyss" of the inner city.

This new scale of slum developments elicited a second response described as "scientific philanthropy." Most urban social problems were concentrated in cities and especially the inner cities, but most of these problems were directly attributed to the environmental disabilities of the slums. It was assumed that once the environmental obstacles to self-improvement were removed, it would be possible to identify a "residuum," or lowest stratum of the poor, for whom only punitive social policies were appropriate. Frequently, the social problems of this lowest stratum were judged to be derived not only from their degraded environment but also from their damaged heredity. The limited gains of moral reform provoked inquiries into the relative contributions of environment and heredity to the moral and physical disabilities of the poor. In the United States changes in the composition of foreign immigration compounded these anxieties about a residual impoverished and defective population. Newly arrived immigrants from southern, eastern, and central Europe were considered less compatible with the host society than were established immigrants from northwestern Europe. Under these circumstances the poor were defined by indicators other than income and were subjected to informal and institutionalized discrimination. When ethnic or racial prejudice exacerbated the social problems and environmental disabilities of the slums, the term *ghetto* was employed to describe slums in which minorities were segregated from the remainder of urban society. Like the term *slum* in the antebellum period, the term *ghetto* was not used with any consistency to describe segregated residential quarters until after World War II, when it was used to describe the extensive concentrations of blacks in northern cities.

During the prolonged depressions of the midseventies and midnineties of the nineteenth century, interpretations of the slums explored not only the environmental but also the economic predicament of the poor. Only after the turn of the century did those public policies described as "progressive" attempt to confront economic insecurity. Although there was no lack of public initiatives to address the social problems of industrialization, progressives judged these earlier efforts to have been inadequate and misguided. Consequently the inner-city slums came to symbolize the social costs of laissez-faire policies during the expansion of industrial capitalism. By 1900 the necessity for a more ambitious and professional level of public intervention was apparent, and social reform was increasingly dependent upon a cadre of trained professionals. These specialists no longer attempted to restore the unified moral order of the past but rather attempted to confront the complex interdependencies of the modern city. Initially this third response to the slums explored some of the ways in which migrants coped with their adverse environment and the degree to which this environment was itself derived from structural sources of poverty. In their efforts to avoid single-factor deterministic explanations like those of their predecessors, many progressives lost sight of some early insights into the structural nature of poverty. Instead they viewed social problems as the product of an infinite number of complex interdependencies that required lengthy investigations before action could be contemplated. New public policies were formed to harness the methods and findings of science, but debates about the policies themselves were often less critical than were discussions of the degree of independence an expert bureaucracy would have from legislative direction and popular sentiments.

Throughout the nineteenth century the obstacles to the self-improvement of the poor were increasingly attributed to the deficiencies of the urban environment, and eventually the progressives included among these obstacles the unregulated impact of industrial capitalism. Until about 1920 interpretations of the migrant experience had been inextricably connected to these debates about the level and kind of public and private intervention. Thereafter, this connection between problems and policies diminished, and despite spasmodic revivals, generalizations about migration and urbanization have subsequently been grounded in theories of social change that reveal a growing confidence in the potentialities of the second stage of industrialization as a source of social mobility and higher living standards. In the second half of the nineteenth century a preoccupation with the environmental deficiencies of the slums had obscured the structural obstacles to self-improvement. Similarly, the decentralization of employment and the material gains symbolized by the vast expansion of suburbs in the twentieth century have obscured the structural sources of social mobility.[3]

The inner-city slums were now judged to be temporary residential quarters of the migrant generation, and eventually the role of ethnic resources in coping with the adverse environment was elaborated. The environmental obstacles to mobility were judged to be less critical than the need for slum residents to assimilate to the host society. Ethnicity rather than poverty became the leading issue in interpretations of the migrant experience. The ghetto was a temporary phase of a social transformation that began with emigration and ended with assimilation. Part II examines how reinterpretations of the migrant experience have viewed the urban environment and specifically the immigrant slums as expressions of cultural and structural processes. Chapter 5 explores the development of interpretations of migrant experiences that stress the complexities of assimilation and the changing role of ethnicity in that experience. Chapter 6 discusses interpretations of migration that have amplified the degree to which ethnic resources facilitated adaptations to the urban environment, but as part of a broader interpretation of the relationships between ethnicity and the sequential, uneven structure of industrialization.

The relationships reformulated

The Chicago School of urban sociology set the agenda for the reconsideration of the migrant experience in cities. Its interpretation of urban society, like that of the progressives, was more complex than its critics have acknowledged. The Chicago School rejected the scientific claims of earlier reformers and argued that its own style of detached academic research was necessary to avoid the moralism of investigations motivated by reform objectives. In fact, the first generation of the Chicago School owed much to the insights of earlier reform perspectives.[4] The most perceptive of the progressives had qualified assumptions about the pathological aspects of the migrant experience, and the Chicago School certainly tempered its focus on the blighted environment of the inner city by an awareness of ethnic community.[5] Its interpretation of the ethnic social order of the inner city was, however, based upon residential propinquity, and accordingly the suburban dispersal of ethnic groups was viewed as a measure of assimilation. Although its interpretations of assimilation and suburbanization have been questioned, the Chicago School did recognize that the discomforts and exclusions of the inner city were not necessarily direct causes of pathological social conditions but rather a setting in which most migrant groups made remarkable accommodations. Initially these accommodations were thought to be derived from direct transplantations of the traditional social order of village life. These transplanted communities served as a decompression chamber for the migrant generation; however, for the second generation they often created obstacles to assimilation.

Subsequent research has revealed major adaptations among the migrant generation and slower rates of assimilation in the subsequent generations.[6] The social fabric of ethnic groups was based upon both institutional and familial arrangements. This social order was not necessarily dependent upon highly concentrated residential patterns but rather upon discrete patterns of several clusters that served as nodes of more dispersed populations. In the short run these arrangements facilitated adaptations to an adverse environment, and in the long run they served as a "ramp" for economic advancement. The coping capacities of the vast majority of migrants modified the impact of those obstacles to self-improvement that had formed the basis of the original definitions of the slums. The selectivity in the rate at which the obstacles to social mobility were overcome was accordingly linked to the cultural resources of various ethnic groups. These ethnic communities have collectively been linked to an apparently "exceptional" American way of coping with industrialization. Some observers have demonstrated how ethnicity and neighborhood rather than class and employment were the predominant sources of political loyalties and actions.[7] Others have argued that the ethnic adaptations of the migrant generation and the subsequent mobility of their descendants reveal a predominant commitment to a middle-class consciousness.[8] In contrast, an adverse environment and residential segregation are major constraints on the advancement of the minorities who dominate the inner city today, but sometimes it is implied that limitations of ethnic resources magnify these constraints. This view of the predicament of current residents of the inner city resembles not only the original negative formulation of the immigrant slum but also the now rejected defamatory distinctions between the "old" and "new" immigrations, upon which the immigration restriction legislation of 1923–4 was based. The immigrant slum was initially defined as a ghetto at a time when the so-called new immigrants from southern and eastern Europe were unlikely or undesirable candidates for assimilation.

Alternative approaches to these differences in the migrant experience have stressed the degree to which ethnicity is an expression of the structural relationships between migration and industrialization. A preoccupation with the varied cultural adaptations of family and community has somewhat obscured broader class-based efforts to retain or obtain control of the workplace.[9] From the structuralist perspective, environmental and social problems that have been attributed to the damaging impact of migration and urbanization are viewed as secondary consequences of the capitalist political economy.[10] Like cultural interpretations of migration, structural interpretations of urban society rarely elaborate the contingent effects of the relationships between the migrants and their urban environment. The negative social consequences of capitalism do have an unusual virulence amongst some migrant groups and they do have an unusual intensity in the inner city, but they are not necessarily confined to segregated minorities. Cultural interpretations of the migrant experience have great difficulty in specifying the environmental restraints on economic advancement and assimilation, whereas structural interpretations consider these restraints at a level that discounts the varied consequences of ethnicity. Environmental constraints may, however, be redefined so that the immediate environs of the inner city are seen as part of a national economy within which the migrant experience was constrained by rates of regional economic development and decline, as well as by levels of residential segregation in a particular city.

The inner-city slums, as a distinctive expression of the uneven patterns of industrialization, were part of a more complex and contingent set of environmental restraints on economic advancement and assimilation.[11] As migrants encountered the inner city, or any other generically defined destination, their ethnicity was redefined. The ethnicity of the immediate ancestral generations of migrants was an identity directly rooted in diverse local cultures. The ethnic traits of most of the descendants of the migrant generation do not differ markedly from each other or from those of the host society. In contrast, the "emergent" ethnicity of the migrant generations defined their capacities to cope with the disruptive consequences of industrialization.[12] The uneven and varied course of industrialization altered the constraints of the urban environment and these structural changes amplified ethnic identities. For some groups this experience remains a source of ethnic pride, but as a fragment of a larger identity rooted in the host society. For other groups, this experience remains a persistent source of frustration, and their minority status describes their deprived relationship to the remainder of society.

Unlike those interpretations of the slum and the ghetto that were derived from the underlying ideas of contemporary reform movements, reinterpretations of the relationships between migration, industrialization, and urbanization have stressed their detachment from the presuppositions of public policies. Detachment has not, however, diminished the degree to which interpretations of social processes remain a matter of debate. In both the original formulations of the slum and the ghetto and the subsequent reevaluations of those original perspectives, geographic considerations of culture and environment and of people and place constitute a common thread in a shifting set of interpretations of migrants in the inner city. This book is about how changing conceptions of the relationships between migrants and their urban environment influenced interpretations of that experience.

PART I

The relationships formulated

2

The slums discovered: 1840–1875

By the end of the nineteenth century the term *slum* expressed the relationships amongst the environmental limitations, the spatial isolation, and the social problems of the largely immigrant populations of the inner sections of large American cities. At that time immigration from southern and eastern Europe intensified the debates about the direction of the relationships amongst social problems, environmental conditions, and residential segregation, but these discussions were also an integral part of the initial definition of urban slums during the middle decades of the nineteenth century. As at the turn of the century, anxieties about urban society were exacerbated by an increase in the rate of foreign immigration, but the responses to the immigrant poor closely resembled those to the poor in general. By the time large numbers of Irish and German immigrants began to settle in substantial numbers in American cities, responses to poverty were already preoccupied with the effects of the increased rate and enlarged scale of urban growth on the stability of American society.

During the same decade in which Disraeli described the social and spatial divisions within English cities as "Two Nations," William Ellery Channing, a leading Unitarian minister concerned with the moral implications of recent social changes, independently applied the same metaphor to conditions in Boston.[1] The term "nation" implied territorial interests, and the most notorious expressions of this insurgent or contagious interest were described as slums. The social indifference and the ostentatious profligacy of new wealth aroused as much concern, as did the problems of poverty.[2] Channing's student Joseph Tuckerman, a leading proponent of the reform of poor relief, applauded experimental British social policies toward the poor and stressed that in rapidly growing cities of newly arrived migrants, social isolation afflicted most urban residents. In cities, he argued, "men are not only divided and separated by the very great inequalities of their condition in respect to property, by the

13

diversity of their interests, and by their various inclinations and tastes, but by the very fact of the extent of their numbers. Every individual in the different classes may . . . be unknown to many even of the class to which they belong."[3]

These anxieties about urban society publicized the coincidence of depravity, destitution, and horrific living conditions in highly localized notorious slums. In many cities the most extreme examples of moral and environmental degradation set the tone for discussions of the poor in general, and consequently it is not always clear whether the term *slum* referred to specific notorious localities or to the vast sections of the city where the poor lived under adverse environmental conditions.[4] The slums were defined as those parts of the city where the removal of the affluent had left behind a concentration of impoverished people. It was assumed that, once isolated from the moral influences of their social superiors, the poor would fall prey to the most depraved among them and thereby threaten the moral fabric of urban society as a whole. Notwithstanding the precise configuration and extent of the slums, they represented a contagious moral and physiological threat to the remainder of urban society. Although residential segregation protected the affluent from this threat, most urban residents lived near, if not interspersed with, those who were presumed to be the sources of contagion. Charles Brace, for example, founded the Children's Aid Society (CAS) in order to remove children from the contagious concentrations of the depraved poor within the slums, where "The very condensing of their number within a small space, seems to stimulate their bad tendencies."[5]

A classic English summary of this argument concluded:

The great cause of human corruption in these crowded situations is the contagious nature of bad example and the extreme difficulty of avoiding the seductions of vice when they are brought into close and daily proximity with the younger part of the people. Whatever we may think of the strength of virtue, experience proves that the higher orders are indebted for their exemption from atrocious crime or disorderly habits by their fortunate removal from the scene of temptation. . . . [I]t is the peculiar misfortune of the poor in great cities that they cannot fly from these irresistible temptations, but that, turn where they will, they are met by the alluring forms of vice, or the seductions of guilty enjoyment. . . . There is a certain degree of misery, a certain proximity to sin, which virtue is rarely able to withstand, and which the young, in particular, are generally unable to resist. The progress of vice is almost as certain and nearly as rapid as that of physical contagion.[6]

American complaints about urban life also expressed fears about the replication of Old World conditions. In 1846 conditions amongst the poor of Boston were described as "a true social barometer" revealing "a downward movement of the poorest classes . . . which if it not be checked, must sooner or later lead us to a condition like that of the Old

World where the separation of the rich and the poor is so complete, that the former are almost afraid to visit the quarters most thickly peopled by the latter."[7] Old fears about social privilege were modified by new fears about the potential insurgency of a permanent wage-earning class. Despite determined paternalistic efforts in New England to contain the social tensions and environmental degradation of industrialization, the growth of factory-based urban settlements raised questions about the compatibility of industry and the egalitarian and proprietary values of the new republic.[8] In the northeastern seaports, ever-larger concentrations of wage earners were employed in the expanding "sweated trades," which produced nondurable consumer goods for domestic and foreign markets. Nevertheless, most observers believed that the damaging effects of industrialization and urbanization were less severe in the United States than in European society.

Fears about the replication of European conditions were also sustained by the rising tide of foreign immigration. The rapid increase in the volume of emigration from the German states and more particularly from famine-stricken Ireland was judged to be an additional source of strain to municipal and state institutions and services, as well as a threat to the economic security of native wage earners. As a political movement nativism was successful during brief periods when the major parties were disrupted by internal dissension and eventually the sectional sources of these political conflicts deflected attention from the problems of the immigrant in American society.[9] During the middle decades of the nineteenth century, concern about immigration was necessarily a secondary political issue in a nation that confronted secession, war, and reconstruction. At the same time a pervasive faith in social mobility, economic opportunity, and political equality greatly subdued the impact of anxieties about urban society. A confidence in the American mission to serve as an asylum for the oppressed and persecuted of the Old World also moderated these anxieties, but this cosmopolitan individualism assumed that eventually most immigrants would assimilate into American society.[10]

Although muted prior to the Civil War, there were already signs that the host society was developing a sense of nationhood or an American ethnicity that was linked to an Anglo-Saxon genealogy.[11] Popular attitudes were also clearly revealed in the stereotypical American image of the Irish immigrant.[12] Since American nationality had been founded on the idea of political participation rather than on common origins, it was expected that newcomers could be readily assimilated according to this new principle of identity; however, confidence diminished during the course of the nineteenth century as various immigrant groups were presumed to possess different innate or hereditary aptitudes for democracy.

Immigrants were also especially prominent in their support for the new urban political machines; accordingly they were often held accountable for the "corruption" of American democracy. These attitudes were revealed in the language of popular culture, which provided stereotypical images accepted by many who had no direct encounters with immigrants. The term "Paddy," for example, was a code word that implied irresponsible delinquency, and when accompanied with pictorial representations, the term explicitly projected an image of a distinct physical or, in contemporary terms, phrenological type. Unlike the more decisive racial boundary between blacks and the remainder of American society, the one that defined the Irish was much harder to maintain, but the experience of the Irish clearly indicates that the ethnicity of the immigrant was a direct consequence of an increasingly ethnic view of American nationality itself.[13]

Although a growing sense of an ethnic American identity obstructed the assimilation of the Irish, the growth and organization of the Roman Catholic hierarchy and the emergence of numerous Irish–American voluntary associations were viewed as unacceptable claims to ethnic and religious autonomy. Similar institutional developments among German-speaking immigrants were regarded with less concern. Although they were often highly clustered both in frontier settlements and within cities, they were initially less visible in urban politics. Unlike the Irish, only a minority of German immigrants was Roman Catholic and German communities included lower proportions of destitute newcomers.[14] Newly arrived immigrants were certainly blamed for importing the social problems of the Old World, but most midcentury reactions to the immigrant poor tended to amplify well-developed judgments about the poor in general. Not only stereotypical images of the Irish poor became harsher and explicitly racial, but those of the poor and of the slums in general.

The association of immigrants with the slums was complicated by ethnic heterogeneity and a substantial native-born element in the most notorious slums. Brace described immigrants as "The refuse of Europe [who] congregate in our great cities and send forth ... wretched progeny, degraded in the deep degradation of their parents ... to be scavengers, physical and moral of our streets," but he also emphasized: "Mingled with these [immigrants] are also the offcast children of American debauchery, drunkenness and vice. A class more dangerous to the community ... can hardly be imagined."[15] Five Points, New York, was a national symbol of the worst slum conditions, but "[e]very State in the Union, and every nation almost in the world, have representatives in this foul and dangerous locality."[16] By the second decade of the nineteenth century Five Points was a symbol of poverty and squalor, but contemporary engravings tended to portray the disorderly street life rather than the slum environment (Figure 2.1).

Figure 2.1 Five Points, New York, 1827: the center of poverty and squalor
Source: Valentine's Manual, 1827.

By midcentury contemporary descriptions of notorious slums emphasized the association of depravity and poverty in a style that suggests that
they were unknown to the remainder of urban society. In New York the
first chief of police, George Matsell, was a participant and patron of this
sensational publicity. Journalistic explorations revealed in macabre
detail discomfort, degradation, disease, and death under the most horrific
living conditions.[17] E.Z.C. Judson, writing under the pseudonym Ned
Buntline, described "The Mysteries and Miseries of New York," and
George Foster excavated through the "slices" of New York life. Foster
penetrated "[b]eneath the thick veil of night [to] lay bare the fearful mysteries of darkness in the metropolis – the festivities of prostitution, the
orgies of pauperism, the haunts of theft and murder, the scenes of
drunkenness and beastly debauch and all the sad realities that go to make
up the lower stratum – the underground story of life in New York."[18]
Engravings of the slums also shifted their focus from the main streets to
unpaved and poorly drained alleys and yards enclosed by delapidated
buildings connected by fragile stairways. These efforts to represent the
horrific environmental conditions of the slums implied an inevitable
depravity amongst their residents, but this assumption might have been
questioned, had one of the dominant compositional elements of many
engravings attracted more attention. Although their titles often emphasized the residents' filthy habits, these representations of the slums were

Figure 2.2 Boston, Burgess Alley, 1849
Source: Boston City Document, No. 66, *Report on the Asiatic Cholera, Together with a Report of the City Physician on the Cholera Hospital,* 1849.

dominated by recently washed laundry hanging out to dry (Figures 2.2 and 2.3).

These literary and pictorial representations of the slums were not necessarily of remote sections of the city. The proximity of these unknown slums to other more respectable or positively affluent precincts often heightened their sensational tone. In New York the slums around Five Points were relatively close to such symbols of wealth and status as Broadway and Wall Street, and consequently the affluent were con-

Figure 2.3 New York, typical court, 1865

Source: Council of Hygiene and Public Health of the Citizens' Association of New York, *Report upon the Sanitary Condition of the City* (New York: Appleton, 1865), 8.

demned precisely because they were blind to the depravity and destitution around them. The most notorious slums had, however, been discovered in rear yards and back alleys that were hidden from view by a frontage of substantial dwellings or business premises. In addition to these symbols of the extremes of wealth and poverty, the Bowery, which later was to rival Five Points in notoriety, became the symbol of the substantial native working class.[19] This group appears to have developed a way of life and, in particular, recreational patterns that also offended the moral sensibilities of reformers.

Places within New York and other cities provided a symbolic geography of urban society, but the extent of slum conditions was rarely specified with any precision. Generally the term referred to the most unsanitary and therefore the most poorly drained sections of the city, which were inhabited by the depraved poor. While the residential quarters of the affluent "nation" were well defined, large sections of the remainder of the city housed relatively heterogeneous populations within which the slums represented the most extreme conditions of environmental and social degradation. The worst sanitary conditions were associated with highly localized notorious sites, although inadequate drainage and sanitation were widespread in most cities. Similarly, the depraved poor were associated with the most notorious centers of vice and disorder, despite concerns about the diffusion of these conditions among the poor at large. The depraved poor were a threat to the remainder of urban society precisely because they, unlike the affluent, lived in close proximity to the remainder of the poor.

Reactions to the immigrant poor were, in fact, firmly based upon earlier anxieties about the effects of the rapid increase in the cityward movement of young single people from rural America. No longer under the natural restraints of their families and local communities and free of any compensating moral influences, youthful migrants were unprepared to confront the temptations of urban life. New frontier settlements were also judged to be far removed from the moral influences of established communities, and evangelical efforts to confront the presumed social isolation of migrants both in the cities and on the frontier were often similar in style and content. Although many reactions to the social problems of the city were part of broader anxieties about the mobility of American society as a whole, most observers linked the most critical social problems to the presumed peculiarities of urban society.[20] Consequently, crime, depravity, drunkenness, popular disturbances, religious infidelity, and pauperism were all viewed as a greater threat to social stability in rapidly growing cities than in well-established rural settlements.

In the new republic there was considerable ambiguity in the role of the state in protecting public morality.[21] As long as the Protestant churches were judged to be an effective vehicle for the discharge of social policies, public assistance was often viewed as a spasmodic supplement to these voluntary philanthropic efforts. Consequently, the dominant sources of contemporary images of the slums were derived from the assumptions of evangelical philanthropy, and the "urban geography of vice charted by the ministers and tract visitors was neither an accurate rendition of plebian reality nor a figment of an anxious bourgeois imagination. Rather it represented the charities' hostile perception of certain kinds of working-class assumptions and associations."[22] The focus of evangelical philanthropy was the delinquent poor, and much more care and attention was devoted to the moral classification of the poor than to the specification of their environs. These efforts to reform the poor did, however, provoke spatial strategies of contact and removal that were derived from assumptions about the contagious nature of depravity and destitution.

The residents defined: moral isolation

By the end of the second decade of the nineteenth century, attempts to classify the poor retained the long-established moral distinction of the worthy and unworthy poor but had rejected long-held assumptions about the endemic nature of poverty.[23] While families whose poverty resulted from sickness and misfortune were judged to be "worthy" and eligible for relief, most poverty was attributed to moral defects of character and failures of individual self-discipline. The "unworthy" poor were undeserving of charity since they were pauperized rather than impoverished. In a society in which the bonds of community had been weakened, self-discipline was judged to be an indispensable virtue. Efforts to inculcate individualistic values were most forcefully revealed in asylums and reformatories, where the most serious deviants and delinquents were to be firmly instructed in the discipline of self-improvement.[24] Draconian policies of removal and incarceration were presumably designed to eradicate the contaminating influence of the delinquent poor on their more worthy neighbors. In particular, emphasis was placed upon the removal of delinquent children to reformatories where they might be protected from the "haunts of vice from which they had been taken" and from "a common prison with other culprits to mingle in conversation and intercourse with them."[25] These actions presumed that in the absence of appropriate parental control, the state might assume parental obligations. In 1838 the State Supreme Court of Pennsylvania upheld these claims in a decision that argued: "The object of the charity is reformation, by training its inmates to industry; by imbuing their minds with principles of morality and religion; by furnishing them with means to earn a living; and, above all, by separating them from the corrupting influence of improper associates. To this end, may not the natural parents, when unequal to the task of education, or unworthy of it, be superseded by the 'parens patriae', or common guardian of the community?"[26]

Other efforts were designed to maintain or revive the informal social controls of smaller communities by facilitating more frequent social interactions between the poor and the remainder of urban society. Missions and Sunday schools were established amongst the poor, while volunteers distributed moral advice in the form of religious tracts. Their visitations were presumed to counteract those deviant tendencies that were left unchecked in growing and increasingly segregated cities.[27] In New York the Ladies' Home Missionary Society purchased a tenement at Five Points that had previously served as a brewery (Figure 2.4). The use of the Old Brewery as a mission was symbolic of efforts to replace the contagious influences of intemperance and depravity with those of moral improvement. From the perspective of contagion, propinquity of influence was absolutely critical. Most missionary efforts were, however, aimed more generally at urban society and usually had their greatest impact amongst the economically more secure strata of urban society rather than amongst the destitute.[28]

These responses did, however, assume that there was a considerable

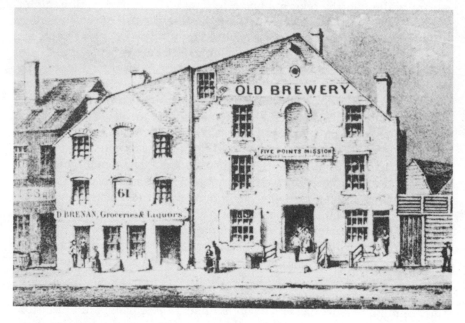

Figure 2.4 Five Points, 1852: from brewery to mission
Source: Valentine's Manual, 1853.

range of moral potential amongst the poor and within the slums. Efforts to check the deteriorating conditions of the poor were profoundly influenced by British precedents, and social policies designed to reduce the social isolation of the poor became a dominant component of philanthropic thought on both sides of the Atlantic.[29] The most ambitious of these missionary efforts, initially developed in Glasgow by Thomas Chalmers in 1819, was based upon explicit spatial strategies to control the delivery of poor relief by means of moral influence. Although there had been similar ventures in Hamburg in the late eighteenth century, it was Chalmers who insisted on the connection between missionary activity and relief by means of a Ministry at Large. This system was designed to involve the sympathies of the wealthy in the plight of the poor in order to reach those not served by the usual parochial system, including those incarcerated in public institutions. Charitable ventures were to be based upon personal visitations of the poor, and relief was considered the response of last resort.[30]

   After visiting with Chalmers, John Griscom proposed a similar system for New York in 1819, but the first American Ministry at Large was formally established in Boston in 1828 by Joseph Tuckerman and adopted

with somewhat less success in New York in 1833.[31] While the system did
not endure in its original form, it formalized assumptions about the relationships of society and space that were the foundations of philanthropic
efforts for the remainder of the nineteenth century. Tuckerman did not
serve a well-defined and highly localized congregation; rather, in the
words of an admirer, he "had the whole city for his field; the poor to
relieve, the degraded to raise, the well-to-do and benevolent to bring into
communication and sympathy with the poor."[32] These ends were, however, achieved by dividing the city into districts over which a deacon or
assistant to the Minister at Large could exercise personal influence by
means of what Chalmers called the principle of "locality." This principle
permitted thorough involvement in the entire life of the families in a limited district for "[t]here is a charm in locality, most powerfully felt by
every man who tries it; but which, at the same time, it is most difficult so
to seize upon as to embody it in language. . . ."[33] Chalmers felt that this
district system would build upon the local sentiments of neighborly
benevolence and also upon a more detailed understanding of local needs
on the part of philanthropists. Under these circumstances poverty would
be diminished initially by frugality and thrift, secondly by the kindness
of relatives, thirdly by the sympathy of the wealthy for the poor, and
finally by the sympathy of the poor for one another.[34]

Tuckerman also attempted to improve the coordination of the growing
number of specialized charities by means of a system of central records.
Despite their imaginative and altruistic purpose, these social policies
were based upon a firmly stated relationship between poverty and individual delinquency, and Tuckerman, like most philanthropists, believed
that this benevolent communication would directly reduce intemperance
and thereby remove the leading cause of poverty. In his judgment, "It
certainly would be a wise principle in legislation never to attempt the
attainment of moral objects by law, till it shall have been proved that
moral means are insufficient for their attainment; and, even then, that
such objects should be made the aim of law, not by assuming the power
of enforcing moral obligation, but by removing, as far as they are within
the fair scope of law, the impediments which are in the way of a free
moral action in society, – the outward and visible facilities and excite-
ments to evil."[35] The law might deter immorality by the removal of environmental nuisances, but not by the legislative enforcement of morality.

The prolonged economic depression that began in 1837 and persisted
until 1843 undermined the moral assumptions of these social policies and
revealed the degree to which poverty was linked to downswings in an
increasingly complex national and international economy. Widespread
unemployment made necessary a broad range of spasmodic and uncoor-
dinated private and public relief efforts, and the optimistic expectations

of evangelical philanthropists became somewhat less than unanimous.[36] The economic recovery had not eliminated social tensions or distress, and the conditions in the slums were now receiving wide if sensational publicity. By midcentury the leadership and support of reform had broadened beyond the evangelical community. The focus of this expanded interest was the contrast between an idealized bourgeois domesticity and the immorality of the slums.[37] Consequently, the connection between poverty and depravity retained its hold over philanthropic thought. Indeed, the expansion of relief and the multiplication of charities during the depression were judged to have encouraged dependency. In the absence of any coordinated procedures, the poor were presumed to have abused the relief system by making multiple applications to different charitable agencies. Although the personal influence of voluntary visitors was still viewed as an indispensable means of reducing the social isolation of the poor, a more professional style was introduced into the relief of poverty.[38]

The most influential expression of these ideas was the New York Association for the Improvement of the Condition of the Poor (NYAICP). In order to ensure the application of strict and standardized principles of eligibility, the AICP dispensed relief by means of paid managers and trained voluntary visitors.[39] Relief was considered a solution of last resort, and visitation was primarily designed to serve an educational purpose. Like the earlier Ministries at Large, these procedures were dependent upon a close and direct knowledge of local conditions, and accordingly relief was administered at the scale of relatively small districts. By 1853 the AICP had divided Manhattan from the Battery to Eighty-sixth Street into no fewer than 337 districts and was serving over 6,500 clients.[40] Like Tuckerman, Robert Hartley, the corresponding secretary of the AICP for over thirty years, viewed intemperance as "the master vice, exerting above all other evil influences a steady and determined opposition to every good word and work."[41]

These efforts to avoid the unnecessary duplication of charitable services by a more systematic organization of contacts were paralleled by a growing awareness of the limited and damaging effects of incarceration. In the absence of adequate management, overcrowded reformatories had become, like the slums, dangerous congregations of the needy and the depraved. Children in particular were regarded as critical targets of reform since they had not fully assimilated the deviant values of their parents and might, therefore, become a positive influence on the behavior of adults. The poor, and especially their children, infested the city streets, thereby extending their immoral world into public space. Since their homes lacked those properties of domesticity upon which moral order was based, "a particular geography of sociability – the engagement of the poor in street life rather than in the home – became itself evidence of a pervasive urban pathology."[42] Accordingly, under the leadership of Charles Brace, the Children's Aid Society made arrangements to remove children from the slums of New York to the farms and small towns of the West, where their instinctive talents would flourish in the natural setting of their adopted families.[43] Unlike earlier strategies of removal to public institutions, these new responses stressed the innate potential of the young poor to respond to the demands of modern society once they were placed in the natural setting of a secure family. These reform efforts were based on the hopeful assumption that the street wisdom of the children of poverty was a form of self-reliance that would ensure success if only they could escape from the contaminating influences of not only the slum, but the city as well.

In part because the placement of "unreformed" delinquent children merely exported the social problem, the NYAICP believed that well-managed reformatories were a temporary necessity, but by 1869 their recommendations for child care included the following:

First, the separation of children from vicious associates and contaminating associations; second, no concentration of large numbers in one institution or long detention therein; third, the family system, that is, segregation by indenture or otherwise, to respectable families in rural districts – in order to avoid the corrupt and corrupting moral atmosphere which was generated by, and inseparable from the congregated system.[44]

In retrospect Brace described these changes in the form of benevolence as

. . . a breaking away from the old method of religious influence, and the adapting themselves to the practical wants of these classes. This has now become so general a principle . . . that its novelty can hardly be recognized. But at that time it met with great opposition. To give a poor man bread before a tract[,] . . . to urge the entire change of circumstances and the emigration to country homes, as of far more importance to a certain class of vagrant children than any possible influence of Sunday-schools or Chapels, to talk of cleanliness as the first steps to godliness – all this seemed then to have a humanitarian tendency, and to belong to European socialism and infidelity.[45]

These procedures retained the spatial strategies of removal and contact, but the specific character of the moral influences was somewhat modified. Like the NYAICP, the CAS organized the city into districts "so that hereafter every Ward may have its agent, who shall be a friend to the vagrant child."[46] But contact now involved more than evangelical exhortation and included the establishment of vocational or industrial schools, and removal involved the restoration of a natural family setting rather than the inculcation of self-discipline. Despite their espousal of the moral values of natural family settings and their efforts to circumvent the agencies of municipal government, philanthropic reformers also believed that new institutions would be needed to facilitate a desirable level of social contacts under urban conditions.[47] Older institutional responses to social problems had not only become part of the patronage apparatus of urban politics but also represented an inappropriate setting in which to inculcate the values of family and community. These aspirations shifted attention to avenues and arenas in which communication and influence would be more natural. In addition to industrial or vocational schools, reformers also envisaged and proposed recreational facilities, including parks, that would serve to elevate popular taste and to provide for natural encounters with consequences as beneficial as the free market itself.[48]

The concentration of many newly arrived immigrants in northeastern cities certainly complicated these efforts to confront poverty and foreigners, who were judged to be a cause of the deteriorating condition of the poor in general. In 1851 NYAICP complained that the character of the poor had "deteriorated of late years in this city from the immense influx of foreigners, many of them being of the most thriftless, degraded class, with whom begging is a trade[;] . . . [only] the counteracting influence of such an Association as this could check the growth of pauperism, or prevent the community from being overrun by swarms of the idle and dissolute."[49] A year later the same association amplified its reactions:

The worst part of the refuse class which is thus thrown upon our shores, here clan together and remain in the city, nor can they be persuaded to leave it. These mostly consist of imbecile and thriftless parish paupers and dependents, the former inmates of poor-houses and even of prisons, who being unwilling or unable to gain an honest subsistence any where, have been sent here, in order to rid the country from which they come of their support. . . . Many of them are afflicted with pestilential diseases, more or less developed, which, as they wander about in search of shelter, are disseminated through the city to the manifest detriment of public health and to the destruction of life.[50]

Under these circumstances serious concern was aroused by the burden that impoverished immigrants placed upon the newly developed and often experimental agencies of relief and correction. Many Irish immigrants, especially during the famine emigration of the late forties, were destitute and sick upon arrival, and eventually a disproportionate number made claims upon relief, medical care, and charity.[51] In 1850 over 45 percent of Boston's population was foreign-born, and this group accounted for half the inmates of the lunatic asylum, 58 percent of the paupers, 63 percent of those sent to jail, 70 percent of the dramshop keepers, 90 percent of the patients in the dispensary, and 97 percent of the residents of the almshouses.[52] As the leading recipients of newly arrived immigrants, New Yorkers felt that their city, "operating like a sieve, lets through the enterprising and industrious, while it retains the indolent, the aged, and infirm, who can earn their subsistence nowhere, to become a burden, and often because of their vices, a nuisance to the community." This burden of pauperism "consists mainly not only of immigrants, but of the accumulated refuse of about two and a half millions of that class. . . ."[53]

Philanthropic reactions to social problems were also based upon assumptions about the Protestant values and cultural homogeneity of American society. Since the identity of the new republic was deeply rooted in Protestant tradition, Roman Catholic immigrants, especially from Ireland, provoked the greatest concern.[54] Despite efforts to diminish the explicit denominationalism of charity, the Protestant tone of private and public social policies necessitated the development of autonomous Catholic charities. The Roman Catholic Church believed that Brace's organization was intentionally taking Catholic children and placing them with Protestant families. In fact, there were inadequate numbers of Catholic households with the resources to provide foster care; institutional facilities like the New York Catholic Protectory remained essential to Catholic social policies. These responses to the predicament of destitute and sick immigrants in northeastern cities also provoked demands for some kind of regulation and restriction of immigration.

Fortunately, most philanthropic agencies were confident that they could restore a unified moral order in the American city, and their optimism softened nativist demands. Indeed, they justified their demands for reform by demanding that "we must, as a people, act upon this foreign element, or it will act upon us. Like the vast Atlantic, we must decompose and cleanse the impurities which rush into our midst, or . . . we shall receive their poison into our whole national system. American social virtue has deteriorated . . . through the operation of influences connected with the influx of foreigners, without corresponding precautions to counteract them."[55] In 1860 an anonymous advocate of improved housing observed that the social and environmental problems of large cities "have become more apparent during the last twenty years than before, and it has been the fashion to attribute their increase, with their frightful consequences, mainly to the enormous Irish immigration. . . . This view is no doubt in part correct; but the larger share of the evils in our cities is due to causes unconnected . . . with immigration[,] . . . causes contemporaneous with it in their development, and brought into fuller action by it, rather than consequent on it."[56] The old view, which blamed the immigrant, was not to be rejected but rather modified in a fashion that attributed some of the blame to the urban environment.[57]

This sensitivity to environmental as well as moral causes of poverty

depended upon new discoveries about the physical processes of contagion. Despite a growing understanding of epidemiology, older concepts
of moral contagion were retained. These environmental interpretations
of the social consequences of the slum also reinforced negative images of
the poor, since it was assumed that an adverse environment inevitably
yielded a delinquent and dependent population. The dominant philanthropic interpretation of antebellum urban society was based upon moral
rather than economic characteristics, and judgments about the pathological behavior of slum residents were reinforced once medical opinion
diagnosed the pathology of the slum environment. The term *pathological*
described by medical analogy an immoral society, but to sanitary reformers the term succinctly expressed both a moral and a medical condition.[58]
Accordingly, philanthropic efforts to rescue the poor from depravity now
included efforts to remove the environmental conditions that contributed
to that depravity.

The environment defined: sanitary indictments

The concepts of contagion that dominated interpretations of the spread
of delinquency were based upon analogies drawn from prevailing medical
opinion about epidemic diseases. Scientific understanding of the processes by which diseases were transmitted remained incomplete until late
in the nineteenth century. By midcentury, however, the connections were
made amongst accumulations of filth, impure water, and the origins and
diffusion of epidemics. The virulence of the 1849 cholera epidemic, in
particular, was interpreted from this sanitary perspective.[59] In contrast,
the earlier epidemic of 1832 had only a temporary influence on prevailing
attitudes, which judged premature mortality to be divine retribution for
moral failings. Popular views were sanctioned by medical opinion, which
stressed the relationship between mortality and predisposing behavioral
causes. Although these predisposing causes were associated with the
depraved poor, whose susceptibility to epidemics was judged to be divine
retribution for their delinquencies, epidemics did spread, if with less virulence, to the remainder of urban society.[60] For those who were unable
temporarily to abandon the city, quarantine was the major public
response.

In 1849 the failure of quarantine to combat the spread of cholera from
its source areas in the filthiest and usually worst-drained districts gave
credibility to an alternative procedure of removing those nuisances from
which the disease seemed to spread.[61] In Boston it was recorded that
"with few exceptions, the disease was confined to the unhealthy, ill-ven-
tilated, and crowded localities. The lower parts of the city, where the
drainage is difficult and the cellars more or less invaded by the backwater,

those reclaimed from the ocean, and those in the vicinity of the marshes were invaded by the pestilence."[62] Despite this emphatic connection between environment and virulence, the same report concluded: "Personal habits seemed to be quite as important as locality, in determining an attack of the complaint. For the most part, the temperate, the moral, the well conditioned, escaped; whilst the imprudent, the vicious and the poorly fed, succumbed to its insidious influence."[63] Nevertheless, cholera was now associated not only with well-publicized notorious locations but with the unsanitary sites that abounded in many sections of most cities. The intermixture of residential and industrial land uses was an additional source of noxious conditions, and relatively few urban residents escaped the emanations of slaughterhouses, breweries, stables, dairies, and piggeries.

The National Quarantine and Sanitary Convention of the late fifties, which was to be the precursor of the American Public Health Association, attempted to publicize the necessity for "internal" rather than "external" hygiene. Most sanitary reformers were convinced that quarantine, or "external" hygiene, had become an inconvenient and ineffective response to epidemic disease and that "internal" hygiene or civic cleanliness was now more critical.[64] As fertile sources of epidemic disease and centers of extremely high mortality, the slums could be defined on the basis of their site characteristics, since in cities with inadequate sanitary arrangements the worst living conditions were to be found on poorly drained and recently filled land.[65] Indeed, under conditions of poor sanitation, it was the occupation of cellars that provoked the most outraged reactions. Environmental deficiencies were clearly revealed in the variations in mortality within most large cities. This variation was judged to be one measure of the high toll of preventable disease and a direct cost of delays in the removal of their environmental causes.[66]

These indictments of the slum environment were not restricted to matters of inadequate drainage and accumulations of filth, for the more immediate housing environment also attracted much critical attention.[67] The partitioning of single-family dwellings into tenements, the infilling of their grounds with cheap new multifamily structures, and the conversion of institutional or industrial buildings into housing blocks were all viewed as a threat to light and ventilation. The conversion of old buildings was considered a temporary adaptation to an unusually large influx of immigrants at a time when many of these neglected structures were destined to be demolished in the face of expanding business needs. In contrast, the construction of new tenement blocks covering almost an entire lot set a new and more permanent standard of housing density. "Such crowding," wrote Stephen Smith in his recollections of the early days of the housing reform movement, "amounts literally to packing."

He argued for a more precise association of environment and mortality when he concluded that "the excess of mortality is not even equally distributed over these populous poor wards, but is concentrated upon individual tenant-houses."[68]

Most indictments of housing conditions also made extremely direct assumptions about the effects of room overcrowding on promiscuity and thereby consolidated the link between the slums and immorality. In the words of Horatio Wood, a leading advocate of the Ministry at Large, "many of these morbid appetites and unnatural desires that seek to assuage their longings by indulgence and excess, have their origin in the action of a distempered body upon the mind rather than of the mind on the body."[69] The environmentalist position was most completely advocated in Chapin's work on New York, which stressed the moral gains to be derived from the improvement of housing and sanitation.[70] In 1853 the NYAICP added its influential voice to the demands for the improvement of housing conditions amongst the poor. Their justifications included, firstly, the reduction of crime, pauperism, immorality, and intemperance; secondly, the diminished threat of contagious diseases to the remainder of the population; and thirdly, the alleviation of taxation by providing conditions under which self-improvement was possible. In 1857 the same organization reported that "if some of the numerous causes of poverty and wretchedness are fairly attributable to the follies or vices of the poor, there are others [i.e., environmental causes] of a different nature which from their importance deserve special consideration."[71]

This fusion of environmentalism and moralism was more emphatically expressed in the findings of a Select Committee of the State Legislature when it concluded that "each startling fact of misery was speedily paralleled by some close-following example of a kindred vice or crime, until the conclusion forced itself on the reflection of all, that certain conditions and associations of human life and habitations are the prolific parents of corresponding habits and morals."[72] In his recollections Stephen Smith declared that tenement dwellers "eat, drink, sleep, work, dress and undress, without the possibility of that privacy which an innate modesty imperatively demands." He described these social and moral consequences as "tenant-house rot" or "slow decomposition":

... a true eremacausis, as the chemists term it. ... Vice, crime, drunkenness, lust, disease and death, here hold sway, in spite of the most powerful moral and religious influences. ... Their intellects are so blunted and their perceptions so perverted by the noxious atmosphere which they breathe, and the all-pervading filth in which they live, move, and have their being, that they are not susceptible to moral or religious influences. ... [This is] a depraved physical condition which explains the moral deterioration of these people and which can never be overcome until we surround them with the conditions of sound health.[73]

While the problems faced in New York were on a scale unparalleled in other cities, the responses there were extremely influential in setting the moral tone and administrative practice elsewhere. In newer cities congested lots were less critical than in New York and Boston. Even in Philadelphia single-family row-houses rather than tenements were the rule. Nevertheless, room overcrowding and inadequate sanitary arrangements plagued most large cities, and these environmental conditions were directly linked to destitute and depraved immigrants. The social degradation of the poor was now linked to their appalling environment, and despite a sensitivity to the moral distinctions amongst the poor, an environmentalist philanthropy was both inclusive and deterministic in its assumptions about the pathological social consequences of overcrowding. John Griscom judged zymotic or filth-borne diseases to be not only a measure of sanitary conditions but also "the hygienic barometer, whose figures on the scale denote the state of physical health, derived from the modes of life, the character of the dwellings, the condition of the streets, the attention given to the removal of filth, the extent and perfection of the sewerage, and the degree of intelligence and supervision of the health officers. The higher the figures, the more degraded are the people in all those circumstances."[74]

It was assumed that many necessities of life that were properly left to individuals in rural areas would have to become the obligation of municipal government.[75] Most sanitary reformers were, however, extremely cautious about the extent of these municipal obligations. Increasingly, professional medical opinion came into conflict both with city governments, which were reluctant to insist on environmental regulations, and with landowners, who resented any infringement of their property rights. Apart from short-lived emergency efforts to remove notorious nuisances, muncipal authorities were initially unable or reluctant to respond to the suggestions of sanitary reformers, and municipal neglect and incompetence became one of the reformers' major complaints.[76] The responsibility for street cleanliness was often under the control of political appointees who relied upon unsatisfactory private contractors for removal services and rarely enforced existing laws pertaining to nuisances. Under these circumstances sanitary reform became part of a broader attack on the competency and integrity of city governments. The inadequacies of civic government became a major argument in proposals to create a cadre of trained specialists who would be responsible for the management of urban services.

The search for civic order

For much of the first half of the nineteenth century responses to urban social problems had relied upon an informal alliance of public and private ventures proposed by political leaders who were usually major patrons of philanthropy.[77] Although this arrangement persisted in efforts to provide charity and relief, by midcentury municipal governments had begun to extend their authority into matters of public order and safety, education, and public health. Philanthropic reformers had already expressed reservations about the damaging effects of public relief, and they were apprehensive about the expanding role of civic authorities in the necessary tasks of creating an institutional environment appropriate to urban society. City government was judged to be under the control of fiscally irresponsible professional politicians and their "machines." These "corrupt" political arrangements were viewed as another indication of the diminished influence of established wealth and status in urban society during a period when both the social origins of elected representatives and the terms of suffrage were decisively broadened. The degree to which these political developments, combined with increasing levels of residential segregation, diminished the moral leadership of old elites over urban society were probably exaggerated. Recent interpretations of the changing political regimes in antebellum cities have also demonstrated that most established political leaders deliberately shared their power with professional politicians whose manipulative and managerial styles were dependent upon political machines rather than on social deference.[78]

Popular disturbances, which had for long been regarded tolerantly as legitimate expressions of collective resentments, were increasingly viewed as a serious threat to social stability.[79] This changing role of civic government was most clearly expressed in the reorganization of fire protection. The memberships of voluntary fire companies had originally included a broad range of social strata, but by midcentury they were associated with disorderly and intemperate artisans. Fires became the occasion for riotous intercompany rivalries and, in the absence of effective police forces, constituted an additional threat to civic order. The spasmodic introduction of professional police and fire services and the more decisive establishment of public school systems drastically altered local government, but they were clearly designed to reorganize urban society as a whole rather than a highly localized delinquent population.[80] In Philadelphia the political jurisdiction of the city itself was extended since the problems of social order were as critical in the adjacent suburbs as in the city itself.

Quite apart from the desirability or capacity of city governments to provide professional services, their efforts revealed a less definitive image of the slums and the poor than that of the philanthropists. In practice, moral classifications of the poor presented many difficulties. Most wage-earners were poor and frequently suffered from unanticipated unemployment, yet philanthropic policies presumed that they were able to distinguish the respectable working people from those who were delinquent.[81] In fact, the security and status of the artisans and mechanics of large northeastern seaports had been threatened by fluctuating market conditions since before the Revolution, but these economic changes were of less concern to philanthropists than was a growing fear that urban communities were losing their cohesiveness.[82] The growth of an immigrant Catholic population provoked religious conflicts, and as a source of cheap unskilled labor that facilitated the conversion of skilled crafts into sweated trades, the Irish were also viewed as a threat to the American artisan. Labor competition was, however, a decidedly spasmodic issue in dialogues about the desirability of immigration. Most popular protests were, in fact, expressions of the economic resentments of artisans and mechanics, whose distinctive and highly organized social world was often confused with that of the slum.[83] For these reasons, disruptive conflicts that threatened civic order have been related to the close proximity and interspersal of a heterogeneous population rather than the isolation of a well-defined depraved group from the remainder of urban society.[84] In any event the new scale and density of urban life had greatly strained effective local communications to the point that older informal patterns of politics were virtually impossible.[85] In contrast to earlier philanthropic efforts to restore a recently lost moral order, the more broadly based civic governments began to cope with the need to provide services and maintain order in an increasingly differentiated society.

Efforts to respond to the deteriorating condition of the urban environment increasingly stressed the need for a health department staffed by experts trained in sanitary science and endowed with discretionary powers to insist on the removal of threats to public health. After several futile attempts to establish a professional state board of health in New York, reformers initiated a comprehensive inquiry into the living conditions of the poor that confirmed in meticulous detail the conditions that had been a source of complaint for over two decades.[86] Although this survey included references to the moral condition of the poor, its primary emphasis was the imperative need to confront the serious defects in the urban environment. The leading causes of environmental defects were abundantly and effectively illustrated with maps, diagrams, and engravings of overcrowded lots (Figure 2.3), the intermixture of stables and other noxious land uses with residences (Figure 2.5), inadequate drainage, accumulated filth, and improper privies or sewerage arrangements. As in earlier indictments, reference was made to the uncleanly and intemperate habits of the residents, but their illustrations continued to feature laundry and laundry lines (Figure 2.6).[87] The report concluded that a professional cadre of medical practitioners, independent of local political influences, would be essential to administer and propose laws that man-

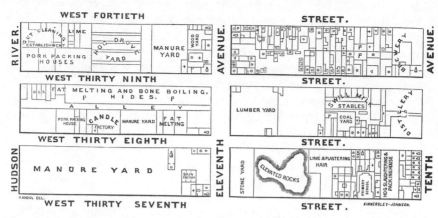

Figure 2.5 Noxious land uses, New York, 1866

Source: Council of Hygiene and Public Health of the Citizens' Association of New York, *Report upon the Sanitary Condition of the City* (New York: Appleton, 1865), 266.

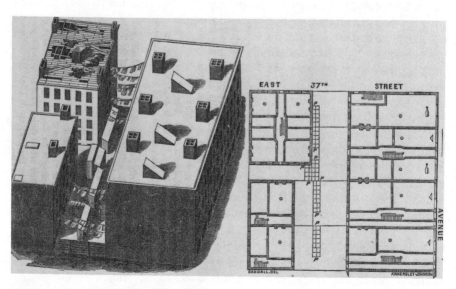

Figure 2.6 Lot congestion, New York, 1866

Source: Council of Hygiene and Public Health of the Citizens' Association of New York, *Report upon the Sanitary Condition of the City* (New York: Appleton, 1865), 266.

dated the minimum standards for the sanitary environment of any building.

Other circumstances enhanced the impact of this survey of sanitary conditions. The draft riots of 1863 had been attributed to the "elements of popular discord . . . gathered in these wretchedly constructed tenement houses, where poverty, disease and crime find an abode. . . . Everything within and without tends to physical and moral degradation."[88] Although these conclusions were erroneous, they did provide momentum for sanitary reform, which reached a peak with the outbreak of another major cholera epidemic in 1866.[89] The newly established Metropolitan Board of Health had an immediate impact on street cleanliness and noxious sites, and new tenement construction would be regulated for the first time. These regulations had only a limited impact on living conditions. They did, however, establish the right of public intervention in private property rights, since the new Boards of Health obtained limited restrictions on the overcrowding of lots and the ventilation of interior rooms in new structures. Not only the depraved poor but also a substantial proportion of the entire urban population was condemned to live in congested and unhealthy quarters. A survey of housing in Manhattan by the Metropolitan Board of Health concluded that of over 18,000 structures, which housed more than three families, over half were judged to be in bad condition, and in one third of the tenements neglect was held to be responsible.[90]

Although most of these sanitary deficiencies were to be found in the lower sections of Manhattan, almost every ward had pockets of unhealthy housing, and the local reports suggest that inadequate drainage and overcrowded lots were a source of unsanitary conditions. Complaints about the sanitary environment, like those about social problems, emphasized some highly localized notorious slums, but clearly these extreme conditions were but a small fragment of more complex and extensive patterns of environmental deficiencies. Overall improvements in public health were primarily derived from improvements in the sanitary environment rather than from decidedly ineffective efforts to regulate housing quality. These sanitary improvements did not extend into extensive shanty developments on the urban periphery, but since these developments were assumed to be temporary, they rarely attracted the attention of sanitary reformers (Figure 2.7). Shanties were often displaced by substantial affluent residential developments, and for brief periods these circumstances resulted in some of the most striking social gradients in the city (Figure 2.8).

Although housing was not one of the leading issues of popular protest, some observers did recognize the underlying economics of property investment, which set rent levels for adequate housing well beyond the

Figure 2.7 Shanty squatters, near Central Park, New York, 1869

Source: Engraved from a drawing by D. E. Wyand, *Harper's Weekly,* June 26, 1869.

Figure 2.8 Polarization on the urban fringe, New York, 1889

Source: Frank Leslie's Illustrated Newspaper, September 7, 1889.

means of the poor. In 1857 it was reported that "in its beginning, the tenant house became a real blessing to that class of industrious poor whose small earnings limited their expenses and whose employment in workshops, stores or about the wharves and thoroughfares, rendered a near residence of much importance. At this period rents were moderate, and a mechanic with family could hire two or more comfortable even commodious apartments, in a house once occupied by wealthy people, for less than half he is now obliged to pay for narrow and unhealthy quarters."[91] Overcrowded rooms, subdivided buildings, congested lots, and inadequate utilities were all strategies to lower rents without reducing the return on the property. Frequent mention was also made to the subletting of property to an agent for a fixed return; the agent obtained a maximum yield by neglecting repairs and services and extracting the highest possible rent, and the absentee owners ceased to have any direct responsibility for their property or tenants.[92]

The difficulty of establishing new standards was emphasized by the failure of several ambitious proposals to erect tenements that would serve as "models" of improved housing but that proved to be exercises in the creation of new slums. Because of the conflicts provoked by threats of public regulation of private building, model tenements were intended to demonstrate the possibility of providing adequate housing at a reasonable rent and with an adequate return on capital. The majority of these ventures provided some early publicity for improved housing, but they failed to sustain their hopeful intentions. As new structures they were rarely offered at rents that would have opened them to the most needy, and as cheaply built structures they deteriorated rapidly to the level of the slums around them.[93] Philanthropists condemned the avarice of property owners and the negligence of municipal authorities, and although the new Boards of Health were able to improve the general sanitary environment of cities, they were unable to resolve the housing problems of the poor. The impact of housing reforms on overcrowding was decidedly modest. Regulations of new buildings took the form of restrictions on the proportion of a lot that a new structure might occupy. Interior windows were also recommended for the improved ventilation of old buildings, and occasionally some selective demolition reduced congestion and improved access to some of the worst slums. Unfortunately, these sanitary gains often increased the level of overcrowding, because the displaced poor moved into adjacent buildings. Large-scale urban improvement schemes, like the leveling of Fort Hill in Boston, were also celebrated because they combined commercial development with the removal of unsanitary quarters, but their devastating effect on the supply of low-rent accommodations was only rarely appreciated.

The newly formed Massachusetts Bureau of Statistics of Labor concluded that "low-paid laborers are not earning sufficient wages to justify their living in [improved] tenement houses . . . and, as there are no intermediate houses between these and the lowest class of houses . . . the laborers of this class are practically compelled to crowd into the miserable refuges in which they now congregate. In fact, so far as we have been able to ascertain, there are no places within the settled portions of the city of Boston, where the low-paid toiler can find a house of decency and comfort."[94] Similar observations were made about the tenements of New York: "The tenement houses are occupied mainly by the honest laboring population of New York, who receive fair wages for their work." Consequently, "The laboring class, who should constitute the backbone and sinew of the community, are thus degraded to a level with paupers, forced to herd among them, and to adopt a mode of life which is utterly destructive of the characteristics which should distinguish them."[95] Discussions of the sanitary problems of midcentury cities reveal considerable ambiguity about both their target populations and the degree to which these delinquent individuals were concentrated in well-defined sections of the city.

A "scientific" moral order

Despite observations that reveal that the impoverished residents of the slums were not necessarily depraved or delinquent and might have constituted the majority of urban residents, the new agencies of reform were concerned:

In providing for the poor, the dependent and the vicious, especially for the young, we must take the ordinary family for our model. We must in a general view of them, bear in mind that they do not as yet form with us a well marked and persistent class, but a conventional, and, perhaps, only a temporary one. They do not differ from other men, except that, taken as a whole, they inherited less favorable moral tendencies, and less original vigor. Care should be taken that we do not by our treatment transform the conventional class into a real one and a persistent one.[96]

These attitudes to poverty were based upon assumptions about the special relationships between capital and labor in the United States, for in Europe labor was "a member of a distinct order in society, engaged in a sort of legal war with the other orders and . . . bound to his fellows, not simply by community of material interest, but by sentiments of caste pride and fidelity, [whereas] the social line between the laborer and the capitalist is here very faintly drawn."[97] Social injustice did not, therefore, provoke an indictment of the social order itself, since reformers were confident that expertise, efficiency, and disinterested inquiry were capable of solving problems.[98]

The development of an executive body of health experts to control the environment owed a great deal to procedures adopted during the Civil War to cope with casualties and disease. The Sanitary Commission established during the war and administered by pioneers of environmental reform, relied upon volunteers to raise funds but utilized trained, salaried professionals to provide for the efficient management of the medical and sanitary needs of the army.[99] Without the justifications of wartime conditions that made possible the organization of over 7,000 completely voluntary auxiliaries dedicated to raising funds for the commission, newly established state regulatory agencies had to rely more on the authority of science and to protect their expertise from the contaminating involvements of politics.[100] The founding of the American Social Science Association in 1865 symbolized a combination of science and reform in the interests of moral order.[101] In the words of a leading publicist of new agencies of reform, "the next great political revolution in the western world [will give] . . . scientific expression to the popular will, or, in other words . . . place men's relations in society where they have never yet been placed, under the control of trained human reason."[102]

Initially this new science of society presumed that the identification and investigation of social problems would automatically reveal their solutions. The sanitary reform movement, in particular, was a leading advocate of this new style and scale of intervention. Initially sanitary reformers believed that their recommendations would be quickly adopted once the public and the legislature understood the scientific principles that specified the damaging effects of an unsanitary environment. John Griscom reminded the Third National Quarantine and Sanitary Convention that he was

. . . a thorough believer in sound republican democracy (in its technical sense); I hold that no amendments in this, as on other subjects, can be satisfactory or safe, without instructions to the legislators, from an instructed people. The masses being those who alone are interested in questions of public health, it is they who must first be moved to demand reform, and their servants, the legislature, will – they must – then grant it. And from whom are the public to receive the necessary enlightenment to justify them in demanding the proper measures of self protection? Clearly, the initiative . . . for this purpose must be taken by members of the medical profession; but their labors, when once begun, will not long be unshared by the laymen."[103]

Since many legislatures were skeptical of centralized administrative authorities and were reluctant to provide substantial funding, it was fortunate that many pioneers of the new social science believed that most problems would be solved rapidly and that some agencies might indeed be temporary. Once defined and reported in statistical terms, public opinion would direct a legislative response to a specific social ill. Researchers believed in the principles of objectivity and impartiality, and their faith was based upon the healing power of statistical facts. A benevolent and omnipotent providence was obstructed only temporarily by evil and discontent.[104] These values were especially prevalent amongst those appointed to administer a newly formed State Board of Health in Massachusetts. Their limitless goals were clearly stated in their first annual report:

The general court has assumed to itself the right to prescribe rules for the intellectual and moral health of the people. But it may well be doubted whether, in the earnest desire to stimulate the intellectual powers of its people, the State has not neglected somewhat the moral, and almost wholly lost sight of the physical nature of man. . . . [I]f in this or any other future report, it should study any supposed evil upon man, it will adopt the fine old maxim, pagan though it may be, that nothing which pertains to humanity, in its widest sense, will this Board deem foreign to its aims.[105]

Somewhat later the same board declared: "To submit quietly to any remediable evil, as if to the will of Providence, is not now considered an act of piety, but an unmanly and really irreligious act. It is the part of error and stupidity, which does not believe in the duty of studying into the physical causes of disease, and . . . to crush out these originators of pest and of death."[106]

Although the role of the state agency was to "instruct," the frustrations of an inadequate response led to speculations about an appropriate "deterrance" to environmental negligence. Nevertheless, the newly formed American Public Health Association was described as an "alliance of earnest men in a voluntary system of organized inquiry and conference" devoted to education rather than legislation.[107] Social and scientific expectations were sustained by "the idea that perfect health was an attainable goal, exceptional in its virtue, and equally available to all who subscribed to the maxims of an orderly, harmonious life."[108] These boundless objectives did, however, provoke more interest in the institutional forms of intervention than in the social problems they were intended to resolve. The new environmental and institutional needs of the city would have to be met by a more bureaucratic and administrative interpretation of democracy that lifted the public interest above the obscuring particularism of daily politics, but this new democracy would apparently "best serve the people by paradoxically being occasionally removed from direct contact with them."[109] This viewpoint proposed the paternalistic and even autocratic intervention of public agencies for the purposes of not only sanitary regulations but also a wide range of other matters, including charities, corrections, and the condition of labor.

This specialist and authoritarian style contrasted with the lax administration and decentralized organization of American cities and suggests a confidence in public intervention closer to the progressives than to mid-century reformers.[110] Reformers phrased their moral purposes in a scientific language in order to resist the centralization of power in the legislative arena, and consequently, although their efforts yielded institutions that were precursors of progressivism, their motives were much closer to the moralism of antebellum philanthropy.[111] Bureaucratic strategies were designed to facilitate the role of experts, and it was the degree to which these agencies should be centralized and autonomous rather than their existence that provoked most debate. The Massachusetts State Board of Charities, which after its formation in 1863 set the pattern for developments in other states, declared that their "great work may be done, not solely, nor even mainly by delegating it to special establishments and to agents set apart for it; but, so far as possible, by the people themselves in their families." The same report did, however, plead for greater executive discretion in order to carry out a uniform policy. The board acknowledged:

Decentralization is conformable to the spirit of our political institutions, and to the genius of our people. It is important for the life and efficiency of local charitable institutions; and desirable for the sake of distributing the duties of charity widely among the community, and so bringing them home to the hearths and heart of the people. But, on the other hand, centralization of some kind is absolutely necessary for accomplishing the objects aimed at by the establishment of the separate Institutions.[112]

Reformers did indeed believe that government had an obligation to use scientific knowledge to improve the urban environment, but by the more technical standards of a later age; they were also generalists who remained deeply conscious of participating in a moral crusade.[113] In New York the fiscal crisis precipitated by the Tweed Ring provided reformers with a clear justification of the need to remove public services from the political arena, but in smaller cities this conflict was less critical than the pragmatic responses of city authorities to the changing needs of urban society. In Springfield, Massachusetts, for example, the development of a Board of Public Works "to separate administration from obstructive politics" was attributed not to struggles for political power among competing interests but rather to a city government in the process of being "pushed forward by the logic of their search for comprehensiveness, order and efficiency, [and] . . . coming to believe that to govern a more complex urban community required a separation of politics and administration that would at once insure the competence of the latter and the democracy of the former."[114]

These improvements of the urban environment raised issues about the kind and control of public intervention, but it was proposals for sanitary reform in the interests of public health that heightened the debate. A growing sensitivity to the social costs of inadequate sanitation and over-crowded housing did not lead to a rejection of established moral inter-pretations of poverty. Justifications of reform were based upon an under-lying assumption that a new scale of urban growth had disrupted the moral order of urban society and that increased residential segregation had exposed a vaguely defined social group described as the poor to the contaminating influences of the most depraved amongst them. Destitu-tion was still firmly linked to depravity or at least to a failure of self-discipline, but since the urban environment intensified the process of degradation and obstructed efforts directed at self-improvement, social policies were required to address the environs as well as the behavior of the poor. Once it was assumed that the poor might be "reformed" by appropriate social policies, the term *slum* became an indispensable image of the social degradation that was presumed to be the primary cause of poverty. The moral purposes of reform were increasingly connected to the need for a scientific understanding of social problems, and conse-quently experts rather than legislators would be the key to further improvements. These experts sensed that they were confronted with the management of a more complex urban society, but their vision of this complexity was inhibited by their desire to restore a unified moral order within cities.

By 1870 the investigations and aspirations of new agencies of reform revealed some of the complexities of the relationship between social problems and the urban environment. During the following decade grow-ing doubts about the pioneering ventures in state intervention were for-mulated in relation to changes in the extent and perception of slums. These doubts were especially prevalent amongst those who had at one time the greatest confidence in reform. The prevailing tone of Godkin's *Nation,* for example, shifted from the advocacy of state intervention to apprehensive fears of the growing political power of the "masses."[115] Despite their belief in the capacities of new public institutions to respond to the needs of a rapidly expanding city, contemporary observers of New York expressed apprehension at the polarization of urban society. They no longer recognized the differences in the social character of the Bowery and Five Points.[116] In the antebellum city certain localities were identified with specific social groups, but these discrete sociogeographic patterns were not only very close to each other but collectively described only a small fragment of cities that were not yet highly segregated, except per-haps at an extremely small scale. By 1870 the inner sections of large cities were increasingly described as a vast, unknowable "wilderness" housing a "mass" that threatened to engulf the remainder of urban society.

Slums were no longer described as scattered pockets of deprivation and vice set within unsanitary and congested yards and courts that were perilously close to respectable districts; they were seen as extensive sections of the city. The preoccupation of antebellum reformers with the contagious threat of slum conditions appeared to be prophetic, for despite new public policies, the slums were described as increasing on a new and more menacing scale. For these reasons there was a growing concern about the development of an alternative and deviant pattern of life in the slums, and once the worst slums were identified with immigrants, it was possible not only to define the residents with more conviction but also to connect social problems to an alien group. In 1868 the annual report of the NYAICP complained:

... the social relations of the foreign to the native population [has] ... materially changed. They no longer as formerly melt away, or so blend with the native stocks as to become incorporated with it. So large are the aggregations of different foreign nationalities, that they no longer conform to our habits, opinions and manners, but, on the contrary, create for themselves distinct communities, almost as impervious to American sentiments and influences as are the inhabitants of Dublin or Hamburg. This principle or tendency of segregation extends to their private, social and public life. ... They have their own theatres, recreations, amusements, military and national organizations; to a great extent their own schools, churches and trade unions – their own newspapers and periodical literature ... as if they were still subjects of a foreign power.[117]

Another indictment of immigrants complained:

Noisy trade goes on in the quarters where the foreigners live, and the Sabbath is filled with noisy, wanton, and drunken violators. ... Every wave of foreign immigration lessens the dry land of religious observance. Churches are swept away, and none arise to take their place. The infidel German, the undevout Jew, the illiterate foreign population, led by an omnipotent press, unite to create a popular sentiment that is pushing out gradually but surely, the observation of the Sabbath. ...[118]

Since the author also makes strident complaints about the strength of the Catholic Church in New York, it is clear that he is distressed by the declining influence of the Protestant denominations rather than a decline in religious observance in general. Destitute immigrants had been judged, like the native poor, as individual delinquents, but eventually it was their clannishness that was viewed as an unanticipated threat to assimilation and a more serious social problem than were mere concentrations of delinquent individuals.[119] In 1872 Brace described the residents of slums as a dangerous class, and despite a growing sense of frustration at the slow progress of reform, in their justifications and their expectations of intervention the social policies of reformers remained firmly grounded in the moralism of antebellum philanthropy.

Scientific investigations had revealed the environmental deficiencies of many sections of the city, and moral interpretations of slums and poverty had been modified to account for the damaging effects of the urban environment. From this perspective the slums were an indispensable image in justifications of the reform of urban society. The slums were symbols of a level of social degradation to which an entire city might be reduced. When, despite much experimental public intervention, these fears appeared to be prophetic, the moral logic of the original image was retained. While the administrative forms and scientific approaches of these new public agencies were innovative, their policies remained grounded in moral explanations of poverty. By 1875 their original expectations of rapid success were drastically curtailed and they became agencies for the administration of regulations.[120] A vision of urban society had been formulated during the boundless optimism of antebellum reform, but the depression of the midseventies revealed not only the limitations of their policies but also an increasingly polarized society.[121]

3

The slums defined: 1875–1900

Fears about the expanding mass of slums were part of a growing concern over the threats posed to American social ideals by the growing scale of urbanization. To the degree that American culture was identified with small towns and petty proprietorship, the growth of large cities was viewed with apprehension. The immense influence of Turner's frontier thesis drew attention to the reports of the 1890 Census which had documented the "closing of the agricultural frontier." Ten years earlier, however, the reports of the 1880 Census had stressed the urban destiny of American society. Quite apart from the diminished availability of cheap land, the vast majority of Americans would live in cities. Prior to the Civil War the most critical social problems and the most menacing threats to American culture were associated with the northeastern seaports and especially New York. By 1880 it was clear that major midwestern cities, which had long been "boosted" as symbols of growth, were increasingly afflicted with the problems of the older northeastern ports. This growing consciousness of an urban destiny was accompanied by a fuller awareness of the extent to which this new scale of urban life was linked to the changing forms of urbanization.

During the prolonged depression of the midseventies (1873–8), unemployment was identified as a leading source of poverty. Ira Steward, a leading labor advocate affiliated with the Massachusetts Bureau of Statistics of Labor, extended the problems of economic insecurity to include the "great middle class." He concluded: "The poverty of the great middle class consists in the fact that they have only barely enough to cover up their poverty, and that they are within a very few days of want, if through sickness, or other misfortune, employment suddenly stops. No one can describe the secret feelings of insecurity that constantly prevail among them concerning their lives, and how it will be with them in the future; and while actual hunger and want may never be known, their poverty is felt, mentally and socially, through their sense of dependence and pride."[1]

These fears were exacerbated by changes in the scale and organization of several major industries which were reducing the chances of advancement from wage earner to independent proprietor and threatened to polarize urban society into antagonistic classes. The social composition of this large class of permanent wage earners became a matter of considerable debate, usually referred to as the "Labor Question." The question addressed the degree to which poverty afflicted a residual depraved minority or included wage earners in general.[2]

As in the antebellum period this metaphor of polarization was graphically expressed in relation to residential segregation, but the new scale of urban life had dramatically increased the degree to which the poor were isolated. Improved local transportation had opened up suburban areas to those whose working hours and secure salaries made the journey to work and home ownership possible. This tendency for the upwardly mobile to move to new housing on the edge of the city was viewed as a heartening trend that would ease the problems of congestion within cities.[3] Suburbanization was, however, based upon selective social mobility, and consequently the older housing stock of the inner city was likely to house a homogeneous remnant population of those who were unable or unwilling to improve themselves. In 1882 Helen Campbell complained: "The middle class have been driven to the country, and it is this middle class on whom any hope of proper municipal action depends. The poor are too poor, the rich too rich, to be anything but indifferent as to whether the city government is administered economically or otherwise. Rapid transit you will say will solve this problem, but there must always be a large class of day laborers too poor to afford the daily fare who will crowd into the regions near which their work lies."[4] Campbell later organized the Consumers' League of New York, an organization devoted to those middle-class values that were especially threatened by social polarization.

Only the extremely affluent were able to maintain their original inner-city precincts. Since the late eighteenth century this stratum had pioneered the development of exclusive residential quarters on desirable sites, but as the suburban movement became more inclusive, these earlier ventures were often left embedded within the inner city. Now historic, some of these neighborhoods retained their prestigious status, and large cities were thus destined to become concentrations of the very rich and the very poor. New wealth was also increasingly associated with industry and domestic consumption rather than with foreign commerce. Industrial plutocrats were thought to lack the paternalistic sensibilities of established mercantile wealth, and their ostentatious materialism was judged to be as serious a threat to the moral order as was abject destitution. In particular, the failure of reform was attributed to an alliance of selfish business interests and their agents, the corrupt machine politicians.[5]

Urban society was portrayed as a contrast of extremes of wealth and poverty, or of "sunshine and shadow" (Figure 3.1), but popular indictments emphasized moral and personal relationships rather than structural and social conditions (Figure 3.2).

The social problems that provoked reform were, however, presumed to be generically urban, and to the degree that cities were primarily comprised of migrants and especially foreign migrants, social problems were linked to unrestricted immigration. Recovery from the depression of the midseventies failed to diminish social unrest, and a new surge in the volume of foreign immigration during the mideighties heightened speculations on the damaging effects of unrestricted immigration. These connections amongst social problems, the city, and the immigrant were also influenced by changes in the source areas of foreign immigration. Most negative reactions to immigration expressed concern about the growing proportion of the total foreign influx that came from east Asia and from southern and eastern Europe. Immigration from these new sources compounded anxieties about unassimilated, and especially Catholic, immigrants from northwestern Europe, who continued to distress those who identified American values with Protestantism. Josiah Strong's widely read indictment of urban society included the city and immigrants, along with Romanism, Mormonism, intemperance, socialism, and wealth as the seven great "perils" to American society. Strong, a leading figure in the Evangelical Alliance of Protestant ministers, was dedicated to an assertive participation in the political debates about the stability of American society. He questioned "whether this in-sweeping immigration is to foreignize us, or are we to Americanize it?"[6]

The overrepresentation of the foreign born and their children amongst those categories of deviance and delinquency that most threatened the moral order of society was also widely publicized by secular critics who relied upon scientific rather than divine truth. Frederick Sanborn, the key organizer of the American Social Science Association, complained that "this whole segment of our people – those of foreign birth or parentage – furnishes far more than its due proportion of illiteracy, of poverty, insanity, infant mortality, vice and crime when compared with the native population of Northern, Western and Pacific States."[7] Van Wyck Brooks attempted to capture in retrospect these reactions to immigration and urban social problems when he described New York as "the almshouse of the poor of half the planet, and foreign countries were deliberately dumping their paupers and criminals in the United States, their blind, their crippled, their insane. Several of the continental nations were making the town a penal colony, and its slums were rapidly approaching the European level."[8] Class conflict might become more serious in America than in Europe since the social gulf between the working class and those

Figure 3.1 Polarization: sunshine and shadow in New York, 1868
Source: Matthew Hale Smith, *Sunshine and Shadow in New York* (Hartford, Conn.: J. B. Burr, 1868), frontispiece.

Figure 3.2 Polarization: sidewalk contrasts, New York, 1876
Source: Sol Etinge, Jr., *Harper's Weekly,* February 12, 1876.

above it was intensified by differences of race, language, and religion.[9] At a time when changing economic conditions had altered the security and prospects of the native-born labor force and appeared to have provoked levels of antagonism that resembled those reported in European cities, social agitation was linked to foreign-born radicals.[10]

Despite fears of radical insurgency on the part of some immigrants, the dominant complaints were about criminality and pauperism. Strong concluded: "The typical European peasant, whose horizon has been narrow, whose moral and religious training has been meager or false, and whose ideas of life are low, not a few belong to the pauper and criminal classes."[11] The concentration of immigrants in new, large-scale industries provoked the observation that the "simple, routine tasks of the factory only matched the dull faces and sloping brows they thought characterised the immigrant peasant."[12] Some invidious distinctions were made amongst the established immigrant groups: "Thrift seems to be the birthright of both the French and German peasant . . . and their careful habits, joined with the better rate of wages in America, soon make them prosperous and well-to-do citizens"; in contrast, tenement dwellers were seen as "a class apart, retaining all the most brutal character of the Irish peasant at home, but without the redeeming light-heartedness, the tender impulses and strong affections of that most perplexing people."[13] In general, established immigrants from northwestern Europe, including the Irish, were more frequently grouped into a more desirable category than newcomers from southern and eastern Europe. According to the leader of the Knights of Labor, the nation owed its greatness to "the brain, bone and muscle" of immigrants who had arrived before the Civil War. In contrast, he found, "the population that is coming today is semi-barbarous. They are willing and used to living in filthy, crowded conditions"; he saw them as constituting a "menacing eruption."[14]

Richard Mayo-Smith summarized the arguments against unrestricted immigration and provided the agenda for the Immigration Restriction League, but he also praised the strength of mixed races and envisaged a future American population possessing the best characteristics of each element.[15] This viewpoint was based upon a growing confidence in an American national identity, which faced no immediate threats from the changing ethnic composition of foreign immigration. Prior to the Civil War American civilization was thought to have been formative and in dire need of Protestant missions, but by the late nineteenth century, it was assumed that the United States was clearly established as a Christian civilization. The new Protestant mission was committed to the removal of residual and imported infidelities. Increasingly, American values were linked to an Anglo-Saxon heritage from which republican institutions and democratic values were derived. An arrogant confidence in the superiority of an Anglo-Saxon heritage presumed that inferior cultures would be speedily assimilated into the host culture, but as the source areas of foreign immigration shifted, it was argued that the assimilation of incompatible groups would damage the established culture.[16] Given the ethnic heterogeneity of the Anglo-Saxon heritage, the hybridization of closely related cultures was not necessarily undesirable, but the inclusion of unrelated and presumably incompatible cultures would clearly jeopardize the achievements of the original mixture.[17]

The most extreme reactions to the effects of exotic cultures on American society were based upon studies of the birth rates of newly arrived immigrants, which, because the immigrants were primarily young adults, were considerably higher than those of the native born. Although Steward had perceptively identified the breadth of economic insecurity, he also concluded that "the most alarming fact concerning the poverty of the native middle classes in this commonwealth is that, for two or three decades past, marriages and births have so far decreased among them that we are nearly or quite justified in saying that they are dying faster than their children are being born; and that it is to foreign sources (and to American born in other States), and to the lower class of native born, we must credit the present increase in our census returns."[18] Despite the demographic basis of differential birth rates, some alarmists publicized the prospect of "race suicide," whereby the proportionate contribution of the native-born stock to the host society would be overwhelmed by the fecundity of the newcomers.[19] The arrival of cheap unskilled labor from new and unfamiliar sources in southern and eastern Europe and in the West from East Asia was certainly viewed as an additional threat to the living standards of American workers, but judgments about these immigrants often echoed attitudes to the poor in general. During and after the Civil War, legislative actions were partly designed to protect immigrants from exploitation, but eventually the exclusion of "defectives" likely to become public charges was followed by efforts to discriminate against immigrants of specified national, ethnic, or racial origin. The Chinese were the first victims of exlusionary legislation, and proposals to discriminate against south and east Europeans were blocked by executive vetoes.

The poor had for long been viewed as delinquent individuals who were potentially an alien outcast society. During the last quarter of the nineteenth century the enlarged expanse of slums and the exotic migrants who come to populate them amplified these reactions. The expanding mass and increasing density of the slums were directly linked to the combined impact of industrialization and immigration, and they were frequently described as a social "abyss." These conditions did provoke a growing advocacy of remedial social policies, but the responsible public agencies were under the decisive influence of the prevailing ideology of scientific philanthropy. While the slums were judged to be the most disturbing consequences of social polarization, their residents became the subject of intense scrutiny as social policies continued to be preoccupied with the need to distinguish delinquent pauperism from legitimate dependency. By the mideighties the social problems of the city had become inextricably connected with foreign immigration but, as in the antebellum period, most reactions to the immigrant poor were elaborations of attitudes to dependency and delinquency. But unlike the antebellum situation, the enlarged extent and increased density of the slums made it possible to equate the slums with the inner city.

The residents defined: social polarization

At a time when economic conditions created an increasingly homogeneous "mass" of impoverished workers, public agencies were preoccupied in developing scientific bases to distinguish paupers from those who had justifiable claims for assistance. After a decade of high expectations, state agencies dedicated to the improvement of health, charity and corrections, and the conditions of labor qualified their ambitious objectives, and to this end several legislatures curtailed their appropriations and mandates. By 1877 Carroll D. Wright, who directed the Massachusetts Bureau of Statistics of Labor from 1873 until 1888 and served as the first U.S. commissioner of labor from 1885 to 1905, concluded that his agency could "not solve the labor question, for it is not solvable; it has contributed and can contribute much in the way of general progress. The labor question, like the social problem must be content to grow towards a higher condition along with the universal progress of education and broadened civilization." The report continues with the hopeful observation that "history shows the social structure to be constantly on the brink of destruction, and that it has, on the contrary, as [sic] constantly risen to a higher and better condition."[20] From their inception, the commitment of state agencies to public intervention was decidedly restrained, for they believed that "society may yet find the means of contravening in some measure the operation of this natural law of the benefit of its feebler and less fortunate members ... without starting evil forces which will more than neutralize the expected good."[21]

It was still an article of faith that those who would not work were "impoverished by their indolence and vices, for which they are responsible [but] the involuntary poor have been reduced to distress by unavoidable or providential causes."[22] Relief was still seen as a dangerous expedient since "temporary aid might end in permanent support and ... the habit of receiving without rendering an equivalent might sap the foundation of that independence of character and one's reliance on one's own resources."[23] Indeed, relief was judged by some observers to be an unfair subsidy to labor in its struggle with capital. Within a year of the onset of the depression of the midseventies one observer complained: "Labor was in a struggle with capital against the lowering of prices. Charity assisted labor in the combat. The soup-kitchens and relief associations of various names became thronged with mechanics. Some of the best workingmen in the city ate and lodged at the public expense. Thousands of able-bodied artisans, young and skillful, were fed by alms. The idleness and dependence injured many among them irretrievably. The whole settlement of the labor question was postponed by the overgenerous charity of the city."[24]

Despite the self-evident impact of a lengthy depression, attitudes to poverty were also influenced by the publicity given to tramps or vagrants.[25] Presumed to be devoid of any local or familial attachments, vagrants were regarded as outcasts who had abandoned the values of society at large and ought, therefore, to be ineligible for assistance. Although they were only a small minority of the total residents of the slums, the pathological social conditions associated with itinerant able-bodied but unemployed adult males were often assumed to be typical of the slums in general. Itinerant pauperism cast a shadow over efforts to confront poverty. Dependency was decisively linked either to the physically handicapped or to moral delinquency. In addition to its focus on urbanization, the 1880 Census also responded to this growing interest in the relationship between dependency and those who were mentally and physically handicapped. Describing them as "defectives," the Census collected information on "deaf-mutes, the blind, the insane, prisoners, idiots, paupers and homeless children." These categories reveal a continuing effort to distinguish able-bodied paupers who refused to work from the handicapped, the aged, and the young, who were unable to be self-supporting. Curiously, however, the accompanying commentary implies that a disposition towards deviancy may take any form and that, in any given generation, it was a matter of accident as to whether the problem was criminality or insanity.[26]

These responses were also associated with explorations of the role of heredity in the persistence of dependency.[27] Attempts to provide definitive statistical resolution of the relationships between deviancy and dependency were complemented by similar investigations of the respective contributions of the environment and heredity to pathological social conditions. Hereditary disabilities had concerned antebellum reformers, but although heredity might create its own environment and perpetuate adaptations to that environment, reformers were optimistic about the mutual and progressive adaptations of environment and heredity.[28] In a comprehensive review of dependency, the second annual report of the Massachusetts Board of State Charities acknowledged the contribution of heredity to social problems but felt that the problems were compounded by socially blighted conditions and that natural correctives would restore the harmony of natural laws without repressive genetic measures.[29]

Within a decade of that report, optimism had waned and the high expectations of behavioral responses to decidedly limited environmental improvements in living conditions were increasingly qualified by a concern with the generational transmission of dependency.[30] Under these circumstances it was believed that there were relatively few individuals reduced to poverty by causes beyond their own control. A classic example of the new statistical approach to social problems concluded:

... by far the greater number of paupers have reached that condition by idleness, improvidence, drunkenness, or some form of vicious indulgence.... [I]t is equally clear that these vices and weaknesses are very frequently, if not universally, the result of tendencies which are to a greater or lesser degree hereditary. The number of persons in our poor-houses who have been reduced to poverty by causes outside of their own acts is, contrary to the general impression, surprisingly small. These two classes of persons ought not to be confounded; nor ought they be compelled to associate with each other. The whole policy of the State should move in the direction of caring for the really unfortunate and worthy sick poor in hospitals, while a vigorous system of labor should be organized and administered for the vicious and unworthy.[31]

These findings implied that competency to perform in the labor market was a matter of innate capacities, and to the degree that depravity was inherited, the underlying moral causes of poverty would not necessarily respond to environmental improvements.

A theory of degeneracy now complicated discussions of poverty, and an old distinction based on worthiness to receive charity was reinforced by hereditarian ideas. Unlike a narrow Spencerian liberalism, which recommended the absolute minimum of public intervention, some Social Darwinians, perhaps better described as "Social Lamarckians," could condone certain kinds of public intervention on the hereditarian grounds that nature itself had been enriched by education and breeding.[32] In order to protect the progressive consequences of both cultural and biological evolution most obviously reflected in the competence of those of Anglo-Saxon origins, specific measures would have to be taken in the form of restricting the immigration of defectives and of races with a high proportion of defectives. For those presently threatening the nation's cultural and eugenic character, incarceration was the preferred solution. Regulations founded on the findings of science were accepted as legitimate forms of intervention in the natural or normal workings of society. To that end, efforts were made to provide centralized and specialized state facilities for the physically and mentally disabled and to separate the most depraved from the young, the old, and others with legitimate claims on charity and institutional care.[33] Although these reforms may have improved the care of the handicapped, they were also closely related to efforts to abolish outdoor relief and to confront the able-bodied poor with their moral limitations. If those who were unable to work could be distinguished and separated from those who refused to work, and if it could be established that the latter group was a small and irresponsible minority, then appropriate social policies could be developed for each category.

The development of social policies designed to confront those who did not require institutional care remained firmly in the hands of voluntary charitable organizations. Like the state agencies with whom they consulted and often served, philanthropists attempted to reform existing policies on the basis of the new, scientifically grounded interpretations of dependency. Indiscriminate and poorly coordinated relief had for long concerned philanthropists, since it was assumed that the system actually supported pauperism by providing assistance to those who preferred not to work. This assumption had provoked the reform of private charity before the Civil War, but under the leadership of the Charity Organization Society these ideas were restated as a system of scientific philanthropy. Introduced from England and initially established in Buffalo in 1877, this system had spread to no fewer than twenty-five cities by 1883.[34] In many cities agencies other than the COS were responsible for similar changes in the organization of philanthropy. The Detroit Association of Charities, established in 1879, initiated many of the practices of the COS.[35] In Chicago the novelty of the COS was vigorously contested by an earlier charitable organization whose leader certainly echoed the COS when he argued: "Public outdoor relief tends to separate society into classes. It aggravates a peril which is already great. It accentuates the differences of rich and poor. It makes the only bond between the prosperous and the broken that of the officials who dole relief from a treasury. When those who give to the poor visit them in their homes, there is a personal tie of humanity; but, when the State interferes to do this work, that tie snaps."[36] The promise of economy also attracted support, especially after the spectacular savings made in Buffalo were publicized, but in Cincinnati, for example, the financial commitment to charity was more modest, and the savings were correspondingly smaller.[37]

Since the Civil War private philanthropy had tended to specialize in target groups under the benevolence of remote patrons, whereas the COS revived the aspirations of earlier efforts to limit the abuse of charity by using trained visitors to determine the circumstances of dependency and to provide beneficial influences rather than alms.[38] The aims of the COS were succinctly defined by Josephine Lowell, the leading advocate of scientific philanthropy: "Three things are necessary: (1) Knowledge of facts; (2) adequate relief for the body; and (3) moral oversight for the soul. The

COS should supply the knowledge of the facts. All relief giving is such an unnatural way of remedying the evils from which our fellow creatures suffer that, even when it is necessary, as it too often is, it tends to pervert and injure the character of those who receive it."[39] Critics of the COS have suggested that their image of urban society was based not upon the friendly neighborliness of small towns but rather upon the sacrificial demands of war, "with vice and poverty as the enemy, the virtuous poor as infantry, and the upper-class charity workers as generals or 'natural' leaders, giving strategic and tactical guidance . . . like the military commander."[40] The search for community was ultimately a search for order.[41] Quite apart from these matters of style, efforts to distinguish the poor on the basis of their deviancy were intended to bring the rich and the poor into friendly contact in order to reverse or to modify the effects of the polarization of urban society.

It was felt that the AICP had lost direct touch with the poor and was in danger of becoming a professional relief agency, and the COS attempted "to discharge more effectively the social obligations of neighborliness incident to citizenship even in the complex and unneighborly city."[42] Like the AICP, the COS organized visitation on a district basis, but in some cities the administrative arrangements were highly centralized since there were too few resident volunteers and virtually no local resources in some sections of the slums.[43] Concern was also expressed about the tendency for visitors to become agents of relief rather than of investigation; consequently, efforts were made to "fortify the Visitors against too urgent appeals, and to strengthen their own judgement by the necessity of rehearsing the situation and reconsidering the case with others[;] it was made a rule that they should give no aid, except in extremely pressing circumstances, until they had carefully reported the case and judgement to the General Agent of the Committee."[44] The NYAICP had a different interpretation of their use of paid visitors. In 1893–4 the semicentennial volume of the association reported that the original system of relief had been "revolutionized" in 1879 when a shortage of experienced visitors forced the appointment of trained, salaried visitors rather than untrained volunteers. The transition was also associated with the substitution of women for men as visitors, and the advantages of this change were extolled: "Their patience in making inquiries, their sympathy with the needy and suffering, and their general readiness to follow the instructions given to them, seem to qualify them especially for this work; while their practical acquaintance with household duties, and their habit of trained and quick observation enable them to test the character of the women whom they visit, as well as enter into their difficulties."[45]

In many respects the new charities exaggerated their difference from their antebellum predecessors. They stressed the moral influence of contact and the need to divide the city into districts "corresponding to police precincts. We avoided ward divisions, considering that they were the worst that could be adopted . . . [and believed] the District Office should be near the centre of the District, in order to be easy of access to the poor. . . . [The office was] in the dwelling house of the paid Agent . . . so that the poor might come to a real home, with home surroundings, and thus be, perhaps unconsciously, bettered by contact."[46] In his recollections of the differences between the old and new philanthropy Alexander Johnson acknowledged: "The old societies recognized the evils of duplication almost as clearly as we did, but their remedy was by what seemed the simple way of concentration, the less direct method of association did not occur to them. They had no conception of any social gulf between rich and poor so they not only made no effort to bridge it but many of their methods might have been deliberately intended to widen it. They said to the benevolent wealth let us distribute your gifts for you; relief for the poor is a difficult task and sometimes does harm; we know how to do it wisely and you don't. They declared 'the less the rich have to do with the poor the better.'"[47] Johnson was especially active in Chicago and later in Indiana as a patron and employee of scientific philanthropy. He became president of the National Conference of Charities and Corrections (NCCC) in 1897 and by that time this organization was clearly dominated by the values and methods of the COS.

Scientific philanthropy was also committed to the meticulous collection of statistical information; consequently, the poor were described in greater detail, but the bulk of the data was left without interpretation. These data were gathered both by the bureaus of state labor statistics of several states and by the increasingly coordinated charitable agencies of large cities. As early as 1875 Carroll Wright had organized a pioneering survey of household budgets that revealed a remarkable range of subsistence in relation to income and showed that most families could not survive on the wages of the principal wage earner. Wright initially contemplated the need for a minimum wage but despite several subsequent surveys from which similar conclusions might have been drawn, interpretation of statistical records were avoided in the interests of scientific and political neutrality.[48] To the degree that the findings were publicized, there was a tendency to direct attention to the misguided consumption of the poor.

The charitable agencies were less restrained in this criticism than were the state agencies. Increasingly, philanthropic organizations relied upon a standardized schedule of those causes that were responsible for applications for relief. Although several causes were involved in the majority of cases, it was usually a single most influential cause, in the agent's judgment, that was recorded. Quite apart from the tendency of agents to emphasize the most immediate personal causes of poverty, the direction of the relationship – delinquency leading to poverty – was rarely questioned. Increasingly, the "causes" of poverty were grouped into two categories, generally described as "misconduct" and "misfortune." The former causes were dominated by excessive use of alcohol; the latter were more complex. Misfortune was usually described as the lack of normal (male wage-earner) family support, unemployment, and the disabilities of sickness or age. Children under fourteen represented an especially large proportion of all cases. A tabulation of over 28,000 applicants investigated by several Charity Organization Societies in 1887 revealed that about 20 percent of the cases were unworthy of relief. Approximately a third of the cases were in need of relief, but neither friendly counsel nor restraint would provide a resolution. The remaining applications, accounting for about 40 percent of the cases, needed work rather than relief.[49] In 1892 an examination of over 8,000 cases in Baltimore, New York, and Boston concluded that over 40 percent needed assistance and 35 percent needed employment; the remainder were ineligible and in need of visitation or discipline.[50] In the same year a survey of a sample of 475 families living in the worst slums of Boston concluded that 42 percent of the families were forced to live there because of intemperance but there was an equal proportion of families that lived there because of economic necessity. An additional 11 percent declared that their residential choice was based upon a desire to live amongst their compatriots.[51]

Despite quite striking variations in the precise contribution of these different causes of poverty from city to city, comparisons not only among American cities but also among West European cities, too, were assumed to reveal that approximately a third of the requests for relief were justifiable and that the remainder were caused by unemployment or misconduct. Although "discipline," including incarceration, was proposed to confront misconduct, the solution to unemployment was less clear and certainly presumed to be the responsibility of labor. State agencies increasingly served the needs of so-called defectives; however, most municipal authorities ceased to provide outdoor relief. Officers of state agencies also actively resisted efforts to expand the role of government in the provision of relief or employment, for "relying on the municipality to do those things which may be accomplished through persistent individual effort tends to become chronic, weakens character, and might easily be carried so far as to cause serious social evils."[52]

The new statistical basis of investigations into social conditions and the growing involvement of the states in the custodial care of defectives was based upon a well-developed judgment about the causes of poverty and the predicament of the poor. Although there were several broad indictments of American society that stressed the underlying economic causes of poverty, most philanthropists derived their views of poverty from "the inductive study of concrete masses of dependents, or case counting, as it may be called, [which] grew naturally out of contact with relief work."[53] The increasingly systematic record keeping of the COS provided details of the immediate causes of requests for relief. Elaborate tabulations of over twenty behavioral and environmental factors assumed to be the immediate causes of poverty became a new and more "scientific" basis to judge eligibility for relief.[54] No generalizations were derived from these data, which confronted the impact of general economic conditions on the scale and extent of poverty. Although some removable causes of poverty were common to large numbers of households, the solutions were judged to be primarily within the capacities of the family. In 1886 a participant at the meetings of the NCCC insisted: "The poor, and those in trouble worse than poverty, have not in common any type of physical, intellectual, or moral development, which would warrant an attempt to group them as a class."[55]

The material predicament and social problems of the poor continued to be interpreted as individual moral failings, but efforts to distinguish the diverse sources of dependency often included hereditary defects. Although discussions of eugenic issues were part of the debate on immigration restriction, it was only in the second decade of the twentieth century that they attained a dominant place in legislative arguments. There was, of course, no immediate threat of contamination, since intermarriage was rare during the first generation. Attempts to preserve ancestral cultures were condemned as a threat to a unified national community, but since most observers linked immigrants to the social problems of the city, their ancestral heritages were judged to be cultural if not hereditary disabilities. While fears about the impact of immigrants on American culture were built upon a hereditarian foundation of attitudes toward defectives and delinquents, the persistence of environmentalist perspectives softened and qualified attitudes toward the immigrant poor. Those who aspired to prevent the propagation of defective heredities usually believed that environmental reforms would strengthen future heredities.[56]

An awareness of the environmental conditions of the slums had qualified interpretations of poverty and the moral order of urban society was increasingly based upon the need for a decent home for every family. This fusion of environmentalism and morality was described as the "new" philanthropy. "On the philosophical side" the new approach "studies causes as well as symptoms, and it considers classes as well as individuals. On the practical side it tries to improve conditions, thus changing the environment of the defective. It tries to build up character as well as to relieve or punish, believing that the essential cause of pauperism or crime is usually some defect inside the pauper or criminal as well as bad conditions around him; and it seeks for prevention as well as cure."[57]

Many social problems were assumed to be exacerbated by the environment of the slums, and this sensitivity to living conditions sustained a housing reform movement that set the agenda if not the procedure of progressive reforms. The responses to these conditions were, however, increasingly directed at the presumed moral costs of overcrowding rather than at their economic causes.[58]

The environment defined: indecent homes

The tenement became the symbol of pathological social conditions as well as a source of sickness and death, and long after major reductions in death rates, overcrowding was viewed as a source of a host of social problems. In 1882 it was reported: "It is in the tenement-houses that we must seek for the mass of the poor, and it is in the tenement houses that we find the causes which, combined, are making of the generation now coming up a terror in the present and a promise of future evil beyond man's power to reckon."[59] Lyman Abbot explicitly linked the perils that Josiah Strong had identified with the city to the environment of the slums: "poverty, ignorance, intemperance, and crime, the four great enemies of Republican institutions, thrive in the frightfully over-crowded districts."[60] In the absence of comfort and privacy, the family was unable to serve its moral purpose.[61] Most descriptions of the tenements also emphasized the threat of "boss" politics, the popularity of the saloon, and the immoral street life of the child to the republican form of government. These conditions were thought to be contagious, and consequently the social environment as well as the living conditions of the slum became a focus of concern.[62]

The tenement, and especially its extreme form on Manhattan, was certainly not typical of immigrant housing.[63] Multistory tenements constituted a major portion of the housing stock in New York and to a lesser degree Boston. Elsewhere the tenements were created from single-family houses, and the problems of congestion were created by the removal of a small original dwelling to the rear of a lot to permit the construction of a larger structure on the street frontage. Under these circumstances the extreme conditions of New York were avoided, but room overcrowding and congested lots remained a serious problem in all major cities. In Cincinnati, for example, it was reported that between 1877 and 1882 the proportion of the working class living in single-family homes declined from 23 to 9 percent, and the proportion living in tenements housing three or more families expanded from about one half to 70 percent.[64] To Jane Addams the dominant elements of the Chicago slums were not high tenements but open garbage boxes overflowing with refuse and providing a major source of childhood recreation (Figures 3.3 and 3.4). As an extreme example of the more general problem of overcrowded rooms and cong-

Figure 3.3 Garbage box, First Ward, Chicago, ca. 1900
Source: Chicago Historical Society, Chicago Commons Collection, ICHi 03808.

Figure 3.4 Immigrant slums, near West Side, Chicago, ca. 1900
Source: Report of the Investigating Committee of the City Homes Association,
Chicago, 1901.

ested living conditions, the tenement captured the imagination as the most serious threat to social stability.[65]

The direction of the relationship between pathological behavior and a deficient environment was the subject of a debate that was often phrased quite bluntly as the question whether "the pig made the sty or the sty, the pig."[66] Immigrants in particular were judged to have exacerbated the environmental problems of the city, since it was assumed that they had previously lived under appalling conditions and were therefore attracted "by the congeniality of surroundings to cellars and the crowded rookeries and, not alone as a temporary expedient until they can afford better things, but because also they have just left homes in nowise [*sic*] superior to these."[67] A census of Boston in 1875 reported: "Morbific tendencies of foreigners [are] so marked as to outweigh, and to a great extent to mask the conditions of soil, of exposure, of drainage, or of climate to which we might look for the causes of endemic disease." Furthermore, "The inhabitants of these districts are for the most part poor, ignorant, and thriftless; they live in crowded homes, moreover, being very prolific, they comprise a large proportion of infants and children. Under such conditions, high rates of mortality must prevail among populations of this class, wherever they dwell and however naturally salubrious the locality into which they have transported their constitutional infirmities, and their characteristic modus vivendi."[68]

The assumption that newly arrived immigrants viewed inferior housing in American cities as an improvement over their former homes became an explanation of the failures of housing reform.[69] An Italian precinct of New York was described as "unhealthy and unpleasant, arguing defective drainage, but those of Venice are equally so, and exist for the Prince no less than for the beggar. As for overcrowding, no one who, for example, has spent a summer in Genoa . . . can find food for sensationalism in the manner of life common to Baxter Street."[70] The tenement system was thus judged to be "an upward step in evolution so far as many foreigners are concerned, quite as much as an accidental and unfortunate crowding in a restricted area. Indeed, in the last analysis, many of the worst social conditions we see are really stages of an upward advance."[71] A growing awareness of the immediate living conditions of the poor did, however, qualify some of the more extreme judgments of scientific philanthropy concerning the moral causes of poverty. As early as 1879 Henry Bellows, one of the pioneers of sanitary reform, questioned the value of a scientific charity that failed to improve the housing environment and to confront the immediate wants of the poor.[72] In 1888 the NYAICP felt that there "was no social question, except that of labor itself, of deeper interest to the community at large" than the improvement of the housing of the poor.[73]

Housing reform was inextricably connected to philanthropic anxieties about the damaging effects of any form of charitable relief, and the restraining impact of these values was most apparent among those committed to the construction of model tenements. Justifications of this procedure provided not only the most articulate expressions of the moral benefits of an improved home environment but also an image of the slum that was consistent with their reform objectives. Just as efforts to confront dependency and especially pauperism had a decidedly limited impact on poverty, related measures to improve housing conditions were also only partially effective.[74] Despite their failure to serve as an example of minimum housing standards during the middle decades of the nineteenth century, model tenements remained a highly publicized strategy for housing improvement (Figure 3.5). Their environmentalist qualifications aside, most proponents of housing improvement assumed that poverty was a self-inflicted moral failing and that the poor were disinclined to respond to the opportunities for improved living conditions.

In 1873 a survey of model tenements concluded that "the chief obstacle to suburban homes for the working classes is the disinclination of the laborer, – of the very poor and unintelligent class, – to accept such an opportunity when it is offered. . . . For the present, he waives considerations of neatness, of convenience, or of comparative comfort, and takes the cellar or the attic, esteeming the immediate necessity as of greater consequence than any prospective advantage."[75] Moreover, those who attempted to overcome the trials of their environment were invariably dragged down by those around them; housing improvements were therefore essential to help the poor to resist the contagious influences of those among them who lacked moral stamina.[76] Intended to demonstrate the profitability of well-constructed and efficiently managed tenements, some ventures did indeed provide adequate housing; however, their rents were certainly far beyond the means of those whose need was greatest. They were designed for "model" tenants who would usually be able to make prompt rental payments and whose domestic management was of the most meticulous efficiency. The underlying assumptions of these ventures were similar to those of scientific philanthropy in that every effort was made to ensure that they were not another unnecessary duplication of charity. Their proposals were therefore another key source of more general attitudes on the relationship between the housing environments and social conditions of the slums.

Many ventures specified an upper return of 5 or 6 percent on invested capital, and their experiments demonstrated that adequate housing could be built under these conditions; however, small capitalists, who dominated the housing industry, expected over 15 percent to compensate for the highly speculative nature of the return, and large capitalists had many

Figure 3.5 Model tenements, New York, Improved Dwellings Association, 1879–82

Source: James B. Ford, *Slums and Housing,* vol. 1 (Cambridge, Mass.: Harvard University Press, 1936), 241.

less troublesome investment alternatives to low-rent housing. Consequently, model tenements were actually a form of "investment philanthropy" by which capitalists agreed to accept a fair return on a socially desirable investment.[77] These efforts to improve housing by example received the active support of the scientific charity movement, and like that movement, proponents of model tenements viewed those unable to respond to an improved environment to be morally delinquent or defective. The model tenement movement was widespread, but the undisputed leader was Alfred White of Brooklyn, who complained that "unless the intelligent and wealthy portion of the community do provide homes for the working classes, the want will be continually supplied by the less intelligent class and after the old fashion."[78]

White's commitment to model tenements was based upon his indictment of existing tenements, which were "badly constructed, unventilated, dark and foul ... nurseries of epidemics which spread with certain destructiveness into the fairest homes; they are the hiding places of the local banditti; they are the cradles of the insane who fill the asylums and of the paupers who throng the almshouses; in fact, they produce these noxious and unhappy elements of society as surely as the harvest follows the sowing."[79] In Boston Robert Treat Paine's efforts were motivated by a belief that tenements were a "poisonous influence which the bad boy or girl or adult exercises over the whole population, crowded together into relations of constant contact and intimacy [and which] ... leads necessarily to extravagant expense, encourages rivalry of display between tenants in modes of life, and dress and food, and is fatal to the independence necessary to enable workmen, out of their small earnings, to save and lay up a part." In contrast, small houses "promote the independence of character and life, which lies at the root of thrift, and they offer the safest investment, easiest to understand, acquire, preserve and improve." He concluded that "the great end to aim at is that each family shall live in an independent home, with their children safe from the contagion of a crowded tenement house; and shall own a part of the soil of their country."[80]

Supporters of model tenements rarely had any sensitivity to the predicament of the truly impoverished. Not only "incorrigibles" but also those whose casual or seasonal employment exposed them to abrupt suspensions of income were excluded from the sanctuary of model tenements. One highly publicized attempt to confront this problem was a related system of housing improvement first developed by Octavia Hill in London. The destitute poor required not only improved dwellings but also the advice of visitors. Rehabilitation was combined with instruction in a system that secured "the lease and control of existing dirty and neglected tenements; to have them thoroughly cleansed; to fix moderately remunerative rents, to collect the rents herself and insist upon prompt payment, and by personal influence on tenants to elevate the family step by step to self-respect and the health and virtues which attend it."[81] Despite their limited contribution to the housing problem, model tenements remained an influential reform strategy until well after the turn of the century.

White's leadership passed to Elgin Gould, whose monumental survey of housing for the U.S. commissioner of labor in 1895 rejected European experiments with municipal housing and concluded that the housing problem could be solved on a strictly commercial basis. Like White, he justified his actions by indictments of existing tenements as a menace to family, morality, health, and civic integrity and by a belief in the home as the characteristic unit of society.[82] The home was the cell of a moral society, and a well-constructed, efficiently managed building provided the environment of this social order; appropriately, many of Gould's ventures were in suburban settings. Suburban proprietors, he argued, became "reflective, careful, prudent, wedded to order and rational conservatism and usually turn[ed] a deaf ear to specious isms."[83] A belief in the beneficial effects of rapid transit in opening up cheap suburban land for development was a critical source of confidence in the so-called commercial solution to the housing problem.

These activities, however, not only failed to establish rents that were appropriate for the vast majority of the poor but also made only an infinitesimal contribution to the total urban housing stock. In New York by the end of the century the model tenement movement was responsible for the construction of 2,000 dwelling units that housed no more than 10,000 people, but during the same period, the housing industry built no fewer than 20,000 units that accommodated at least three quarters of a million people.[84] The majority of urban residents depended upon the slow improvement in the regulation of new construction, and these efforts were directed at reductions in the proportion of a lot that could be covered by a building in order to ensure that light and air would reach each room in a tenement.[85] Fortunately, the limited impact of efforts to improve the structure and spacing of dwellings was somewhat offset by the transformation of the sanitary environment of many cities.

Despite the contribution of improved sanitation to the reduction of the mortal toll of high levels of population density, overcrowding became the leading edge of the housing reform movement and the persistence of inadequate sanitary arrangements under low-density conditions was often ignored. The first surge of sanitary reforms during the decade following the Civil War did include regulations on the spacing and interiors of multifamily structures, but these laws were in many respects symbolic of the right rather than the ability of local government to regulate housing. The exercise of these public rights awaited the more ambitious housing reforms of the progressive era, and their limited impact prior to the turn of the century was further diminished by problems of enforcement. The creation of a cadre of professional housing inspectors was slow and expensive, and their actions were always subject to litigation and political interference. Although the health authorities usually required the removal of nuisances, street cleanliness remained a serious problem in the slum districts.

Until the turn of the century most reformers sought the stricter application of existing laws and relied upon model tenements to demonstrate the presumed profitability of adequate housing. Efforts to enforce adequate light, air, and ventilation within dwellings proved to be extremely difficult. Indeed, in 1879 those committed to the reform of charity joined with those dedicated to housing improvement to sponsor a Sermon Sunday in which major New York philanthropists and reformers attempted to provoke public opinion by stressing the moral consequences of overcrowded housing. Their efforts provided further support for model tenements, but more critical was the response of the board of health, which for the first time made serious efforts to enforce the tenement house code of 1867. The issue of enforcement, however, remained a major obstacle to improvements throughout the remainder of the century. Moreover, the regulations were not always relevant to existing conditions. For example, earlier regulations had mandated interior windows in rooms without external windows, but adequate ventilation required adjustments in the arrangement of buildings on long, narrow city lots.[86]

In New York this goal provoked a competition to design a building that would provide adequate light and ventilation within the limits of a lot that measured one hundred feet by twenty-five feet. The award-winning design made use of so-called air shafts to light and ventilate interior rooms and set the design of tenements for the last twenty years of the nineteenth century. Since these air shafts were completely surrounded, they provided little light, and as repositories of refuse they yielded contaminated ventilation (Figure 3.6). The sponsors concluded: "It has been satisfactorily demonstrated that it is impossible to build a tenement house on a city lot of 25 × 100 feet, in such a manner as at the same time to secure for its owners a profitable investment, and for its occupants all the requirements of physical and moral health."[87] The disadvantages of this unit of development had begun with the infilling of the rear yards of the original dwellings, but the restrictions on the construction of tenement blocks on adjacent lots proved to be an exercise in the regulation of congestion (Figure 3.7).

Despite their declarations about the critical importance of housing in their efforts to improve the poor, the NYAICP withdrew from tenement

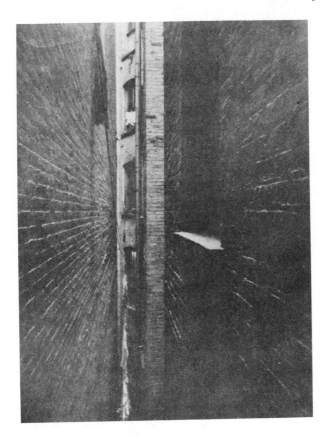

Figure 3.6 Regulated congestion: "Old Law" air shaft, ca. 1900

Source: James B. Ford, *Slums and Housing,* vol. 1 (Cambridge, Mass.: Harvard University Press, 1936), 221.

house inspection in 1886 on the grounds that the public sector was now adequately enforcing minimum standards. Although the regulation of new construction improved, the benefits of legislation were still confined to about one fifth of the tenement population; thus more than 800,000 citizens lived in homes more or less unsanitary and unhealthy. As early as 1887 New York's Board of Health offered an explanation of these limited gains. Those evicted from the worst dwellings were usually the poorest of the poor who had no alternative to substandard housing and the only solution was to compel them "to abandon their unsuccessful effort at self-sustenance and become at once a public charge. But public opinion will scarcely sustain one department of the city government in thus mul-

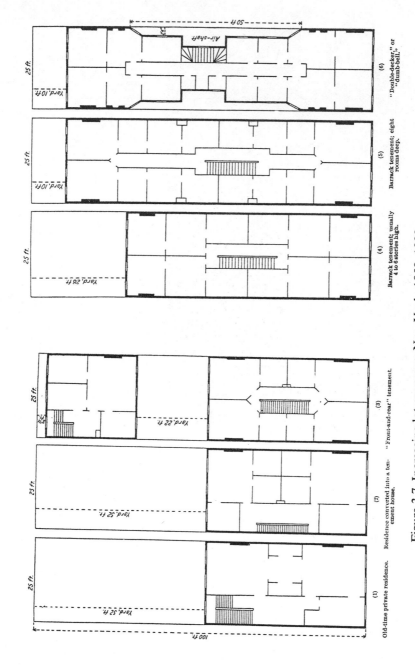

Figure 3.7 Increasing lot coverage: New York, 1850–1900

Source: New York City Health Department, *The Tenement House Problem in New York,* 1877.

tiplying the expenses and responsibilities of another." Despite this sensitivity to the devastating effects of displacement, the same observer concluded with an affirmation of the prevailing moral interpretation of poverty, for "so long as intemperance, vice, unthrift, sickness and death remain with us, so long will it be impossible to completely eradicate the worst of the evils pertaining to the tenement house system."[88]

Toward the turn of the century demands for improved inspection and enforcement of existing regulations became the basis of a major and eventually successful effort to regulate tenement house construction according to more desirable minimum standards. Reformers most directly committed to housing reform publicized the material predicament of the poor in a style that was capable of arousing public sympathy. Although the poor were viewed as a remote and threatening mass, this image was a background that was tempered by a more sympathetic foreground of the poor in the setting of their overcrowded living conditions. The magnification of this foreground proved the most effective means to provoke and mobilize housing reform and related efforts to improve the urban environment. This sharpened image of the slums was provided by journalistic exposés dramatically illustrated by engravings and later photographs. They presented the slums as indecent homes, and large-scale illustrations of families and especially of children in congested alleys or overcrowded rooms aroused public interest in the moral consequences of the environmental disabilities of the slums.

Jacob Riis, who pioneered the use of photography in his efforts to reach the conscience of his readers, was the most influential practitioner of this style of advocacy.[89] Other observers made similar use of this visual magnification of the predicament of the destitute, and for two decades this form of communication was critical to the reform agenda. Before Riis offered his photographic essay, the medium had been used to celebrate the coming of age of the American city. Photography had dramatized the transformation of the wilderness into booming cities and of frontier cities into centers of civilization in the form of monumental public buildings and opulent residences. The city was projected as an image that was more awesome, more orderly, and more civilized than in reality.[90] In contrast, Riis explored the sights of the underside of the city, and he also manipulated his frames to emphasize the negative aspects of slum life. The effects of flash photography on the faces and settings of his subjects exaggerated the sense of helplessness he so evocatively captured. The problems of the slums received wide publicity, and the photographic realism of Jacob Riis did much arouse public consciousness (Figure 3.8). Overall, Riis completed the Victorian image of the slum and through the creative use of photography introduced a profound sense of social realism into discussions of housing, poverty, and social problems.

Figure 3.8 Shanties in a rear court: New York, ca. 1900
Source: Jacob Riis, Museum of the City of New York.

Although he was troubled by the antiseptic methods of the COS, Riis shared many of the assumptions of the scientific charity movement about the restoration of an idealized community. The city was still viewed as a unified moral community into which the residents of the slums had to be integrated, and in the formal education and organized leisure of children he hoped to reunify urban society. His efforts were a "bridge" founded upon justice and built of human hearts.[91] Like Brace, he was aware of the survival instincts as well as the demoralization of the poor and placed great emphasis on efforts to reach the children of the slums before they were tragically damaged by its influences. He described the slums as "centers of disease, poverty, vice and crime, where it is a marvel not that children grow up to be thieves, drunkards and prostitutes, but that so many should ever grow up to be decent and self-respecting. . . . [That virtue] should blossom in such an atmosphere is one of the unfathomable mysteries of life."[92]

His environmentalism was rooted in a deep belief in a community grounded in republican moralism. He warned Philadelphians to look beyond their apparently favorable housing conditions and to examine their "pauperized citizenship," which made possible the social divisions of their community and their indifference to boss politics. He concluded that "the peril of the home is not the only one that besets our Republic. But I still believe that the home is the mainstay; that it proves the home to be beset with perils not in the city only."[93] Occasionally Riis fused his environmentalism with hereditarian ideas, for the slum, he argued, "makes its own heredity. The sum of the bad environment of to-day becomes the heredity of to-morrow, becomes the citizenship of to-morrow. The lowered vitality, the poor workmanship, the inefficiency, the loss of hope – they all enter in and make an endless chain upon which the curse of the slum is handed down through the generations."[94] Riis recognized the social patterns of immigrant communities, but he viewed them as a clannishness that delayed assimilation. His sympathetic sentiments were grounded in a concept of assimilation to a community, which had long since passed away. His vision of a unified moral community was an ideal rooted in his sentimental recollections of his own Danish childhood rather than a coherent description of the realities of the American city.

These ideals did broaden the scope of housing reform efforts to include neighborhood facilities. The provision of bath houses and parks was an attempt to provide collectively what could not be provided individually. The establishment of physical facilities was often accompanied by programs to organize the recreational life of the children of the poor and to use local public schools as a focus of neighborhood life.[95] Schools, playgrounds, and clubs were indispensable to the self-advancement of the poor, but these institutions were not really indigenous to the slum, for they were intended to serve as a bridge between the slums and the remainder of urban society. Other movements attacked the "sweatshops," which were a threat not only to the health of the residents but also to the consumer at large. At the same time, moral crusades were mounted to eliminate the saloon and the brothel, which were associated with the slums. Riis was also never quite clear on the relationship between poverty and the slums; in 1899 he wrote: "The poor we shall have always with us, but the slum we need not have. These two do not rightfully belong together. Their present partnership is at once poverty's

Figure 3.9 Block model of maximum lot coverage: the Tenement House Exhibition, New York, 1900

Source: Robert W. DeForest and Lawrence Veiller, eds., *The Tenement House Problem,* vol. 1 (New York: Macmillan, 1903), 10.

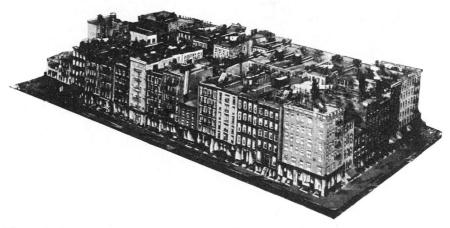

Figure 3.10 Block model of actual lot coverage: the Tenement House Exhibition, New York, 1900

Source: Robert W. DeForest and Lawrence Veiller, eds., *The Tenement House Problem,* vol. 1 (New York: Macmillan, 1903), 112.

worst hardship and our worst fault."[96] His ideas were built on the visual and experiential image of the slum environment, and like the model tenement movement, this vision aroused sympathy for the poor but obscured the critical issue of poverty itself.

The transformation of the publicity of slum conditions into a legislative program of housing reform required the skills of Lawrence Veiller. In 1885 and again in 1894 the State of New York conducted major investigations of housing conditions, but despite recommendations for the stricter enforcement of more demanding regulations and advocacy of the moral benefits of environmental improvements, the legislative consequences were extremely modest.[97] Veiller's command of the technical details of tenement construction and of the legislative process resulted in the establishment of an effective tenement house department within the government of New York City. The amalgamation of the boroughs of New York City provided an opportunity to prepare a new tenement house code. Veiller's response to initial failure was to organize an exhibit that extended the impact of well-established visual images by means of block diagrams and maps. The most celebrated item in the exhibit was a model of a block of tenements that revealed the magnitude of overcrowding and the inadequacies of air shafts (Figures 3.9 and 3.10). Within a block measuring 200 feet by 400 feet there were thirty-nine tenements with a combined total of 605 dwelling units, housing 2,781 people, with no baths and only 264 water closets. The relationship between this environment and claims for relief, sickness, and death were revealed by dot maps and together with carefully chosen photographs provided a synthesis of slum conditions (Figures 3.11 and 3.12).[98] Veiller's exhibit was a landmark in the history of housing reform, and along with his colleague Robert W. DeForest, he expanded his efforts to include other major cities and provided a voluminous survey of the national scale of the housing problem.[99]

This environmental approach to the slums was paralleled by British and German efforts to confront their own slums, and although many American reformers shared the European commitment to the expansion of municipal services and regulation, they remained skeptical of proposals to provide public or subsidized housing.[100] Both the organization of municipal government in the United States and an underlying confidence in the unique opportunities for self-advancement within American society greatly restrained proposals to adopt more ambitious levels of public intervention. Although Veiller's approach to housing reform was closer to that of progressive reformers than to that of Riis, he was also firmly committed to the moral assumptions of the charity movement for which he initially worked. The specific requirements of tenement house reform involved more than an insistence on adequate light, air, and sanitation.

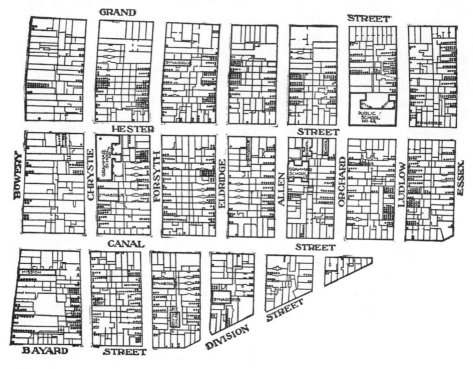

Figure 3.11 Poverty map: the Tenement House Exhibition, New York, 1900
Source: Robert W. DeForest and Lawrence Veiller, eds., *The Tenement House Problem,* vol. 1 (New York: Macmillan, 1903), 114.

Regulations that specified access to bedrooms and toilets were also designed to establish extremely high standards of personal and family privacy, and justifications of inspection were in part linked to efforts to eliminate prostitution. In fact, although prostitution was associated with the slums in general, this activity was highly concentrated in specific slum areas and was certainly not widespread throughout the slums. To Veiller, a small single-family house with a small amount of land was the key to improvements in domestic life:

Under no other method can we expect American institutions to be maintained. It is useless to expect a conservative point of view in the workingman, if his home is but three or four rooms in some huge building in which dwell from twenty to thirty other families, and this home is his only from month to month. Where a man has a home of his own he has every incentive to be economical and thrifty,

Figure 3.12 An old image in a new medium: typical court, New York, 1900

Source: Robert W. DeForest and Lawrence Veiller, eds., *The Tenement House Problem,* vol. 1 (New York, Macmillan, 1903), 16.

to take part in the duties of citizenship, to be a real sharer in government. Democracy was not predicated on a country made up of tenement dwellers, nor can it so survive.[101]

Because of their deep anxieties about the damaging effects of overcrowded dwellings and the institutional deficiencies of the slums, reformers proposed to increase substantially the levels of government intervention in the housing industry. Veiller's insistence on the enforcement of minimum standards of tenement housing provoked confrontations with the speculative building industry and gained him an early reputation as a radical reformer. He was also extremely critical of the model tenement movement, but his insensitivity to the economic implications of housing reform eventually estranged him from later efforts to confront the relationship between poverty and housing.[102] In 1910 his main complaint concerned the inadequate appropriations provided to housing departments, which reduced their capacity to enforce newly established minimum standards.[103] He dismissed as "fallacies" many reasonable reservations about the impact of housing reform on the poor and continued to recommend suburban solutions. Despite the heightened sensitivity to the housing environment and a growing awareness of the need for the enhancement and administrative enforcement of housing regulations, most policies were rooted in the values and policies that had traditionally confronted the problems of poverty. Many housing reformers had actively resisted efforts to expand the role of government in the provision of relief, largely because they underestimated the relationship between low and uncertain wages and inferior living conditions. Veiller's patron and collaborator, Robert W. DeForest, personified this fusion of housing reform and philanthropic moralism when he declared: "Public outdoor relief makes for class separation and enmity of classes. Private charity makes for the brotherhood of man."[104]

While the dominant philanthropic reaction to the poor and their environs was insensitive to the critical relationship between income and rent, more radical indictments connected social unrest and disenchantment to the changing conditions of employment. Henry George complained bitterly about the myopic focus of the highly publicized 1894 tenement house investigation of New York chaired by Richard Gilder, editor of a leading journal of reform thought. Gilder believed that "even the dullest and lowest intelligence will in time respond to an ameliorated environment."[105] His paternalism offended George, who complained that the poor were treated as a "different species from the rich, who are to be inspected and regulated and instructed and kindly helped by their betters."[106] The increased costs of minimum standards resulted in higher rents, and in the absence of corresponding adjustments of wages, families were forced to accept lodgers or double up in single dwellings.[107] The commissioner of labor reported in 1895 that "the percentage of earnings of heads of tenant-families which is absorbed in payment of rent in all large cities is far too high. It is no wonder that overcrowding within the dwelling as well as overcrowding on space becomes an almost universal practice."[108] There were no provisions to supply alternative housing for those displaced by slum clearance. Both Jacob Riis and Jane Addams experienced at first hand the pain of displacement when they were involved in the demolition of tenement blocks that were beyond rehabilitation in order to create small parks and playgrounds.[109] Riis campaigned for the creation of a park in the midst of the slums of Mulberry Street; the park was a remarkable achievement but won at the cost of many painful displacements (Figures 3.13 and 3.14).

A contingent environment

As it had been before the Civil War, New York was the leading focus of anxieties about overcrowded tenements, and efforts to regulate multistory construction there influenced the national debate in two ways. Firstly, cities with only limited numbers of multistory structures failed to identify the nature of their own deficient urban environments, and secondly, the moral consequences of overcrowded rooms were emphasized at the expense of the broader issues of poverty and deprivation. Investigations of living conditions in the slums revealed that crude measures of congestion were often unreliable indicators of the most damaging environmental conditions. Room overcrowding and lot congestion were especially severe in New York, but precisely because so much attention was placed on measures of density in judgments of housing conditions, cities with a predominance of single-family homes often neglected to provide adequate sanitary facilities. Consequently, inadequate sanitation and alley housing devoid of utilities or paved access constituted the preeminent environmental deficiency of the slums outside of New York and perhaps Boston. In spite of the limited impact of housing reform, however, the establishment of public health authorities with some degree of control over the sanitary environment did result in decisive reductions in mortality rates. These sanitary advances were decidedly uneven between regions, between cities, and between neighborhoods, but their effects on living conditions were impressive. Running water within buildings replaced wells and hydrants, integrated sewers permitted the abandonment of privies, and noxious industries were relocated away from residential quarters.

The relationship between filth and disease was established in the 1850s, but it was another generation before accumulations of waste were identified as the medium by which living organisms spread disease.[110] Until the discovery of the role of germs in the transmission of disease, epidemiology was dependent upon empirical associations that provided general rather than specific policies to address the impact of the environment on public health.[111] By 1890 public health was increasingly based upon bacteriological laboratories and specialized branches of civil engineering. The growing professional prestige of civil engineering facilitated the establishment of administrative procedures for inspection that proved to

Figure 3.13 Mulberry Bend, before demolition
Source: Jacob Riis, Museum of the City of New York.

Figure 3.14 Mulberry Bend Park, after demolition
Source: Jacob Riis, Museum of the City of New York.

be less controversial than efforts to regulate housing construction.[112] Sanitary provisioning became a specialized element in civil engineering and lost its former connection with comprehensive environmental planning.[113]

On the basis of the data gathered for the 1890 Census, Billings concluded that site characteristics and proximity to noxious activities inflated mortality to a greater degree than did overcrowding and recommended a greater emphasis on street cleanliness and sanitary engineering.[114] The report on slums by the commissioner of labor also revealed the complex relationships between overcrowding, sanitation, and public health within and amongst the four cities under scrutiny. Whereas over half the slum residents of New York had access to water closets, Philadelphia, long celebrated for its single-family row houses, had a system of open drains. Less than a third of Philadelphia's slums had access to water closets, and in Chicago the fraction was barely a quarter. Investigators concluded nearly unanimously in the report that the general level of public health was somewhat better than anticipated. Some of the highest mortality rates were associated with poor sanitation rather than with the highest levels of overcrowding.[115]

These relationships between the slum environment and mortality were also influenced by the ethnic ancestry of the resident groups, since the mortal toll of congested living conditions was much greater on Italian than on Russian Jewish immigrants, although the highest age-standardized death rates for the period 1884–90 occurred among those of Irish birth and parentage.[116] In New York some of the lowest death rates were recorded in wards with the highest levels of overcrowding. These wards were predominantly occupied by Russian Jews whose long experience of urban life had apparently prepared them for the rigors of the American city. Many Russian Jews had in fact migrated from relatively small shtetls, but dietary practices and other customs were clearly influential in their adaptation to the congested world of the American city. In contrast, high death rates amongst Italians were linked to the inadequacies of their preferred diet and their vulnerability to respiratory diseases.[117] Similar conclusions were drawn in Chicago, where the residents of three wards most closely identified with the slums exhibited some startling contrasts in their vital statistics. These contrasts were more closely related to the ethnic ancestry of their residents than to any major environmental differences. Newly arrived Jewish immigrants were afflicted with substantially lower death rates than were the Irish or Italians in neighboring slums.[118]

There was also a growing body of evidence that stressed the ability of the immigrant poor to cope with their adverse environment. The neglected and filthy external conditions of overcrowded housing were not necessarily good indicators of interior cleanliness. Apartment interiors were often described as clean and well organized. The first of the two major state investigations of housing conditions in New York concluded that in 1885 "the condition of the tenants is in advance of the conditions of the houses they occupy."[119]

A survey of Boston's tenements completed in 1892 concluded that even in the so-called concentrated district negative judgments were not to be extended to the inhabitants in general, for "while here may be found instances of poverty, unthrift, uncleanliness and vice such as are at present inseparable from the crowded parts of every large city, nevertheless, by far the majority of the dwellers here are industrious and law-abiding. Many of them do the rough work of the world, and, for the most part, do it well, according to their light. They are, in many cases, slaves of circumstances. In characterizing the conditions under which the inhabitants are living in this or any other district we by no means intend, either directly or indirectly, to characterize the population." This survey also gave an estimate of the relative contribution of economic and moral influences on the necessity of residence in the worst slums and concluded that only a minority of their residents could be described as morally delinquent. Overall the report concluded that "extreme slum conditions have not yet blighted any considerable territory here," and while crowding existed in certain districts, it was not on the scale reported in East London by Charles Booth. Overall, less than 12 percent of the families endured poor or bad outside sanitary conditions and a lack of interior cleanliness, and less than 8 percent experienced poor or bad conditions of ventilation, light, and air. A "concentrated district" was defined within which conditions were judged to be worse than in the city as a whole, but even there less than a quarter of the population endured poor or bad sanitary conditions.[120]

About the same time the U.S. Commission of Labor examined slum conditions in New York, Philadelphia, Chicago, and Baltimore and came to similar conclusions. The report prefaced its findings with the widely accepted dictionary definition of the slums. They were described as "dirty back streets – inhabited by a squalid and criminal population; they are low and dangerous neighborhoods," but the tabular record did not provide a convincing statistical demonstration of this definition. The report attempted to avoid "inquiries looking to causes why people are found in the slum districts of cities, what brought them there, the experience which leads to such a residence" as being "too vague for the application of the statistical method."[121] The data did confirm common assumptions about the unbalanced sex ratios of the foreign born, their overrepresentation in overcrowded housing and in criminal behavior, and the high density of saloons in the slums, but the magnitudes were far from impressive.

Efforts to maintain habitable quarters in the "vilest rookeries" were not uncommon; it was reported that "nobody can visit the tenement dwellers without being struck as much by their hopeful capabilities as by the degrading nature of their usual surroundings, a degradation for which the occupants are often not to blame."[122] One of the most positive descriptions of the social life of the immigrant poor was William Elsing's description of life in a New York tenement in an anthology devoted to the urban poor. He contested the common assumption that conditions were uniformly bad and argued that they provided a better living standard than many rural districts. He stressed efforts to maintain clean quarters despite the congested living arrangements and emphasized that many residents overcame their discomfort and moved to improved housing.[123] Another positive interpretation of slum life argued that one district had "developed a life of its own that is far from being the dull, inhuman thing that popular opinion assigns to a tenement-house district; and this life resembles no one thing so much as the life of the typical New England village." Although the analogy was somewhat exaggerated, the writer attempted to capture the "village"-like society of the slum, based on "custom rather than ethics," and found that slum dwellers' "many splendid human qualities" ought not to be exchanged for "middle class respectability."[124]

Other observers attempted to qualify the negative associations of specific immigrant groups. As early as 1879 the NYAICP reported that although the concentration of Italians on Jersey Street at first sight looked like a "pestilential breeding, law-breaking colony . . . a more intimate acquaintance with it . . . confirmed the first but not the second impression; no more peaceable, thrifty, orderly neighbors could be found than these Italians."[125] Ten years later they were described as "generally peaceable, but, perhaps because of the lawlessness that has prevailed in Italy until recently, nearly all of them carry arms habitually. . . . They do not Americanize easily or quickly, and the immigrant himself is sure to die an Italian whether he returns home or not. His children, however, make bright scholars . . . and grow up with American habits."[126] Descriptions of the Italian populations of Boston and Chicago also expressed similar qualifications of the prevailing tendency to associate Italians and crime.[127]

The "filthy quarters" of Russian and Polish Jewish immigrants were often attributed to their negligent habits. This issue was especially prominent in efforts to regulate the "sweatshop" production of clothing. Clothing manufactured under unhealthy conditions was judged to be a source of contagious diseases. Testimony presented to the Congressional Investigation of the Sweating System in 1893 argued that "the immigration of the Jews has made it worse, in that they are a dirtier class of people, and their tenement houses are dirtier," but the reactions of the staff field investigations were quite different in that "the streets were, on the whole not in bad order; the tenements, half of them at least, filthy to a nauseating extent, though in almost every case the apartments actually occupied

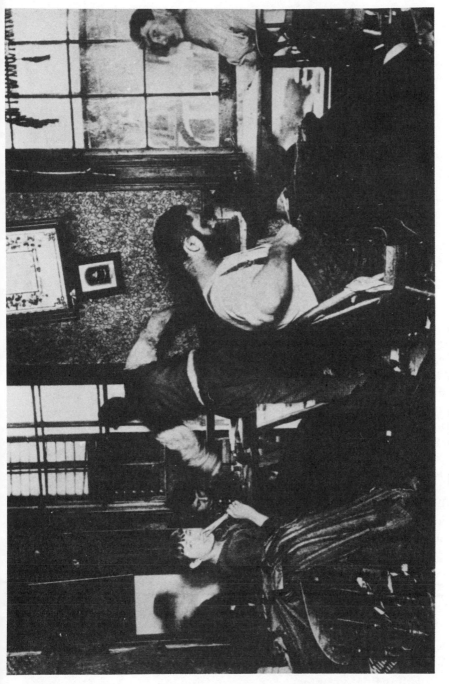

Figure 3.15 Sweatshop interior, New York, ca. 1900
Source: Jacob Riis, Museum of the City of New York.

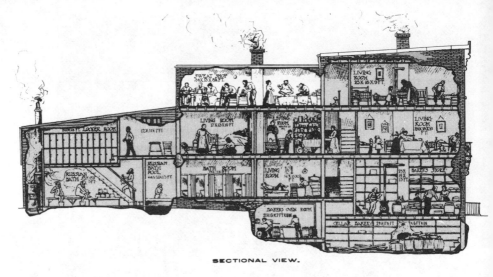

Figure 3.16 Cross-section of a sweatshop, Baltimore, ca. 1900
Source: Bureau of Industrial Statistics of Maryland, *Twelfth Annual Report*
(1903), 69.

by the family were in better condition than the halls and public parts of
the buildings" (Figures 3.15 and 3.16).[128] Other observers highlighted the
positive elements of the Jewish quarters and especially the low levels of
crime and pauperism and the population's responsiveness to public education.[129] The concentrations of Russian Jews were increasingly referred
to as the "ghetto." The term often implied a slum district that happened
to be occupied by Jews rather than by some other immigrant group, but
there was a growing awareness of the indigenous institutions and family
stability of the ghetto, too.[130] In the context of an indictment of slum conditions of Chicago special mention was made of the helpful social institutions of the ghetto, where "it is almost impossible to maintain the old
family life in the environment of the factory system, dependent as it is
on the surrender of the individual to the division of labor, with its long
hours and employment of women. The astonishing fact is the preservation of so much tradition of family in the face of modern social
disintegration."[131]

The submerged residuum

Although there was a growing awareness of the ways in which the poor
coped with their environment, a preoccupation with the size and condi-

tion of the lowest stratum of urban society reinforced the prevailing negative interpretation of the slums. This stratum was described as a residuum that might be beyond the reach of reform. Most housing reformers
believed that there was a stratum of the poor that would not respond to
improved housing, and carefully supervised municipal lodging houses
were recommended for this moral residuum. This residuum presumably
lived in the worst slums, and estimates of the extent of this lowest quality
of accommodation attracted more interest than did the generally low
quality of tenement housing stock. In 1884 the investigation of New
York's tenements suggested that an earlier estimate that 15 percent of the
city's tenements were in a bad or very bad condition was too low and that
the proportion was closer to one third. About a decade later, the second
investigation complained that the Board of Health had recorded only a
quarter of those tenements its investigators believed to be in need of further investigation for code violations. The absolute number was approximately the same as it had been ten years earlier, but the percentage had
diminished in part because a more restricted definition of the slums had
been used.[132]

Charles Booth's monumental survey of London's poor set the agenda
for a more precise definition of this issue.[133] He divided London's population into several strata and then determined that the lowest four represented different levels and kinds of poverty. Together, these four strata
accounted for one third of London's population, and many were impoverished by circumstances beyond their control. Booth had not anticipated
his own findings, for his investigation was prompted by his own assumption that earlier estimates had been too high. There was general agreement about the distinctions of the extremely wealthy and the remainder
of urban society, but the vast majority of the remainder were now divided
into four or five strata on the basis of their level of subsistence. The lowest stratum or residuum was unlikely to be responsive to conventional
social policies.

Israel Zeisloft, like Booth, attempted to place the extremely poor in the
broader context of a stratified urban society. He classified New York's
population into seven strata, stressing that between the two most affluent
groups, which together accounted for only 10,000 families, and the
remaining 1.56 million households, there was a wide chasm. In short, he
retained the sense of social polarization, but precisely because the affluent
minority was so small he examined the distinctions amongst the less
affluent majority. He described his third and fourth categories as
the "prosperous" and "comfortable" middle class, respectively. His fifth
group was "too well off to be classed with the poor [and] . . . miserable
knowing neither luxury nor contentment." The two lowest strata, which
together accounted for one million households, were those who were able

to subsist but had "no aspirations beyond their means" and the "submerged poor," who were mainly foreigners or the children of foreigners. Despite its immense size, this combined lowest stratum was thought to be smaller than it had formerly been, but "since they do not live in the orderly way required of the tenants" of improved tenements, he was skeptical of further reductions.[134]

Although reform had initially been provoked by fears of social polarization, the main focus of concern was with the lowest, most impoverished stratum of urban society, described as a residuum. On the one hand, poverty afflicted an alarming proportion of the urban population, but the dimensions of the problem were redefined by an emphasis on the unreformable residuum. An influential review of American philanthropy described pauperism as "the irremediable residuum of defective character and of social errors; and poverty, [as] the remediable 'disease of destitution' which might incapacitate great numbers of the population."[135] This residuum was identified with the worst slums, often described as a "social abyss" that threatened the destruction of American civilization.[136] This metaphorical abyss was bounded by slopes that were scaled only with extreme difficulty and down which many of the more respectable poor might slip. Although "no sharp line could be drawn between the pauper and the self-respecting poor, . . . [there] stretched between them a vaguely sinister region to which the socialist gave the name 'The Abyss' where charitable societies, as on a field of battle, struggled to rescue the miserable from crossing the poverty line into disgrace and social imprisonment."[137]

Although New York was no more typical of American society than was London of British, by the turn of the century the Lower East Side, like the East End of London, was a symbol of the most extensive and extreme expression of slum conditions. In 1899 the Lower East Side of New York was judged to be "a picture of human misery unparalleled in the world." But that indictment was followed by a curiously hopeful commentary: "New York is grappling bravely with this problem, so suddenly thrust upon it by the enforced exodus from their native lands of the hordes of non-self-supporting and incapable humanity. . . . With the restrictions now placed on immigration, together with the close attention paid to the education of the young, another generation or two may hope to see the East Side undergo a transformation to Americanism only less wonderful than the change wrought on the island itself in the last century."[138] Although American philanthropists were becoming increasingly sensitive to European, and especially to English, responses to poverty, they believed that American society had avoided the class conflicts of the Old World. Despite the tone of anxiety in most social commentaries, American conditions continued to be contrasted favorably with those of England. A seminal review of philanthropy concluded: "The English [charitable] societies have accepted the presence of an hereditary poor class, a class that is static. In America there is too much hope and progressiveness in the atmosphere even of the poor, for such a static condition to endure. The American poor are a dynamic group, nor is the immigrant often found in the pauper class. The universal testimony is that they rise in the social and economic scale with great rapidity."[139]

This confidence was, however, severely tested by the rapid growth of American cities, which presented an environment perilously close to those associated with the worst conditions in Europe while immigration was importing a European labor force. A sensitive observer commented that "problems of destitution, unemployment, and family disintegration . . . have kept pace with the movement of population toward cities and manufacturing centers, and . . . were in part the result of an undistributed foreign immigration. With the beginning of the twentieth century, America has realized the possibility in these congested localities of conditions as desperate as those with which some parts of Europe have long been familiar."[140] Throughout the last quarter of the nineteenth century, there was a growing awareness of the social polarization of urban society, but the dominant responses continued to be guided by the moral precepts of scientific philanthropy.

Most commentators believed that social problems were confined to newly arrived immigrants, and as the focus of both the immigrant poor and the negligent rich, the city was identified as the cause rather than the consequence of social tensions. In Chicago, for example, it was found that the poor "are usually of foreign nationality, and often ignorant and squalid, with little knowledge of, or interest in their civil rights. It is upon this semi-circle of stagnant real estate that the greatest congestion of population is found, and the highest ratio of depraved poverty."[141] William Tolman, a member of the NYAICP and the founder of the American Museum of Safety Devices and Industrial Hygiene, expressed similar anxieties. He complained: "At the present time the social instinct, tending toward congestion in urban centers, the influx of foreign elements, the non-assimilation or resistance of Americanizing influences, new industrial conditions, the failure or indifference of the church to its social mission, make the modern city a storm center."[142] For some observers the labor question had not only been reformulated as the urban question but also as a question of race: "The American City is a conglomerate of all races, nations, tongues, faiths, customs and political ideas; and by this fact, and that of an easily attainable citizenship, it is the menace of the American Church and State. To penetrate this alien mass by an evangelical religion is as difficult as it is imperative. The question of the city has become the question of the race. How to reach the heart of the city and to change its life is, indeed, the question of questions."[143]

As in European cities, this large impoverished population was frequently compared to those in remote uncivilized parts of the world. Visiting the newly established settlement of Graham Taylor in Chicago, Johnson seemed to be questioning his own confidence in the efficacy of personal contacts when he expressed apprehension at the social distance between rich and poor, for he declared that "missionaries in the heart of Africa could hardly present a greater contrast with their surroundings than did these cultured refined people in such a neighborhood."[144] The establishment of settlement houses within the slums was an effort to learn from the poor as well as to assist them, and both the pioneering workers and their supporters stressed the value of neighborly relations:

What the monastery of St. Bernard was to the Cistercians, what the original brotherhood of St. Francis was to the Franciscan order, so Hull House will be to the brotherhoods and sisterhoods of helpers and neighbors, who in increasing numbers will take up their residence in the midst of the crowded and desolate quarters of our overcrowded cities. Only by this means can we hope to reconstruct the human family, and restore something approaching to a microcosm of a healthy organization in every precinct of the city. Mere propinquity counts for a great deal in human affairs.[145]

These efforts to link poverty to an increasingly polarized society necessarily implied that the poor were unavoidably degraded by the slum environment.

During the eighties the protests of those most affected by changes in the economy offered more radical diagnoses of social problems, but the depressed economic conditions of the midnineties, weakened their influence. Their diminished impact has also been attributed to the lack of a "single set of values, [a] commonly accepted vision of the redemption of the republic, [which might have] guided the many streams of working-class struggle into a single-minded flood of protest."[146] Depressed economic conditions in the nineties again raised the specter of downward mobility, but economically grounded indictments of American society were overshadowed by moral resentments about the "corruption" of politics and business. The moral problem of the city was society at large rather than the delinquency of the poor. The social gospel movement, along with more secular utopian reactions to social problems, linked the poor and their environment to the "corruption" of society at large and especially its political and business leaders.[147] In his indictment of Chicago in 1893 William Stead argued that the "disreputable" classes were not the unemployed but the rich who constituted the "plague spot in Chicago which eats far more deeply into the vitals of the community than fifty sporting houses or one thousand saloons."[148] The contrast of the ostentatious White City of the Chicago exposition of the summer of 1893 and the Black City of the unemployed of the succeeding winter symbolized the growing polarization of urban society.

Utopian visions of social justice also explored the paradox of progress and poverty and provided social criticism with both publicity and political influence. Like philanthropic idealism, these broad indictments of American society were also grounded in deep reverence for the the Jeffersonian world of small producers, a harmony of interests, and a general belief in a natural moral order that might be recovered without any fundamental reordering of society.[149] Public and private philanthropy was dedicated to the sustenance of those moral principles of community that would ensure the survival of conditions conducive to self-improvement, but the enlarged scale of both the city and its slums reduced the effectiveness of these efforts. The slums were by now remote from the residential quarters of most friendly visitors, and conceptions of urban neighborhoods as small towns failed to confront the striking heterogeneity of urban populations. Concepts of community presumed natural relationships amongst diverse strata and those of different status, but in the slums most residents were of the same low status. The preference for the pastoral was, however, accompanied by a growing sense that the new world would require not old values but a new social intelligence.

Some elements of the social gospel movement shared the scientific temperament of more secular reformers and believed that social problems should be investigated neutrally, on the assumption that factual knowledge would yield solutions. The new science of Christian sociology combined an awareness of the social roots of poverty and a sensitivity to the complex interdependencies of urban society. The *Andover Review* became the chief organ of this new view, which William Jewett Tucker defined as one that "took account of the individual in his human environment. It viewed him more definitely as a social being, a part of a vast but closely fitting social organization."[150] This pioneer of Christian sociology concluded: "We study pauperism; but we go only a little way before we find that, if we would analyze the poor man's poverty, we must stop and analyze the rich man's wealth."[151] His disciple Graham Taylor aimed to determine these relationships by means of a census including "all classes and conditions of men from all nationalities. Its work is to investigate the conditions of social and personal life, discover the causes of suffering and the sources of inharmonious relations. When Christian sociology has done all this, it will be more possible to adjust differences, and harmonize the varying elements by applying the principles of Christianity."[152]

The yield of scientific investigations of social problems had necessitated the subdivision of their findings into distinct fields of research and the classification and categorization of facts even within those fields. Despite the taxonomic difficulties of describing the worst slums and associating them with a delinquent stratum, economic considerations were qualified by a preoccupation with the moral costs of overcrowding and the moral delinquency of the residuum. Scientific analysis was an effort both to replace moralism and to inform majoritarian will, but in revealing the complexity of urban society, researchers discovered that policy solutions were neither self-evident nor immediately acceptable to the polity.[153] The subsequent progressive response was dependent upon a more complex view of both the slums and urban society as a whole. During the first decade of the new century, attempts to reform urban society modified or abandoned older images of a unified moral order, and described the city as a highly differentiated, interdependent world that, with appropriate controls, offered hope for a new social order.

A growing emphasis on the complexity rather than causality of social problems differentiated the progressives from the more cataclysmic visions of social change that had prevailed during the final quarter of the nineteenth century.[154] The justifications of public intervention were decisively changed, and the environmental and moral underpinnings of earlier policies were reformulated in a more complex system of interdependencies rather than a single principle of causality. To some observers these new ideas were a necessary prerequisite to further progress in social reform, but to others there were already competing ideas that would have made possible a more ambitious and earlier attack on social problems.[155] The progressive movement was itself diverse in its composition and objectives, but most policies assumed a highly differentiated social order that required artificial means to ensure that these separate elements were efficiently coordinated.

Inhibitions about the proper role of municipal regulation were moderated, and the presumed failures of civic government were attributed to a lack of competence as well as to "corruption." Like the complaints of antebellum elites, those of the late nineteenth century exaggerated the extent of influence of the new and less desirable political leaders and underestimated the continuing impact of established elites.[156] Consequently the restoration of paternalistic leadership to government was less critical than the employment of experts dedicated to the efficiency of urban society. These aims proved to be as troublesome as those of their Victorian predecessors, but they did yield a different image and a more complex response to the slums and the poor than those that had prevailed since the early nineteenth century. By 1900 reformers had elaborated their image of the slum to express the social isolation and environmental degradation of the poor, and especially the immigrant poor. This image provoked not only a sustained effort to improve the housing environment but also more radical proposals to ensure social justice.

4

From slum to ghetto: 1900–1925

By the last decade of the nineteenth century the slums were clearly associated with the inner city, where congested living conditions and social isolation deprived the poor of appropriate opportunities for self-improvement. This conception of the slums had aroused major efforts to improve the urban environment and to reduce the social isolation of the poor, but they were grounded in assumptions about the moral causes of poverty and the possibility of restoring a unified urban community. The limitations of these assumptions had been apparent to some social critics throughout the late nineteenth century, but during the first decade of the twentieth century, many of these assumptions were abandoned as several streams of reform thought converged and proposed policies described as "progressive."[1] While retrospective evaluations of the progressives have stressed their weakly defined objectives and limited achievements, it is generally accepted that most progressives shared a common belief in the need to confront the inadequate and presumably negligent social policies and practices of their Victorian predecessors. Older ideas about a unified urban community were elaborated to accommodate the complexity and interdependency of urban life. They retained an organic view of urban society, but the metaphor was adjusted to capture a highly differentiated cellular structure. These structures were, moreover, the creation of human agencies, and as artificial fabrications they would be responsive to human manipulation. In the hands of professionally trained specialists, this manipulation would result in an efficient organization of a highly urbanized society. Under these circumstances, the city became not a threat to an older world but the basis of a more hopeful and "progressive" view of the future of society.[2]

In several states, the need for public intervention to check social evils had found broad acceptance, and after 1894 the National Municipal League attempted to coordinate efforts to confront corruption in municipal government. The league emphasized the need to replace local politicians, and especially mayors, with men of integrity, believing that urban problems were primarily the result of dishonest government. Within a decade it had become clear that effective administration was also dependent upon professional management based upon careful research. Public intervention ought to be based upon an increased reliance on the technical expertise of specialists who were presumed to possess not only the professional training appropriate to solve specific problems but also the objectivity necessary to be independent managers of the public interest. The degree to which the agencies of regulation were to be independent of the legislative process did, however, remain a matter of debate. On the one hand, centralized agencies were viewed as a threat to local control; on the other, local control was usually more vulnerable to manipulation by corrupt political influences.[3]

To a greater degree than with the old immigration from northwestern Europe, the slums were associated not with the poor but with the immigrant poor. Although newcomers from southern and eastern Europe attracted the greatest attention, blacks, Hispanics, and East Asians were also represented in increasing proportions in the inner sections of American cities. The slums housed minorities whose assimilation into the mainstream of American life was likely to be more difficult than that of earlier immigrants from northwestern Europe. Eventually the term *ghetto* was adopted to describe the segregation of minorities who were directly or indirectly excluded from full participation in American life. This generic meaning of the term *ghetto* was not, however, firmly established during the Progessive era, when immigrant quarters were also frequently described as "colonies." The initial American use of the term *ghetto* was associated with the settlement of East European Jews in northeastern cities towards the turn of the century.[4] Since other recent immigrant groups found themselves in similar situations, the term was later adopted to describe the association of deprivation with religious, ethnic, or racial minorities. The slums were now identified with newly arrived immigrants, primarily from southern and eastern Europe, but also from the American South, and the term *ghetto* was increasingly if not consistently used to describe the segregation of exotic minorities in the crowded sections of the inner city.

This tendency for immigrants to cluster in exclusive national or more frequently provincial groupings was usually at a small scale. In New York, for example, there were well-defined concentrations of Jews and Italians and small clusters of Bohemians, Chinese, and Syrians, but in many areas "it would be difficult, if not impossible, to indicate definite localities inhabited by this or that race, and none would be harder to find than that occupied exclusively by the American working man."[5] Jacob Riis captured the complexity of ethnic residential patterns when he insisted: "A map of the city, colored to designate nationalities, would show more stripes than on the skin of a zebra, and more colors than any rainbow. The city on such a map would fall into two great halves, green for Irish prevailing in the West Side tenements, and blue for Germans on the East Side. But intermingled with these grand colors would be an odd variety of tints that would give the whole the appearance of an extraordinary crazy-quilt."[6] The degree of ethnic homogeneity was often dependent upon the rental decisions of ethnic landlords with holdings in several blocks, and ethnic diversity at the local level was frequently increased as the ethnicity of specific blocks shifted from one dominant group to another.[7]

The changing source areas of foreign immigration had provoked proposals to restrict immigration during the last two decades of the nineteenth century, but despite a continuing campaign, these discriminatory sentiments did not receive executive endorsement until after World War I. Persistent demands for immigration restriction were debated with great frequency, but the agenda of progressive reformers tended to place immigration policies in the broader setting of social reform. The discriminatory implications of immigration restriction offended some progressives, but others viewed the regulation of both the inflow and distribution of foreigners as a means to protect immigrants from exploitation.[8] The established language and institutions of the United States did set a dominantly English tone to prevailing interpretations of American identity, but there was also a growing acceptance of the less emphatic but influential contributions of immigrants from continental Europe. Although it never reached a wide audience, Hapgood's *Spirit of the Ghetto,* completed in 1898 and published in 1902, revealed a sensitivity to a counterculture of great value not only to ghetto residents but to America at large. In its second edition, published in 1909, the book implied that this counterculture already displayed the impact of Americanization.[9] Of greater, if rhetorical, influence was the metaphor of the "melting pot" derived from Israel Zangwill's drama. Like earlier conceptions of America as a fusion of several European immigrant groups, it suggested that the particular contributions of each "ore" would vary, but it never made clear the place of blacks, East Asians, and American Indians in this fusion.

Indeed, many observers remained skeptical of the possibility, let alone the desirability, of assimilation. Many who questioned the direct contributions of the different immigrant "ores" to the fused host society were, however, prepared to acknowledge their indirect impact as they adjusted to their adopted country. There were also some advocates of a plural society within which immigrants might maintain some if not all of their ancestral heritage, although some degree of assimilation appeared unavoidable.[10] Only after draconian efforts to reform urban society appeared to have failed or at least to have reached a point of diminishing returns was it possible for the proponents of restriction to deepen their support. By that time the scientific prestige of eugenics was added to the arsenal of arguments in favor of restriction. For the first two decades of the present century it was certainly assumed that the new immigrants exacerbated the social problems of the slums of the inner city, but initially new interpretations of poverty directed attention from immigrant residents to causes beyond their control. Poverty was still attributed to pathological obstructions to self-advancement, but the slums were now viewed as a serious residual element in a more complex vision of urban society. Initially efforts to improve the housing environment became more sensitive to the relationship between rents and wages and recognized the ability of slum residents to cope with their adverse circumstances. By 1920, however, many reform efforts viewed social problems and the urban environment in relation to an organic conception of the interdependent complexity of urban society, and this perspective eventually obscured some promising insights into the cultural and structural settings of poverty.

The residents defined: low and uncertain incomes

Throughout the nineteenth century the slums had been viewed as places where social isolation and environmental disabilities obstructed and discouraged self-improvement. Generally evaluations of poverty were preoccupied with the eligibility of the poor to receive assistance, and in order to limit the presumably damaging effects of relief on able-bodied workers, much attention was given to the size of a morally delinquent residuum. Once the needs of the sick, the young, and the aged were appropriately met, a residual group of intemperate, criminal, or merely lazy ought to be denied relief, since this assistance would subsidize their immoral life-style and discourage those who had taken the route of self-advancement. Throughout the nineties, the resistance of the charity movement to public relief measures provoked criticism from among its own supporters. For example, Robert Paine, a leading advocate of housing reform, insisted, "The problem of employing the unemployed and of relieving distress and treating pauperism had better be . . . kept absolutely distinct [for] it would be unwise to send the unemployed to various societies . . . which are organized to deal with distress and want and suffering . . . to submit to the ordeal of the usual charity approach."[11]

The settlement house movement was more forceful in its reactions, and during the depression of the midnineties, settlement workers distanced themselves from the charity movements.[12] Stanton Coit, founder of New York's first settlement in 1886, "deplored that the people who started the

COS were tainted with laissez-faire doctrines and extreme individualistic theories. . . . [S]cientific philanthropy will some day learn that charity organization is a distinctive municipal function."[13] To Jane Addams, "no point of contact in our modern experience . . . reveals more clearly the lack of equality which democracy implies" than "the difference between the emotional kindness with which relief is given by one poor neighbor to another poor neighbor, and the guarded care with which relief is given by a charity visitor to a charity recipient. The neighborhood mind is at once confronted not only by a difference of method, but by an absolute clashing of two ethical standards."[14]

The early residents of settlements, like many radical reformers, "were convinced of the crude and vast insufficiency of the old industry whose sanctions had been so deeply wrought into all that was American." Some became committed socialists since "there appeared no possibility of amelioration short of the administration of industry by the state in the interests of all citizens," but the "main settlement contingent, holding long-range hopes and postulates of their own as to a better order of society, saw it as a duty and an opportunity to exercise the passion of patience."[15] This "patience" was based upon their confidence in the direction of reform as the vast majority of charitable organizations subdued their longstanding preoccupation with the damaging effects of relief in favor of a more decisive concern with those causes of poverty that were clearly beyond the immediate control of the poor.[16] From this perspective the poor were now defined as "all those who fail to have the means by which they may become assets to the community"; the definition discarded "the sentimental point of view that would exalt poverty as the safeguard of virtues or the self-exonerating position that makes the poor the dumping ground of undesirable vices and ignorances."[17]

By the turn of the century almost all varieties of reform thought had retreated from moral classifications of the poor into two groups on the basis of their "worthiness" for relief.[18] Investigations of poverty suggested that between 20 and 30 percent of requests for assistance could be attributed to personal culpability and that personal misfortune, especially unemployment, accounted for the remainder. The presumption that poverty was largely a matter of personal limitations was qualified into a more complex conception of the relationship between environment, heredity, and behavior. Amos Warner, the author of the first major work to summarize the findings and objectives of the "new" philanthropy, concluded: "We found that disease produces poverty and now we find that poverty produces disease; that poverty comes from degeneration and incapacity, and now that degeneration and incapacity come from poverty. Yet it is not without benefit that we trace the whole dismal round of this vicious circle, for it well illustrates the interaction of social forces. But in tracing the long circle . . . there have been many contributory forces added from time to time which are distinctly preventable."[19]

In 1899 a committee of the National Conference of Charities and Corrections (NCCC) revised the format of case schedules, dispensing with several minor causes and changing the categories of "misconduct" and "misfortune" to "causes within and outside the family."[20] Inferences about personal culpability drawn from the case records of various Charity Organization Societies were also questioned, since all too frequently they became descriptions of the personal limitations of the applicant for relief. In 1907 Lilian Brandt presented a more severe indictment of the case records and, in particular, questioned the validity of "causes" based upon the opinions of agents who continued to stress the most immediate causes from within the family. "The renowned causes of poverty," she argued, were "largely symptoms and results of poverty, . . . potent, to be sure, to produce more poverty, but not the beginning of it."[21] For some time efforts had been made to specify those causes of poverty, which were often beyond the perspective and immediate knowledge of agents.

In 1906 Charles Frankel analyzed applicants for assistance from the United Hebrew Charities and concluded that sickness was the immediate cause of distress in 66 percent of the cases, bereavement in 14 percent, and insufficient earnings in 18 percent. Accordingly he emphasized that "living, suffering human beings [are] . . . submerged not because they are dissolute, submerged not by reason of any evil acts of their own, but because they live in an industrial environment, where it is a physical impossibility to eke out a decent living and to maintain a decent standard of existence."[22] Frankel summarized his findings in the form of a fourfold classification of the causes of poverty: "ignorance, industrial inefficiency, exploitation of labor and defects in governmental supervision of the welfare of citizens." The State Conferences on Charities and Corrections continued to emphasize "the administrative and financial problems of institutions and activities dealing with the wrecked, the broken, the deficient, and those offending the law; but ever increasingly has there developed a desire to get at causes of poverty and crime, to know the reasons for industrial inefficiency, physical infirmities, lack of character and subnormal mental capacity. We know the amount of the bill we have to pay; we want to know why it is so big and why it rolls up in the face of what we call prosperous times."[23]

This emphasis on social "causes" was also reflected in the broader philanthropic community. In 1907, on its twenty-fifth anniversary, the New York COS concluded that "the result to the community in eliminating and diminishing some of the more important causes of pauperism is of definitely greater value than could have been brought about by the same amount of effort and the same amount of money expended for the relief of individual suffering." The society's commitment was now "to lay emphasis on the field of removing or minimizing the causes of poverty, and to firmly establish and extend these forms of work by organizing them into a department for the permanent improvement of social conditions."[24] These conclusions were based upon surveys that attempted to determine a minimum standard of living, "which cannot be violated without the social unit becoming a social deficit." It was necessary to "fix levels below which the exploitation of workers and consumers would not be tolerated, above which the principles of free competition might safely and advantageously be left free to operate."[25]

Once the parameters of this standard were established for a locality, it would be possible to "know the extent to which labor is exploited; and if exploited, we are led to inquire how the deficiency is made up."[26] Since it was assumed that a careful documentation of the minimum needs of a normal working family would provoke appropriate legislative and corporate responses, several surveys of the conditions of the poor attempted to determine not only the causes of poverty but also the minimum wage necessary to sustain a "normal" standard of living.[27] These surveys were indebted not only to the work of Charles Booth and English investigations of poverty, but also to an older continental European tradition of social research. Specifically, the large-scale surveys of Engel and LePlay's intensive examination of household budgets were the models for a growing number of inquiries into American social conditions. In the United States the Settlement House movement had pioneered this survey approach, but more ambitious statistical investigations were sponsored by the U.S. commissioner of labor and the NCCC.

The ability of some families to save at low levels of income was a source of perplexity, but savings were always a trade-off against some current necessity. The adequacy of wages was strongly influenced by family size. Incomes rarely expanded in proportion to the increased costs of a growing family, and poverty was exacerbated at critical stages in the life cycle. The most vulnerable stage occurred when children were numerous but the eldest were too young to work. Those families with some surplus despite extremely low wages invariably suffered some physical deterioration. Deficits were usually alleviated by the help of relatives, friends, and neighbors. Relief and charity were strategies of last resort, and consequently the data on dependency not only understated the dimensions of poverty but also inferred its causes from an unrepresentative sample. For example, a survey of families of German and Irish parentage and birth living in the tenements of New York's East Side described them as "typical" rather than "the most unfortunate, thriftless type," but they were nevertheless "frequently on the verge of distress, for their wages do not enable them to maintain their physical efficiency. They are often unemployed or work at irregular occupations. . . . Nevertheless, they shun charity. In actual need, they first turn to the kinfolk who are better off or they accept the aid of neighbors."[28]

Moreover, it was also argued that a living income ought to include far more than the expenses permitted "normal" wage earners. Beyond the so-called necessities of life, which maintained physical efficiency, it was imperative that wages should provide a margin for sickness, pleasure, emergencies, and savings.[29] In New York several careful surveys were made to determine the income and expenditure patterns of so-called normal wage earners.[30] It was concluded that an extremely high proportion of their income, if not the entire amount, was consumed in subsistence needs, such as food, rent, heat, and clothing. Barely a quarter of these families had any surplus and an equal proportion faced a chronic debt. In short, "a proper and safe standard of living cannot be maintained on the wages commonly received by the great bulk of our day laborers. . . . [U]nskilled labor, even when steadily employed without missing a day through sickness or weather, does not earn these sums. . . . [U]nskilled labor, not at its worst but at its very best, is underfed and in want of necessaries because its wages are too low to buy them."[31]

These shifts in approaches to poverty were clearly reflected in the title and editorial tone of the leading journal devoted to charitable activities. The *Charities Review* had been founded in 1891 and reflected old attitudes until about 1905, when it merged with a more radical publication to become *Charities and the Commons.* The new title was associated with an increased sensitivity to the social rather than personal causes of poverty, and its editor, Edward Devine, defined the old philanthropy as "the mendicant's alms, the pauper's maintenance, the imposter's largesse, gifts even to a worthy cause wrung from an uneasy conscience"; in contrast there was "the new view which makes of charity a type of anticipatory justice, which deals not only with individuals who suffer but with social conditions that tend to perpetuate crime, pauperism and degeneracy." Moreover, he was confident that "behind every form of degeneracy, dependency, and injustice there is apt to be some entrenched pecuniary interest which it is desirable to discover and expose, and with which it is the duty of society to deal."[32] His radical tone was captured when his definition of the goals of modern philanthropy was quoted as "a determination to seek out and strike effectively at those organized forces of evil, at those particular causes of dependence and intolerable living conditions which are beyond the control of the individuals whom they injure and whom they too often destroy."[33]

Throughout the first decade of the present century efforts to confront the complex causes of poverty increasingly emphasized the critical impact of unemployment. Over one third of a sample of almost 25,000 wage earners were unemployed for at least a month, and over a quarter for at least two months.[34] A survey of the standard of living of the industrial people of America in 1911 stressed the damaging effects of unemployment "even in prosperous times," for a sixth of the sampled families contracted debts and almost a half were unable to save for future emergencies.[35] A major commission viewed unemployment as an indicator of "the efficiency or lack of efficiency of social organization and mutual consideration in an industrial community [which] can be measured by the extent to which it is necessary, during a time of business depression, to maintain able-bodied and willing workers out of charitable funds."[36] Estimates of the size of the "submerged poor," or residuum, who were presumed to be trapped by conditions of their own making, were also revised downwards. Robert Hunter's comprehensive survey of poverty at a national scale concluded that of ten million impoverished people only 40 percent could be described as paupers, but Brandt questioned this proportion and argued that "when exploitation of labor and defective government supervision were eliminated, the irreducible minimum of human misery would not be large enough to constitute a serious problem."[37]

Some authorities attempted to link this residual misery and the contaminating moral degradation of pauperism to a reserve army of underemployed workers whose low wages deflated those with more secure jobs. This supply of temporary labor, partly sustained by relief, dragged down the wages of those in the lowest-paid full-time employment.[38] The semiskilled and underemployed labor force of the sweated and service trades were described "as parasites dragging down their more successful fellow stragglers," but the solution now included the provision of some system of public support.[39] Foreign immigrants were assumed to contribute a large proportion of a reserve army of unskilled labor that exerted a downward pressure on the wages of those in secure employment. In 1901 the U.S. Industrial Commission concluded that the downward pressure on wages in several industries had directly affected the immigrants' standard of living, but wage levels in general, and especially among the native-born labor force, were judged to have increased. The deliberate recruitment of single male labor and their exploitation by the agents of steamship companies and industrial enterprises were viewed as a problem confronted by immigrants rather than by the labor force in general.

In any event, data were obtained that indicated that the bulk of newly arrived immigrants were joining friends and relatives who might have assisted in providing their transoceanic fare. Complaints about the drainage of funds from the United States because of the large number of "birds of passage" who returned to their homelands with the fruits of their American sojourn were also questioned. Many of those who returned later reemigrated, often with their families. In general, the conclusions of these reports on the economic effects of immigration implied that there was a greater need for legislation to protect and assist immigrants upon arrival than to restrict their emigration. Reports of commissions of inquiry into the effects of immigration established in New York and Massachusetts came to similar conclusions, and their key recommendations were clearly in the direction of legislative protection of immigrants from exploitation rather than of restricting immigration.[40]

Although the Dillingham Commission on Immigration, appointed in 1907 and its findings published in 1911, stressed the damaging economic impact of immigration, its evidence was inconclusive and misinterpreted.[41] The commission claimed that the lower standard of living of recent immigrants from southern and eastern Europe allowed employers to reduce wages and to keep the labor force of some occupations in a perpetual level of degradation. The commission concluded that immigration "may not have lowered in a marked degree the American standard of living, [but] it has introduced a lower standard which has become prevalent in the unskilled industry at large."[42] These opinions provoked a debate amongst leading economists, and Isaac Hourwich in particular indicated how the data collected by the commission could be interpreted in a way that revealed that the new immigration had only minor effects on wage levels.[43] In any event, business interests, and especially the National Association of Manufacturers, opposed restriction, and apart from determined resistance to East Asian immigration, the opposition of the labor unions became less strident and less nearly unanimous. Although the size and foreign-born contribution to the so-called reserve army of labor continued to be a matter of debate, some economists insisted that the vast majority rather than a small minority of wage earners lived under conditions of irregular employment and uncertain earnings. Fully one half of the labor force was in the so-called reserve army for at least part of the year. On the basis of COS claims Brandt reported that "contrary to what might be the popular opinion," they were not permanently dependent but rather constantly "on the verge of distress."[44] A leading economist rejected the concept of a reserve army: "If we have an army of the unemployed at all it is a citizen army in which practically all serve, and not a standing army, wholly detached from industry."[45] This structural view of poverty questioned the validity of a moral or economic residuum and especially the degree to which foreign immigration exacerbated the condition of the native wage earner.

During the course of the first decade of the twentieth century, several streams of reform thought converged around the need to confront poverty as a structural economic problem or alternatively the need to establish a minimum level of security as a matter of citizenship. In 1910 Jane

Addams was convinced that the objectives of radical social reformers and the charity movement were quite close and that they were now prepared to support similar political goals.[46] Among these goals were proposals to establish employment exchanges, unemployment insurance, and job training.[47] Organizations like the United States Commission on Industrial Relations, the American Association for Labor Legislation (AAL), and the Board of Public Wealth successfully agitated for workmen's compensation and widows' benefits while, after decades of resistance, the mainline charitable agencies supported the formation of employment bureaus and specific state benefits. Although the principle of compensation was firmly established, that of insurance was not. Large-scale industries and major voluntary interests alike envisaged concrete advantages from the substitution of compensation for liability, but this unanimity of conviction was absent in the case of other, more critical kinds of social insurance.[48]

The economic interests of labor and the broader reform agenda of the progressives remained distinct, and their differences were most forcefully revealed in the majority and minority reports of the United States Commission on Industrial Relations.[49] The demand for the commission came from a broad range of leading reformers and labor advocates. The former saw the commission as a means to investigate industrial relations as the basis for some unspecified future reforms, but the latter were convinced that the hearings had revealed self-evident exploitation of labor that required immediate legislative redress. There was, however, no unanimity in the ranks of labor about the kind and extent of this redress, for not only were many reformers skeptical of the capacities of state and local governments to provide social services, but unionized workers also resisted the bureaucratic form of the new services.[50] New responses to unemployment were amongst the most divergent elements of progressive thought, and a growing preoccupation with the interdependent complexity of social problems rather than with predominant causes strongly influenced discussions of poverty.[51]

By 1915 it was reported that although "there has never been more effective cooperation on the part of both public and private agencies in dealing with the problems arising from a period of industrial depression," it was unlikely "that permanent plans for dealing with unemployment on the basis of experience acquired during the past winter are likely to be adopted on the part of the community, either to prevent its recurrence or to deal comprehensively and systematically with it when it does occur."[52] During the depressed conditions of 1921–2, these new efforts to provide public relief and unemployment insurance were largely rejected.[53] For brief periods the debate about economic insecurity accommodated the interests of immigrant workers and the objectives of reformers, but eventually inadequate legislative expression of these interests became part of the adverse environment that continued to afflict the poor.

The environment defined: overcrowding reconsidered

Efforts to link the housing problem to wage levels, like those that confronted unemployment, also failed to have an enduring effect on public policies. Nevertheless, during the first decade of the twentieth century, low wages were identified as the predominant cause of the housing problem, and the environmental deficiencies of the slums were convincingly linked to unemployment and underemployment. Surveys that revealed the relationships between rent payments and wage levels amplified long-standing anxieties about the impact of housing reform on the supply of low-cost accommodations. New standards had for long been opposed because they tended to increase the supply of improved accommodations and diminish the supply of inferior quarters, but many reformers assumed that the response to the availability of improved housing would gradually relieve the pressure on the older, inferior accommodations. In the short run these assumptions were reasonable, but the demand for improved quarters was limited to those whose incomes could sustain the higher rent levels, and the demand for old accommodations was maintained by high levels of foreign immigration. Major sanitary improvements and some modest structural requirements had only minor effects on rent levels, but the rapid elevation of minimum housing standards raised rental levels beyond the means of the lowest stratum of society. In the absence of rising real incomes, it was found that "restrictive legislation has forced the character of multiple dwellings up to a standard that makes it necessary to increase the number of residents and intensify their use to the extent of creating congestion."[54] In New York this problem was especially severe during the first decade of the twentieth century and provoked frequent rent strikes at a time when many better tenement properties had high vacancy rates.[55]

Since efforts to improve the urban environment often exacerbated overcrowding, several well-publicized investigations of the poor attempted to determine the relationships between wages and rents. Low wages and the unpredictability of employment were increasingly identified as the key factors in the housing problem. Surveys of household budgets amongst the poor revealed that accommodations available at affordable rents were inadequate. For many households on Manhattan, three rooms, one of them windowless, a shared toilet, and no bath was the ceiling of their rental expenditures, and the upper limit was either a five-room unit in an Old Law tenement or a three-room-unit New Law tenement. These surveys of the standard of living did not, however, restrict themselves to minimum standards of space but also expressed concern about tenement design. The dwelling had to provide more than minimum needs for light, air, and ventilation, and also some opportunity for personal taste. In particular, great stress was placed on the need for a parlor for individual privacy or special occasions.[56] These sensibilities were somewhat premature, for among newly arrived immigrants expectations of personal privacy were not high, and the willingness to take in boarders to share rental costs certainly exacerbated overcrowding.[57]

Several studies also emphasized the effects of wage levels on suburbanization, since the time and cost of the journey to work was a major restraint in households that were dependent upon the wages of several members: "Any conversation with wage-earners on the subject quickly brings out the importance which they put upon convenience of access to their work."[58] The journey to work was integrally linked to the wage issue in a survey of the South End of Boston that revealed that those who could afford suburban residence had abandoned the locality to the poor. Only 26 percent of piano craftsmen and only 37 of 531 employed at the Elevated Electric plant lived in the vicinity of their place of work in the South End.[59] In Manhattan 31 percent of printers with an eight-hour day lived on the island; 42 percent of leather workers with a nine-hour day; and 75 percent of the food workers with a ten-hour day.[60] This relationship between wages, working day, and the journey to work was quite complex, for the attractions of their social environment discouraged some residents from leaving the discomforts of the housing environment of the inner-city slums.

In any event several investigations of the slums revealed some of the intervening factors that qualified the relationship between various measures of congestion and mortality. In particular these surveys explored the degree to which levels of domestic cleanliness revealed a capacity to cope with overcrowded living conditions. One professional response to the New York Tenement House Exhibit of 1900 warned against making simplistic assumptions about the mortal consequences of congestion: "When tenements are more than three stories high and occupy more than 50 percent of the lot, so shutting out light and air, both poverty and disease are abundant. We are even wont to think that the older tenements, like the wooden shanty and the old two and three storey houses, must be less sanitary than the imposing modern tenements, but such is absolutely not the case."[61] Even Jacob Riis commented that "as the buildings grew taller, the death rate fell. The reason is plain, though the reverse had been expected by most people. The biggest tenements have been built in the last ten years of sanitary reform rule, and have been brought in all but crowding, under its law," whereas old tenements, especially those that were converted from private dwellings, could not be improved.[62] One of

Figure 4.1 Old and new tenements, New York, ca. 1900
Source: Jacob Riis, Museum of the City of New York.

his celebrated photographs clearly revealed that the worst living conditions were in shanty-type structures within the alleys and yards of larger tenements (Figure 4.1).

The overcrowding of lots with multistory tenements was relatively rare except on Manhattan, but room overcrowding and lot overcrowding were widespread in the poorer sections of all cities. In New York multifamily dwellings were built as tenements, but elsewhere it was found that "The old types of one and two family houses are being converted into tenements wholly inadequate for their new use, but which, on account of their cheapness, have become increasingly popular with the lower strata who cannot meet the rent of the legally regulated and controlled buildings."[63] In Philadelphia, it was argued, the same causes that afflicted New York produced a different kind of housing problem. There was a high proportion of home ownership and single-family dwellings, but many structures

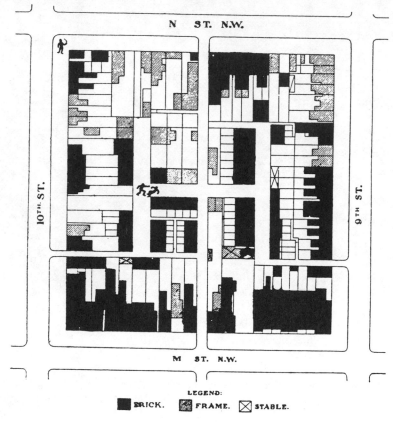

Figure 4.2 Alley property, Washington, D.C., 1912

Source: The Monday Evening Club, *Directory of Inhabited Alleys of Washington, D.C.* (1912), 1.

were poorly built and inadequately provided with sanitary facilities: "The only one-family houses accessible to [the poor] are the court and alley dwellings. These are usually three stories high, having one room on each floor, the houses being arranged in solid rows back to back, leaving only one side for light and air. This side often faces a narrow court or alley in which surface drainage and privy wells are common."[64] By 1910 the focus

Figure 4.3 Alley property, Chicago, 1900
Source: Report of the Investigating Committee of the City Home Association, Chicago, 1901, 29.

of housing reform had shifted to poorly drained, unsewered, and congested alleys and yards, which were to be found in almost all large cities (Figures 4.2 and 4.3).

Nevertheless, the association of congestion and sickness proved to be a powerful image in efforts to improve public health. Ernest Poole publicized the appalling level of tuberculosis in a group of tenements in New York that he called the "Lung Block" (Figure 4.4). He "used this block as a center, not to prove but to image what has already been proved all through the civilized world, to image the three great evils we must fight in the tenements. These evils are congestion, dissipation, infection."[65] Similar graphic conceptions of the mortal and socially pathological consequences of overcrowding were broadly publicized by an alliance of reformers known as the Committee on the Congestion of Population (CCP), which organized a large exhibit in the hope of reviving the interest provoked by Veiller's earlier venture. The traveling exhibit used photographs, graphs, and maps to display and to simplify many of the relationships between the slum environments and the social and health problems of their residents.

The initiative for the exhibit came from Benjamin Marsh, whose myopic views on congestion were shared by his more conservative

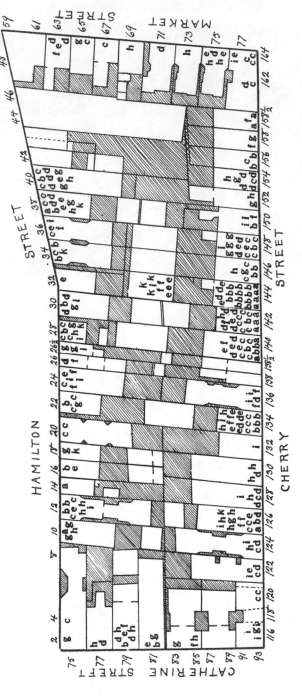

Figure 4.4 Tenements and tuberculosis: the "lung block," New York

Source: Charities and the Commons 11 (1903): 194.

patron, Henry Morgenthau. In a style more reminiscent of the late Victorians than of the progressives, Morgenthau argued that congestion "is an evil which is gnawing at the vitals of the country – an evil that breeds physical disease, moral depravity, discontent, and socialism – and all of these must be cured and eradicated or else our great body politic will be weakened. This Community can only hold its preeminence if the masses that compose it are given a chance to be healthy, moral and self respecting. If they are forced to live like swine they will lose their vigor."[66] This persistence of antebellum anxieties about the contagious effects of the slums was also apparent in Josiah Strong's later works in which he stressed the "moral as well as physical contagion" of crowded tenements. His source was no less an authority than the survey of tenement life by DeForest and Veiller, who described: "The most terrible of all features of tenement life as the indiscriminate herding of all kinds of people in close contact" and "the fact that, mingled with the drunken, the dissolute, the improvident, the diseased, dwell the great mass of respectable working men of the city with their families."[67]

The CCP identified low moral standards and low intellectual standards as well as low wages, long working hours, and land speculation as the primary causes of congestion.[68] Marsh also believed that the relationship between congestion and death rates was "borne out so conclusively that it is not worthwhile to attempt to site [*sic*] the elaborate investigations made by various cities." Marsh specifically emphasizes that "the death rates from consumption in the overcrowded wards in lower Manhattan were even two or three times higher than the death rates in sections of the city that had "a normal density and normal living conditions." To eliminate disease it was imperative to eliminate congestion.[69] Others supported measures to reduce congestion, insisting that although not "the first cause of poverty or disease, it is certainly a factor that very largely emphasizes these evils. Removal of congestion often removes just that factor which has made it impossible for a family to fight successfully with these other evils."[70] Marsh believed that facts were weapons "against which the corporate interests cannot contend," but his facts became a matter of debate.[71]

Critics of the environmentalist assumptions of the exhibit argued that the mortal consequences of overcrowding even at the lowest scale of the room were dependent on access to light and air, hot water, toilet facilities, and playgrounds, as well as on the provisionment of adequate food and clothing. They also questioned assumptions about the "low morality" and "low intellect" of those who lived under congested conditions. Local hospitals would do more immediate good for the health of the poor, they believed, than would measures designed to disperse people: "Until the great economic causes underlying poverty can be studied and remedied we must not abate one whit our endeavors to increase the wholly inadequate hospital facilities for those sections of our cities where both poverty and density per lot exist."[72] Another commentator reminded reformers "that congestion of population is a symptom or expression of a natural tendency, whose growth has paralleled the progress of civilization"; "[reformers'] main function should be ... to transform congestion of population into harmless or even beneficial concentration before we attempt to interfere with a natural tendency of society and employ artificial means to decentralize or to distribute over more extended areas the so called excess of population."[73]

Despite this debate, the New York CCP reiterated these presumed relationships, stating that "congestion is indicative of conditions which are conducive to insanitary and immoral living."[74] The report did, however, acknowledge that the "crude death rate of New York City is not, notwithstanding the conditions of congestion to which attention has been directed, a high one. . . . While, therefore, such conditions of congestion as exist in this city have not had any alarming results upon the health of the population, it is still true that these conditions have unquestionably had a bad effect on public health." The report was, in fact, emphasizing the relationship between overcrowding and the incidence of tuberculosis in the Italian quarter.[75] The campaign to reduce deaths from tuberculosis stressed the need to eliminate overcrowded living conditions, and although the disease was unambiguously linked to notoriously overcrowded blocks, the incidence of the disease varied greatly within the slums. This variation was partly attributed to a low incidence amongst Russian Jews who also lived in some of the most overcrowded quarters. This ethnic immunity was thought to be related to their long endurance of congested living conditions and also to cultural practices that diminished the mortal costs of overcrowding.[76]

Despite their favorable vital rates, Jewish quarters had gained a reputation for low standards of cleanliness; however, this judgment was frequently contested. In 1902 a survey of the Lower East Side complained: "Philanthropists and reformers, particularly those of the fair sex, are apt to regard the immigrant Jewish population of New York as a 'slum' population; as degraded residents of narrow and filthy streets, whose foul general habits are beyond their power to describe. . . . But these ladies and gentlemen have never visited the homes of these apparently uncleanly people. . . ."[77] A review of the living conditions of Italians in American cities concluded:

Any sweeping classification of congested sections as the slums of a city is untenable. Congestion is necessarily a menace to health. It is socially undesirable. It is to be deplored and remedied by every feasible agency. But congestion does not make the slum, necessarily, with its essential characteristics of squalor, degrada-

tion and crime. The congested districts of New York, Philadelphia and other leading American cities today are not slums, though they doubtless contain slums. It
is by its average character that a district must be judged and classified and not by
existing exceptions.[78]

A decade later the British Board of Trade conducted an inquiry into
the cost of living in American cities and warned: "The abnormal density
of the population of the Lower East Side has been emphasized because it
is the dominating fact affecting the local life in its every phase. It would
be very misleading to conclude, however, that, although so crowded, the
picture is unrelieved; that the neighborhood is one from which those living there are anxious to escape; that the general death rate is excessive,
or that it is just a 'poor' neighborhood lacking colour, animation and
brightness. The reverse is the case, and on the surface the impression
often conveyed is indeed stimulating rather than depressing."[79] The same
report examined the West End of Boston and declared: "Outward evi-
dences of poverty were not visible and, even a crowd, including a sprin-
kling of coloured population . . . was free to a noticeable extent from the
poor and ragged element that . . . would have collected in one of the
poorer and crowded parts of London."[80] The social conditions amongst
black families were also applauded, but these positive findings were
attributed to their frequent contact with affluent white families. The main
threat to black families and neighborhoods was their segregation in the
least desirable districts, in which the depraved and the moral were "indis-
criminately mixed."[81]

Throughout the nineteenth century immigrants were also viewed as
contributing disproportionately to social problems like crime, prostitution, intemperance, and pauperism. These social problems were identified with large cities, and most new immigrants did concentrate in the
congested inner sections of large northeastern and midwestern cities. As
it had disputed the impact of immigration on the wages of the native
born, however, the Industrial Commission of 1901 questioned well-publicized relationships between immigrants and pathological social conditions. Data standardized to adjust for the high proportion of young males
in the age–sex distribution of newly arrived immigrant groups did not
confirm popular opinions about the overrepresentation of immigrants
amongst convicted criminals and paupers. Moreover, the crimes of which
immigrants were convicted were petty misdemeanors related to ordinances concerning the conduct of small businesses.[82] Some observers
clearly distinguished immigrant quarters from slums occupied by single
men of mixed ethnic ancestry and including many native born. These
rooming house districts were much more closely identified with those
pathological social conditions that were attributed to the inner-city slums
in general: "The quarters of American cities where the foreigners live are

Figure 4.5 The social world of the tenement, Boston, ca. 1909

Source: Lewis W. Hine Memorial Collection. Courtesy of the International Museum of Photography at George Eastman House.

not the worst quarters; and I would rather trust myself in the dark, to the mysteries of Hester Street than to certain portions of the West Side exclusively populated by a certain type of degenerate Americans."[83]

In Boston a predominantly Italian tenement district was contrasted with a rooming house area containing a diverse native- and foreign-born population: "The problem in the North End is the problem of immigration, to be solved at the ports of the U.S. The problem of the South End is the internal social problem."[84] Similar contrasts were drawn between the Lower East Side and the Bowery in New York.[85] These variations also occurred within districts and among neighbors. As early as 1893 Jane Addams stressed: "Working people live in the same streets with those in need of charity, but they themselves, so long as they have health and good wages, require and want none of it." Settlement workers were especially sensitive to the complexity of social conditions in their neighborhoods since they encountered "either the hopeful, the progressive, or at any rate the normal life of working families – or perhaps dramatic episodes of tragedy or comedy that became a part of neighborhood knowledge. But in the case conference, there was one hard luck story after another. We could not help seeing how fortunate we were to live in a house where all elements of local life were seen. We knew not only poverty and crime, but also the intelligence and ability and charm of our neighbors."[86]

The photographic record of the slums also revealed a more complex interpretation of the immigrants' world; Lewis Hine, in particular, captured the intimacy and vitality of street life (Figure 4.5). A medium that had documented the environmental deficiencies of the slums expanded its vision to celebrate the ways in which the poor used their environment. There were also numerous verbal testimonies to the social and economic vitality of immigrant quarters. In spite of the "double curse of the slum and the ghetto," the Jewish quarter of Chicago, which was perilously close to the "red-light district," had relatively few saloons, and "the people in these districts are for the most part sober and law-abiding citizens."[87] In Boston, too, "neither cramped quarters nor the absorption with business affairs destroys Jewish home and family life."[88] The association of crime with Italian immigrants was also questioned: "According to the police showing, . . . the North End, so far from being exceptionally lawless, is, on the contrary, law-abiding to a degree that is not generally supposed."[89] Another observer praised "the Italian laborer and his family [as] more steady and sober, more provident and more generally reliable than their Irish predecessors."[90]

Perhaps the most striking qualifications of popular views of the living conditions of immigrants in the slums of large cities were recorded in the reports of the Immigration Commission, which certainly attempted to interpret its findings as a justification for immigration restriction. Nevertheless, the commission found that its conclusions tended "to modify impressions based on studies of extreme cases, and brings out the fact that a large majority of the immigrants in cities lead a decent, hard-working life, in homes that are clean, though in many cases poor, and that the undesirable conditions prevailing in congested quarters often are not brought about by the residents, but largely in spite of them."[91] The general cleanliness of the immediate living quarters of the majority of slum residents certainly modified the presumed relationship between overcrowding and mortality. Much contemporary testimony stressed the contrast between the untidy and poor quality of exterior conditions, which were largely under the care of landlords or municipal authorities, and the cleanliness of apartment interiors, for which the residents were responsible.

The Immigration Commission indicted municipalities for many of the undesirable aspects of the slums: "The neglected appearance of a great many of the streets is a result of indifference on the part of the city authorities about keeping out of the way districts clean, rather than carelessness on the part of the residents. In frequent cases the streets are dirty while the homes are clean."[92] Overall, it was found that "average conditions were materially better than had been anticipated, that the worst conditions could be attributed to municipal neglect and that interiors were relatively clean. Conditions in small industrial towns were judged to be worse than in the largest cities and the worst conditions were identified with large boarding houses rather than tenements in general."[93] They also emphasized that "while very many most deplorable conditions were found, the fact is clearly established that a large majority of the immigrants in these great cities lead a hardworking honest life, and that their homes are reasonably clean, and that the undesirable conditions found in these quarters are in many instances not the fault of the inhabitants, but exist largely in spite of them, owing to the fact that the city authorities do not provide sufficient facilities for adequate water supply, for proper cleaning of the streets, and for proper drainage and sewerage conditions."[94]

The commission, despite its preoccupation with the distinctions between the old and the new immigration, concluded that recency of immigration had no relationship to cleanliness.[95] In describing the Italian districts of New York, one observer concluded: "There is not an exalted standard of cleanliness in the congested quarters of New York or other great American cities, but they are not intolerably filthy, except in spots, and the inhabitants are not sunk in degradation beyond any rational prospect of betterment."[96] In her research for the Industrial Commission, Kate Claghorn of the New York Tenement House Department revealed that "No account of filth in daily surrounding among Italians and Hebrews can outmatch the pictures drawn by observations of the habits of immigrant Irish and even Germans."[97] There were many surveys of housing conditions that reiterated these findings about relatively adequate standards of cleanliness in the slums and suggested that they were attempting to modify a stereotypical view that attributed the presumed filth of the slums to the neglectful behavior of their residents. A survey of conditions in St. Louis revealed: "That nearly 70 percent of the 7,458 rooms listed were clean testifies either to the heroic endurance of the weaker sex or to their lack of economic perception."[98]

A careful survey of conditions in Philadelphia highlighted the sanitary problems and room overcrowding in a city that prided itself on the absence of tenements; it concluded, however: "In spite of crowded conditions and the inadequacy of the water supply, the great majority of the rooms investigated were clean, a fact which may surprise those not familiar with the sections of the city inspected."[99] About a decade later the Henry Phipps Institute funded a survey of Philadelphia. The report concluded that about a third of the housing was in good condition and a half was adequate, but measures of environmental quality were not highly related to cleanliness, nor was the incidence of tuberculosis. This discrepancy provoked the author to suggest that tuberculosis might be linked to the strain of maintaining cleanliness under adverse circumstances rather than to some more direct effect of the housing environment.[100] This survey had equally striking findings on the condition of Philadelphia's black population: "To many people who have been accustomed to think of the negro population as living to a great extent in squalid, filthy homes, the findings just given (revealing that 96 percent of negroes lived in clean homes compared to only 85 percent of the total sampled population) must come in the nature of a revelation." The investigator was provoked to reexamine these findings: "thinking that there might be some lack of uniformity in the grading of the homes by different workers, the negro estimates being made by a colored social worker, several workers were questioned on the degree of cleanliness observed by them in the homes of different races, and they all agreed that the above percentages would conform fairly closely to their general impressions."[101]

This complex view of the slums was not, however, broadly accepted, and the prevalence of a negative view was implied by the strident efforts of most sympathetic observers to qualify the image of the slums that had been created in the "popular imagination" by generalizing from exceptional "extreme cases." They contested "the impression that the extreme instances in cities are the whole story, and that the congested quarters of large cities, full of filth, squalor and depraved humanity, are a menace to the nation's health and morals. Moreover, the responsibility for these conditions is almost universally placed by old residents on the immigrant, and primarily on the recent immigrant, from the South and East of Europe. The Italian, the Hebrew and the Slav, according to popular belief, are poisoning the pure air of our otherwise well regulated cities; and if it were not for them there would be no congestion, no filth, and no poverty. . . ."[102] Despite much negative testimony about the social and environmental conditions in the slums, there was a substantial body of commentary that revealed the degree to which the immigrant poor coped with their adverse environment. The impact of these observations on professional and popular opinions was decidedly uneven, but at least many long-held assumptions about the relationship between the slum environment and its immigrant residents were the subject of much discussion and debate.

Reports about the adaptations of the immigrant poor to their housing environment failed to displace prevailing assumptions about the moral damage of congested living conditions. Critics of the mainstream of housing reform claimed that the regulation of new construction "confused the point of view of the philanthropist, who deals with the socially subnormal, with the national problem of housing the working people. This has led to the acceptance of a minimum standard and a complete neglect of a necessary national ideal."[103] Unfortunately the task was formidable, for in 1916 it was estimated that $15 per month, the minimum rent necessary to guarantee a decent home, was greater than the rent-paying capacity of over half the wage earners, whose incomes were less than $800 per year.[104] The housing shortage during and after World War I aggravated this relationship between housing costs and wage levels.

Some of the most perceptive surveys of housing conditions examined the interdependent relationships among innumerable variables that were assumed to define housing quality. This focus on interdependent relationships, rather than seeking a leading cause, was clearly exemplified in a diagram that illustrated the findings of the survey of housing conditions in Philadelphia sponsored by the Phipps Institute (Figure 4.6). Despite its remarkable insights, the survey provided a more complex description of housing conditions that failed to connect these conditions to the low and uncertain incomes of their residents. It became increasingly difficult to make this connection between housing and incomes as conceptions of poverty in general also became preoccupied with a search for the interdependent complexity of an almost limitless array of variables.

Interdependent "complexity"

New interpretations of poverty had shifted attention from a morally delinquent residuum to the unemployed, but a leading proponent of the new philanthropy warned against "interpretations of social problems [or] any specific combination of several such interpretations [that] provided

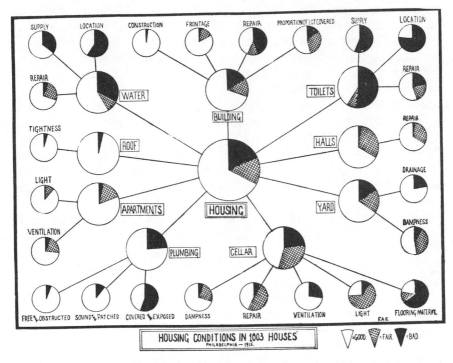

Figure 4.6 Interdependent complexity: housing conditions in Philadelphia, 1915

Source: F. A. Craig, *A Study of Housing and Social Conditions in Selected Districts of Philadelphia* (Philadelphia: Henry Phipps Institute, 1915), 53.

a complete explanation of poverty," for "destitution is bound up with the facts of economic life and modern industrial life is infinitely complex."[105] A leading economist, E.R.A. Seligman clearly expressed this skepticism about simple causation when he wrote: "The Malthusian seizes upon redundant population, the communist upon private property, the socialist upon property in means of production, the single taxer on property in land, the cooperator upon competition, the anarchist upon government, the anti-optionist upon speculation, the currency reformer upon metallic money and so on. They all forget that widespread poverty has existed in the absence of each one of these alleged causes. . . . The causes of poverty are as complex as the causes of civilization and the growth of wealth itself."[106]

As a former president of the American Economic Association, Seligman was deeply committed to the professional competence of his discipline, and as a key adviser to the Carnegie Institute of Washington, D.C., he pioneered the liaison between new research foundations and academic research. The patrons of the research foundations were concerned about the limitations of older ideologies of unrestricted competition and sought to use the expertise of science in matters like labor relations, as well as in technology and management.

This expertise stressed the interdependency of every conceivable component of urban society and overshadowed the more parsimonious concerns of those who were convinced that inadequate housing was primarily a matter of low and uncertain wages. The same insistence on complex diagnoses obscured some of the more forceful arguments, which held the main problem of the poor to be economic insecurity. During the second decade of the twentieth century, the reorganization and professionalization of charitable activities into social work also recorded a shift away from a "societal" explanation of poverty to one based upon "complex and often unique interdependencies" of influences in specific cases. Discussions of the "causes" of poverty emphasized economic rather than moral causes, but increasingly circumstances beyond the immediate control of the household were described as "conditions" rather than causes.[107] Although there was broad support for some public responsibilities to alleviate poverty, it was assumed that individual cases would still be unresponsive to general solutions. Many reformers retained a belief in the value of individual diagnoses and the necessity to combine "on the one hand community wide planning and control, and on the other that approximation to case work treatment of the unemployed which could be secured only through decentralization of the actual administration of relief."[108]

Experimental changes in the approach to juvenile delinquency also revealed new and more complex interpretations of the slum environment. Each individual delinquent had distinctive interactions with the environment that were judged to be relevant to current behavior, as well as to past socialization. The environment itself was redefined as the family setting.[109] From this perspective, case studies revealed an almost infinite combination of factors in the causes of social problems. William Healy, a pioneer of the new approach, stated that his aim was not "the development of any philosophical system or scientific theory concerning delinquency or delinquents. In view of the immense complexity of human nature in relation to complex environmental conditions it is little to us even if no set theory of crime can ever be successfully maintained." He concluded: "The causative factors, as I termed them, were always multiple. Even the same types of factors played their parts in varying degree in different cases and were interwoven, often in intricate fashion."[110] His caution was in part a reaction to the hereditarian arguments, which increasingly were being redefined in the more scientific guise of eugenics, and in part an effort to redefine the way in which individuals were influenced by their environment.

The main impact of the recognition of complex causation was an individual or case response, and efforts were made to decentralize and de-institutionalize existing practices. Some of these workers saw their primary mission as a kind of traffic directing, providing a comprehensive map of social services rather than serving as a specialist clinician. Informed individuals could "direct" clients to appropriate agencies.[111] Others stressed the need to serve clients in their homes by means of a professional cadre of workers organized within a bureaucratic administrative framework.[112] The various Charity Organization Societies sponsored the development of professional casework and invigorated an older style of scientific philanthropy.[113] Therapeutic methods of treating individual delinquents gained an expanded role in social work, initially as a complement to "social treatments," which linked individual problems to their social environment.[114] Eventually clinical psychologists established themselves as the dominant components of professional social work, but initially casework owed much to older styles of scientific philanthropy. These influences were most apparent in Mary Richmond's pioneering efforts to organize the formal training of caseworkers and stressed the need to supplement the so-called wholesale approach of social reform with a "retail" approach of individual casework.[115]

This distinction was reflected in the division of charitable activities into "social welfare" and "family welfare." The former, she argued, tended to generalize and simplify causes, whereas the latter was based on careful analysis and differentiated the causes of distress. Although Richmond regretted the antagonism of the proponents of what she believed to be complementary approaches, she opposed several efforts to provide public welfare in the form of pensions. Her own view of the development of social work stressed its direct links to reform movements and legislation, but despite her recognition of efforts to generate mass betterment during the first decade of the twentieth century, she envisaged future gains by means of individual betterment (Figure 4.7).

Richmond's "social diagnosis" of individual problems attempted to link the details of a personal predicament, including matters of personality described as "characterology," with an array of influences that began with the immediate environs of family, friends, and neighborhood and extended to include the more remote impacts of society at large. "All city families, rich and poor alike," she argued, using the diagram in Figure 4.8, "are surrounded by forces indicated within these circles; in every family asking charitable aid, therefore, the natural resources have so far failed as to send its members crashing through circles B, C, D, to E, the

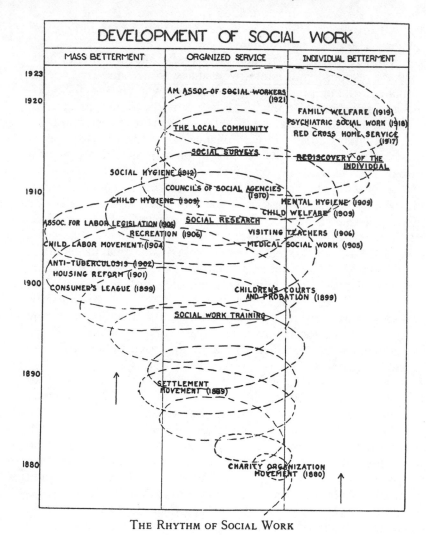

THE RHYTHM OF SOCIAL WORK

Figure 4.7 The changing focus of social work, 1880–1920

Source: Mary Richmond, *The Long View: Papers and Addresses* (New York: Russell Sage Foundation, 1930), 589.

circle of private charity. The problem of charity is to get them back into A again by rallying the forces that lie in between. . . . Other things being equal, the best force to use is the force that lies nearest the family."[116] Her method was primarily an orderly description of the presumed causes of distress; because of the overwhelming burden of detail, she found it impossible to generalize about treatments.

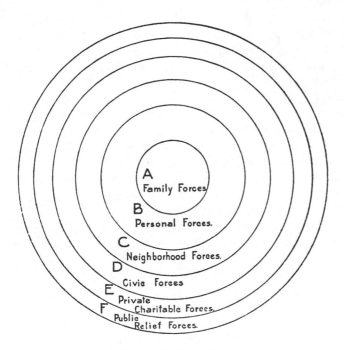

Figure 4.8 The social space of charity work

Source: Mary Richmond, *The Long View: Papers and Addresses* (New York: Russell Sage Foundation, 1930), 188.

Individual treatment and family rehabilitation became the key purpose of social work. In particular, children were a dominant focus of reform since they were presumed to be most promising subjects of improvement. Consequently, "child-saving" rather than any specific ideology of reform was often the source of cooperative efforts to obtain legislative standards for health, housing, education, and working conditions. This concern with casework and a growing stress on problems of socialization eventually overshadowed efforts to create permanent agencies of social welfare and economic assistance.[117] Social work had sought to confront the multiple sources of individual problems and to provide an integrated diagnosis, but the specialization of expertise resulted in the segmentation of different problems and treatments into distinct social agencies.[118] Despite these frustrations, the diagnostic skills of trained specialists were regarded as professional responses to public preferences. These preferences were assumed to be the outcome of public debates to which specialist practitioners lent their own professional authority.

Comprehensive diagnostic surveys of the social and environmental problems of entire communities were the means by which this public debate was to be "informed." In keeping with this growing emphasis on comprehensive investigations, the title of the leading journal of preventive philanthropy was changed once again, from *Charities and the Commons* to *The Survey*.[119] The most ambitious commitment of this approach was conducted in Pittsburgh between 1907 and 1909 and published in six volumes in 1914.[120] Pittsburgh was a center of large-scale industries that had attracted substantial numbers of new immigrants and was therefore viewed as a representative example of the new urban society. Two thirds of the residents were judged to be underpaid and faced exposure to frequent industrial accidents, long hours of work, and inadequate housing. The survey revealed many of the social and environmental problems that had long been associated with the slums, along with the inadequacies of urban government to confront the broader issues of urban life. The analysis and suggestions presented a picture of extreme complexity, in which any problem was related not to a direct cause but rather to an array of interdependent causes.

In the words of the director, the Pittsburgh Survey was "an appraisal . . . of how human engineering had kept pace with mechanical[,] . . . an attempt to throw light on these and kindred economic forces not by theoretical discussion of them, but by spreading forth the objective facts of life and labor which should help in forming judgement as to their results."[121] The survey movement was built upon the foundations of scientific philanthropy. The coordinators of the survey also acknowledged their debt to the case methods of the COS for "bringing problems down to human terms; by figures, for example, of the household cost of sickness – not in sweeping generalizations but in what Mr. Woods called piled up actualities."[122] This expertise, like that of scientific philanthropy, was to be based on sound data, but the revelation of the findings was intended to energize public opinion. One of the leading exponents of surveys compared their role to that of good journalism in the tradition of Riis and Steffans, which had exposed problems and advocated solutions.[123] Photographic journalism was, however, the subject of some debate, since it was felt that "the public soon wearies of pictures of destitute children or desolate tenement interiors. . . ."; the photographer ought rather to capture "the spirit behind the faces which reveal the tragedy and the beauty of these people."[124] Vivid photographs of social and environmental conditions had lost their "shock" value, and illustrations, as in Weller's survey of Washington's "Neglected Neighbors," were increasingly "tailored" to the reform goals of the text.[125] The Pittsburgh Survey supplemented photographic illustrations with several thematic maps designed to show the relationships between social problems and the urban environment, but despite the survey's commitment to complexity, the complexities of the graphic relationships were rarely explored (Figure 4.9).

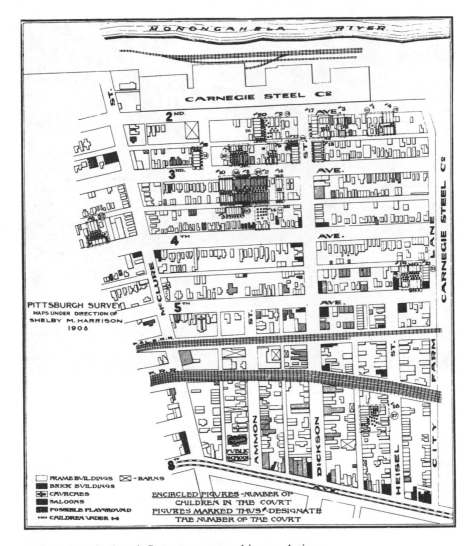

Figure 4.9 Pittsburgh Survey, cartographic correlations
Source: Margaret Byington, *Homestead: The Households of a Mill Town* (New York: Russell Sage Foundation, 1910), 132.

Some critics have argued that the survey researchers had a vested interest in projecting a complex image of the city in part because their diagnoses called for the continued employment of their expertise.[126] The movement certainly shared a desire for efficiency with those who saw the business model as an answer to city government, but it was also vitally

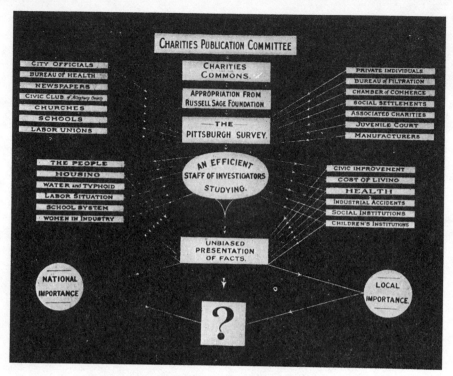

Figure 4.10 Complexity: organization of the Pittsburgh Survey
Source: Charities and the Commons 21 (1908–9): 519.

concerned with the need to invigorate local decision making, for the city
was to be the hope of democracy.[127] Devine, as editor of *The Survey,*
described himself as a social economist who was dedicated to "a well-
ordered community, in which stability and security and equity are
insured. He joins hands with the philanthropic societies, to get out of the
way initial obstacles which prevent natural growth; but he is not at heart
as much a philanthropist as a democrat."[128] A good survey was more than
an investigation of a specific social problem such as housing, working
conditions, or poverty: "The successful working of this leaven of civic
renewal depends upon the correcting power of facts . . . plus such a telling
of facts as will make them common knowledge. It is believed to be the
American experience that communities will act upon facts when they
have them."[129] Curiously, a question mark represented these outcomes in
an elaborate tabular presentation of the complex components of the Pittsburgh Survey (Figure 4.10).

In this way scientific analysis could energize public opinion in the direction of appropriate reforms. A survey confronted the interrelationships of several problems and presented solutions to them in an integrated fashion:

... the survey, by dealing with many subjects, affords a rallying center as well as the so called psychological moment for arousing the whole community to organized co-operative and therefore more forceful action – often along the very lines where intermittent, unrelated efforts had previously been made without result. Thus, the survey through the authority and the authenticity of its facts not only educates the whole community but through its uniting of interests promotes co-operative community action, believing that we have yet touched only the remote fringe of the latent power of the community for good when aroused to think in terms of the whole and to act as an organized unit.[130]

A recent evaluation of these efforts concluded that they engaged the feelings rather than the intellect and "used the symbolic representation of issues to evade the systematic representation of issues. In that respect the publicity efforts of the professionals broke completely from their own commitment to the rational evaluation of scientific data."[131]

The newly established Russell Sage Foundation generously supported the survey movement, including its journal *The Survey,* and, along with other similar institutions, attempted to promote research in the interests of a more orderly course of change than had occurred in the nineteenth century. Partisans of the COS dominated the Sage board, and the survey movement was clearly an effort to set and perhaps restrict the agenda of social reform so that professional social workers could organize "constructive" voluntary philanthropy.[132] The ethical and political implications of this growing connection between philanthropic foundations and public policy research became a matter of intense controversy when the Commission on Industrial Relations publicized the interests of the Rockefeller Foundation in research on industrial relations while the patron of the foundation was deeply involved in a savage industrial conflict with labor unions.[133] The internal conflicts of the commission necessitated majority and minority reports that revealed the impatience of partisans committed to the immediate redress of social injustice with the necessity for the documentation of examples of this injustice by means of careful, lengthy, and often inconclusive research. The corporate philanthropic sponsorship of this research was also judged to be "an effort to perpetuate the present position of predatory wealth through the corruption of sources of public information." The survey was naturally indignant at the tone and content of the majority report and, along with *The Nation,* complained about the lack of careful research and its insensitivity to the complexity of the problem of industrial relations.[134] This debate revealed the degree to which the objectives of reformers increasingly diverged from those of their intended clients and, as in earlier periods, the poor had to cope not only with their material predicament but also with formulations of that predicament that rarely included their own reactions.

Nevertheless, reform ventures celebrated growing agreement regarding purpose among the private and public agencies, which "welded" in the interests of efficiency "the power and prestige" of the former with the "initiative and elasticity" of the latter.[135] In 1909 this kind of arrangement was initiated in Boston, which aspired to create a more desirable urban world within a six-year period.[136] The Boston-1915 movement was, however, conscious of a tradition of urban paternalism and provisionment, and unlike the case in many other cities, local resources appeared to be a source of optimism. Efforts were made to bring together the many kinds of data and expertise and to develop additional information with the cooperation of able people in civic groups. It was assumed that careful analysis of the facts would suggest ways to improve the quality of urban life.[137] A sixteen-point plan was proposed to enhance not only "the unity, convenience and beauty of the city" but also "the prosperity of its industries, the enlightened labor policies of its employers, the efficiency of its city government, the progressiveness of its educational and recreational institutions, and . . . the attractiveness and healthfulness of even its least costly housing." These connections were naively conceived in relation to the automatic and mechanical behavior of several cog wheels (Figure 4.11).

Another expression of this search for interdependency was the formation of the Massachusetts Homestead Commission two years later. The commission was sensitive to the need for some kind of public subsidy to reduce the cost of capital for housing construction or for willingness on the part of public authorities to construct low-rent housing. The commission was responsible for the construction of only twelve homesteads in Lowell, but like several efforts to confront the wartime housing shortage, it moved beyond the limits of restrictive legislation advocated by Veiller and developed proposals to increase the supply of adequate housing for low-income households. Its justifications did, however, retain many old assumptions about the relationship of overcrowding to "disease, poverty, ignorance, vice and crime" and about the conservative social effects of homesteads or cottages set in grounds. Their aims necessitated the establishment of planning boards with purposes very similar to those of the survey movement. Planning was necessary for the promotion of "health, convenience and beauty" and involved all aspects of city life "as component parts of an organic whole, so that each may dovetail into the next."[138]

This organic interpretation of the city was based upon a cellular con-

Figure 4.11 Interdependency: the 1915 Boston Exposition
Source: Charities and the Commons 23 (1909): 328.

ception of neighborhoods, but the metaphor obscured profound differences in interpretations of the political autonomy of neighborhoods.
Originally, the neighborly ideal was intended to facilitate the friendly
relations between different social groups, but in large segmented cities,
neighborhood became the basis upon which to build the social amenities
for relatively homogeneous districts.[139] To one of the pioneers of the settlement movement, Robert A. Woods, the therapeutic actions of neighborly settlements would lead to the creation of hundreds of democratic
villages. He asserted that the residents of settlement houses were from

... the first generation of students whose thinking was molded by the principle of
natural science that the mass is to be identified and affected through the molecule
or atom, and the living organism through the cell. They were prepared for a similar point of view in social science. This appeared in the treatment of the ancient
village community as the nucleus of the state and civilization. Such teaching, far
from minimizing the family, marked it out in its community setting. The city
neighborhood had already been recognized as a distraught survival of the ancient

communes which were in a real sense the menstruum in which family life might float. It was the "family of families," when its present day mysteries were penetrated, that was to become the reinforcement both of character and of citizenship.[140]

Graham Taylor of the Chicago Commons settlement included the neighborhood among his four "life spheres," along with the family, industrial relations, and community service. "Neighborship" was to Taylor "our most ancient treasure, the heritage of the race, the one thing common to all who share the same origin, and to all of different origin who live near each other."[141] Propinquity could apparently overcome differences of origin. Taylor was aware of the uprooting effects of unemployment and mobility, but he believed that new neighborhood ties were being forged by fraternal orders, insurance societies, and trade unions, and he considered these ties to be natural substitutes for the loyalty of the old craft guilds.[142] He also cautioned against the potential isolation of neighborhood, stressing that these communities were an integral part of the city as a whole. Jane Addams was also sensitive to new views of the civic community when she complained that she did not believe in geographical salvation. She argued that "moral disorder resulted not so much from rampant individualism as from the failure of the community to provide an environment that would nourish youths' best impulses and permit them to flourish naturally."[143] Although the immediate family had become the main focus of environmental influences on social problems, more than most progressives, Jane Addams continued to recognize the environmental impact of the larger society.

Some observers were also able to recognize that some of the presumed social problems within the slums were in fact part of the immigrant social order. The adolescent gang and the saloon continued to arouse the anxieties of the majority of reformers, but the imminent threat of a national prohibition provoked several responses that stressed the convivial recreational role of the saloon. In the absence of appropriate alternatives, prohibition was likely to destroy a major component of the social fabric that might be indispensable to the future course of reform.[144] This interest in community also yielded a more complex description of immigrant neighborhoods. The positive role of religious institutions, voluntary associations, and stable family arrangements were recognized, but they were also judged to be relics of the traditional world of rural Europe and inappropriate to the needs of the modern American city. These "transplanted villages" softened the immigrants' painful initial encounter with American society, but by delaying assimilation, they created generational conflicts once American-born children encountered the world beyond. Jane Addams established a labor museum at Hull House "to bridge the past life in Europe with American experiences in such wise as to give them both some meaning and sense of relation. . . . In the immediate neigh-

borhood were found at least four varieties of these most primitive methods of spinning and at least three distinct variations of the same spindle
put in connection with wheels. It was possible to put these seven into
historic sequence and order, and to connect the whole with the present
method of factory spinning."[145] The museum recorded a sensitivity to the
disruptive consequences of rapid assimilation and a preference for a
slower, more deliberate course that recognized the immigrants' heritage.[146]
Moreover, in moving from the slums to the inner suburbs, or "zone of
emergence," many immigrants encountered a decidedly limited environmental improvement and often the loss of a supportive network of neighbors and associations.[147]

In any event, the participation of immigrants in the activities of the
settlement houses was decidedly selective and generally spasmodic.
Many groups replicated many of the cultural and recreational functions
of the settlements within the fabric of their own institutions, primarily
because they were suspicious of the intentions of this most altruistic link
with American society.[148] Most reformers who were sensitive to the indigenous social world of the immigrant were concerned about the immigrants' lack of the democratic foundations of an "American" community.
For these reasons, many progressives hoped that the specialist contributions of architects, engineers, sculptors, and social workers would make
possible a new kind of political process. The social setting of this process
did, however, retain many elements of Victorian efforts to restore a sense
of community in an urban setting. An image of the natural democracy
and "spontaneity" of small-town society continued to influence the direction of reforms. The work of Charles Cooley on the critical role of family
and neighborhood in the socialization of individuals in modern urban
society strongly influenced ideas about community.[149] He explored the
persistence of primary relationships within the framework of a changing
and increasingly regulated social environment, but he also felt that these
primary relationships needed to be reconstituted into community-like
associations. Like their clients, many reformers were apprehensive about
an excessive reliance on paternalistic and bureaucratic measures to
resolve social problems. They were often explicit in their efforts to
"democratize" urban life by distinguishing the execution of the wishes of
the electorate from the debates about those wishes.

The ideal of "neighborhood," which had originally provided an image
for the rehabilitation of slum areas, was broadened to express this desire
for local democracy. The diffusion of these values within urban society
did, however, involve careful manipulation and adaptation.[150] Boyer has
charted this process of manipulation and concluded:

For generations moralists had attempted to use traditional patterns of social
authority. Now, or so hoped the civic loyalty propagandists, it would no longer
be individuals or organizations whose moral force would prevail, but a disem-

bodied collective standard sustained by the psychologically energizing power of urbanization itself. In place of the old order of the village or small town, where moral authority had in fact reposed in tangible institutions and flesh and blood people, they offered a community of the imagination whose authority depended not upon day to day experience but upon the manipulation of ideas and images.[151]

In 1907 the Committee on Civic Centers of the St. Louis Civic League applied these ideas broadly to all sections of the city.[152] They proposed the establishment of socially balanced communities centered on a set of communal facilities that would also serve as an alternative political order to the ward.[153] By 1911 there was a National Conference on Social Center Development designed to adopt the idea to the growing suburbs, and in 1918 a National Community Center Association had 152 members. Over 600 cities utilized local schools as the focus of tax-supported community activities that included evening classes and organized recreation.[154] While the use of schools as social centers was consistent with those reforms that were committed to the use of professional management to attain social efficiency, the social centers were also communities that resembled ideal-izations of the New England town. Edward Ward, the leading proponent of the extended use of school buildings in the interest of fostering local consciousness "in the midst of our complex life," hoped to restore "the community interest, the neighborly spirit, the democracy that we knew before we came to the city."[155] In response to what he described as a "monotonous lack of local structural design and thus of efficient organic character in our outspread cities," George Hooker proposed a new federal department of urban life to standardize the policies of states and cities in order to facilitate the functioning of neighborhoods.[156] Mary Follett extended these ideas beyond the limits of urban society and envisaged a future in which "neighborhood units across the city would unite and then multiply and form people into a state, the New State."[157] Older ideas about the moral order of community were reformulated as an organic metaphor that expressed the need for expertise in the management of the complexities of urban society. There was belief in the fragile possibility that morality and expertise could together create an organized city and a desirable society.[158]

The political form of this combination remained a source of dispute since the new urban professions often sought to establish self-governing associations at a time when population turnover and suburbanization diminished the effectiveness of neighborhood-based organizations. Nevertheless, advocates of the rights of clients and consumers as well as of the deprived based their policies on the presumed vitality and legiti-macy of community councils based upon districts and neighborhoods.[159] In its most radical form, under the leadership of Wilbur Phillips in Cin-cinnati, the neighborhood movement embraced a broader agenda of

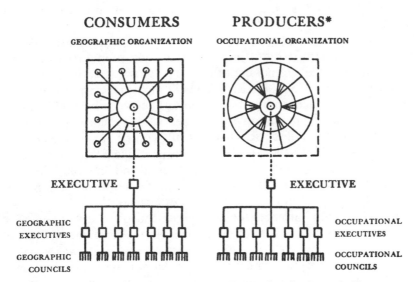

CONSUMERS

GEOGRAPHIC ORGANIZATION

PRODUCERS*

OCCUPATIONAL ORGANIZATION

EXECUTIVE

EXECUTIVE

GEOGRAPHIC EXECUTIVES

GEOGRAPHIC COUNCILS

OCCUPATIONAL EXECUTIVES

OCCUPATIONAL COUNCILS

* The term "producers," as used here, embraces the members of all occupational groups, who, alone and together, "produce" the satisfactions required by consumers.

Figure 4.12 The Social Unit plan

Source: Wilbur C. Phillips, *Adventuring for Democracy* (New York: Social Unit Press, 1940), 379.

socialist idealism.[160] This more ambitious Social Unit Movement proposed, "with the counsel and advice of national social experts, a model program for community organization, the approach being made through the channel of public health with the child as the point of attack."[161] Social Units were an institutional arrangement that facilitated communication between experts and their clientele and made possible the coordination of several services in a comprehensive fashion at the neighborhood level (Figure 4.12). In keeping with the organic metaphors of the broader movement, "block workers were described as the nervous system of the body politic." In Phillips's words the Social Unit was "a plan to hasten the coming of democracy, both genuine and efficient, by building upon a basis of geographical units an organization in which the people could get a clear idea of the common needs and could utilize the skilled groups in society in formulating and carrying out programs to meet those needs." It was, in short, an "intensive and democratic organization on a district basis."[162] The Cincinnati experiment attracted antagonistic reactions during the period following World War I and without the support of the medical and social work professionals fell prey to political pressures.

In the experienced judgment of Devine, the Social Unit was not another "altruistic imposition" but a genuine effort to involve local communities in the decision making of experts. He was convinced that "it was unheard of in current practice to consult the beneficiaries of any program and to train them to become active on their own behalf."[163] In his indictment of the fragmentation of social services, Hyman Kaplan argued that the specialization of services had actually contributed to the destruction of neighborhoods and local communities. Like Phillips, he advocated the need for a buffer between the client and the specialist and argued that this function was dependent upon the political mobilization of these communities into participatory democracies.[164]

Many influential pioneers of social work were also sensitive to the need to consider the social environs of their clients in the formulation of treatment. Despite his emphasis on individual treatment, Healy was sensitive to "the complex of factors which make for delinquency; there are many social elements, deprivations and pressures that cannot possibly be bettered by clinical effort alone." Ultimately, he argued, "any project for the prevention of delinquency will be confronted with the necessity for modification of the spirit or ideology of community life."[165] Richmond reminded social workers that it was not enough for them "to speak the language of democracy; they must have in their hearts its spiritual conviction of the infinite worth of our common humanity before they can be fit to do any form of social work whatsoever."[166] Richmond's work was published just before the new ideas of psychology and the new therapies of psychiatry were to have a decisive influence on social work, and precisely because of the inadequacies of her conceptions of personality, her efforts to understand human behavior in the context of a complex social environment were neglected.[167] She also alerted social workers to their increasing dependence on the regulated disbursements of the community chest, which she regarded as a serious threat to their professional autonomy. Not only incompetent public authorities but also large and often opinionated donors threatened the professional autonomy of social work.[168]

Various efforts were made at the neighborhood level to preserve or to reconstitute primary relationships, but the degree to which these local communities were envisaged as participatory polities was a matter of debate. In any event it was assumed that the coordination of the broader interests of these neighborly cells would require the services of specialists or experts organized as state agencies designed to respond to the particular but interdependent needs of the city. Justifications of public intervention were now firmly grounded in efforts to confront the segmentation of urban society as a whole.[169] Once the problems of segmentation were linked to decentralization, a preoccupation with the suburban destiny of urban society obscured the persistence of many of the social and environmental problems of the inner city.

The panacea of decentralization

These explorations of the relationship between a growing dependence upon the expertise of specialists and the political role of neighborhoods were overwhelmed by efforts to harness the processes of urban decentralization in the interests of efficiency. The shift from a moral to an economic interpretation of housing conditions had initially drawn attention to the issues of inadequate wages and unemployment, but during the second decade of the twentieth century, decentralization within the framework of a city plan was viewed as a more comprehensive solution of the social and environmental problems of the city. Under these circumstances the neighborhood became the social unit defined by the circulatory patterns of the city, and the slums were a residue of an older, less efficient spatial order. After generations of concern with the need to instill in the poor the values of prudence and thrift, Simon Patten's influential economics of abundance explored the social implications of increasing consumption. These ideas stimulated a preoccupation with the recreational activities and service needs of urban society and especially with the creation of an appropriate urban infrastructure to facilitate these needs.[170] The search for a unified approach to the complexity of urban society was initially broadly based on several emerging professions, but efforts to combine environmental improvements with community development were increasingly concentrated in the expanding profession of city planning. At a time when social work moved away from a primary concern with the environmental deficiencies of the slums to a preoccupation with the psychoanalytical foundations of deviant behavior, city planning confronted the need to create an efficient spatial order to facilitate access not only between work and residence but also between residence and recreation.

A major source of this interest in the recreational needs and circulatory structure of urban society was the City Beautiful movement and related efforts to provide parks and other urban amenities at a metropolitan scale.[171] During the last decade of the nineteenth century, following the lead of Chicago's "White City" and the establishment of Boston's metropolitan park system, several municipalities had attempted to restore their physical unity by monuments, parks, and boulevards designed in accordance with a classical motif, but increasingly this search for an urban aesthetic became enmeshed in the need to improve the efficiency of the city by means of land-use controls. These controls were designed to subdivide the city into homogeneous areas or zones.[172] Julius Harder stressed the need to combine city planning and civic beautification in *Municipal Affairs,* the publication of the Reform Club of New York, but it was Charles Robinson who provided momentum for the fusion of reform movements and the efficient organization of the city.[173]

As early as 1903 Robinson had anticipated the necessity of dividing "the city into parts, according to the purposes it serves; and each of these parts has presented a question of development by itself, while the great, all-embracing urban problem has proved to be the co-ordination of these into a single scheme comprehensive and harmonious." Robinson attempted to fuse aesthetic and functional issues: "If the end be to clothe utility with beauty . . . [there are] three requirements: Those that have to do with circulation, those that have to do with hygiene, and those that have to do distinctly with beauty. No hard lines separate these classes. . . . " His book, *The Improvement of Cities and Towns,* published by Robinson himself because of presumed financial risks attending publication, became the agenda for hundreds of local improvement societies, whose membership often overlapped with other reform movements. He concluded: "Personified, modern civic art appears as a sort of social reformer, for if the eye be that of the artist, there yet is surely in it the tear of the philanthropist."[174] This approach was publicized by exhibits at the Louisiana Purchase Exposition in St. Louis in 1904, where displays on matters of social economy and a "model" street were intended to energize reform by means of public education.[175]

Somewhat later the exhibit organized by Marsh and the CCP also recommended the planned decentralization of people and employment as a solution to urban congestion. In 1909 Marsh collaborated with the Municipal Art Society in preparing another major exhibit devoted more broadly to city planning and eventually presented in Washington at the first National Conference of City Planning. Strongly influenced by European and especially German ideas about comprehensive planning, Marsh stressed the need to regulate new building in accordance with a preconceived plan that included specified land-use zones. These ideas were forcefully expressed in his book *An Introduction to City Planning: Democracy's Challenge and the American City.*[176] Frustrations with the older tradition of regulating congestion, along with the growing conviction that the decentralization of employment would enhance the suburban movement, directed the attention of housing reformers towards the need to propose an integrated city plan. Since industry was congested in the inner city, the nascent profession of city planning stressed industrial decentralization as a solution to congestion. Some skeptics argued that ethnic institutions rather than local employment stimulated residential concentration, for many residents of the Lower East Side commuted to work in Hoboken and Jersey City and indicated no inclination to live near to their jobs.[177] The majority view held: "The old theory that congestion is due to the congregation of nationalities which desire to live huddled together in little colonies is fallacious. In studying the distribution of workers in the factories of New York City it has been found that in every instance it is the location of the place of work, and not the nationality group which determines residence."[178]

At a time when most authorities were confident that policies of decentralization required no radical changes in the organization of society at large, Marsh insisted that new tax policies similar to those proposed by Henry George would be required to make the decentralization policies effective. His commitment to the reform of property and land taxation alienated him not only from his patrons but from most other planners too. In brief, he attributed congestion to tax policies that stimulated speculation in land and to the develoment of local transportation without any related measures to decentralize industry.[179] Marsh thought a new principle of taxation was the answer, but most planners were reluctant to separate this one factor from the numerous other factors that contributed to congestion. Veiller and other older housing reformers reasserted their separate identity by founding the National Housing Association. Veiller dismissed Marsh's assertion about the relationship between congestion and exploitation, low wages, and land policies and continued to stress the need to regulate the height and arrangement of buildings. To Veiller, the enforcement of existing regulations would limit lot congestion, and since he believed that room overcrowding was caused by the social habits of tenement residents, he dismissed proposals to "distribute" immigrants in rural areas where, he argued, they would reproduce crowded conditions.[180] At the second National Conference on City Planning held in Rochester in 1910 "congestion" was dropped from the list of issues, and the organization developed policies that were less offensive to business interests.[181]

This perspective was especially prominent in the newly established *National Municipal Review*. John Ihlder, for example, justified planning on the grounds that the elimination of social and environmental problems would diminish future public expenditures. The Philadelphia Housing Commission made similar arguments in proposing new standards of "hygienic efficiency."[182] For several decades the administration of both public health and municipal engineering had become specialized civic responsibilities, and the established expertise of these professions strongly influenced the nascent profession of city planning.[183] The technical and scientific pretensions of the new civic professions were expressed in the form of regulations that were formulated and administered by specialists. For early city planners, zoning regulations became the core of their technical expertise. To be sure, there were many reformers who, like George Ford, viewed planning as a matter of the scientific coordination of specialist services and continued to emphasize the need to confront social problems as part of the challenge of environmental management.[184] Increasingly, however, a preoccupation with the technical and legal processes involved in the facilitation and control of decentralization stressed the specialist rather than the integrative role of planning.

Since decentralization was regarded as the leading solution to urban congestion, it was thought that regulations that interfered with suburbanization would be counterproductive. Housing reformers had become increasingly sensitive to the need to relax or at least modify the regulations necessary in the inner city in applying them to the rapidly growing suburbs. Veiller, for example, argued: "One of the chief problems of any tenement house law is in adapting it to the differing conditions of different parts of our cities, which vary all the way from crowded sections in which land values are so high that only tall buildings can be profitable, to country districts in which land is so cheap that it is only adapted to the two or three storey frame house. . . . Its solution lies in the adoption of the principle of height as the determining factor."[185] There were also efforts to distinguish between the regulation of poorly built tenements and that of elegant apartment buildings, but such a procedure would have acknowledged the existence of class distinctions, which even reformers found hard to accept. As early as 1904 Boston had imposed differential height requirements in the central area on the grounds that higher building densities created a greater fire hazard than in the remainder of the city. In New York the conflicting claims of retail activities, warehouses, and high-rent residences brought a demand for regulation from the world of private property.[186] All streets were allocated to five levels of height restrictions, which were determined as multiples of street width. Each section of the city was also "zoned" to be exclusively devoted to residential, industrial, unrestricted, or undetermined uses. These policies were also extended to include suburban areas, since in rapidly growing cities, new investments in residential areas could be threatened by undesirable neighbors.

Eventually, the principle of zoning made it possible to enforce regulations differentially. The key ideas of comprehensive planning were the enhancement of efficiency by means of a system of circulation and the enhancement of the aesthetic setting by means of parks, which were often integrated into a complex weblike framework of arterial boulevards. These ventures were less attentive to the interstitial areas where housing conditions were extremely varied, and improvements were often part of a "boosterlike" effort to improve a city's image. The most ambitious fusion of aesthetics and functionalism was revealed in Burnham's plan for Chicago, which proposed a system of arterial routes linked to an elaborate lakeside and peripheral park system.[187] The street system was conceived of as three patterns or as one underlying and two superimposed patterns. The older gridiron pattern was overlaid by no fewer than four concentric arcs and by several diagonals radiating out from the hub to intercept the successive arcs. These diagonals were necessary correctives to the gridiron pattern and symbolized a more global view of city structure, and the arcs provided a rationale for functional differentiation, with the inner zones devoted to distribution and the outer zones to recreation.[188] The interstitial areas were not ignored, but their social provisionment rather than their environmental deficiencies became the focus of attention. The framework of transportation defined residential districts, which were to be provided with a focus of social amenities or civic centers anchored to a main civic center adjacent to the central business district.[189]

The playground movement advocated the virtues of recreational open spaces as nodal points of neighborhood activities. Some proponents of playgrounds felt that the therapeutic impact of parks was derived from exposure to their natural settings, but increasingly this faith in the spontaneous effects of the environment was abandoned in favor of instructive play directed by professional recreational managers.[190] The necessity to offer alternatives to the autonomous and spontaneous play of the street and to commercial entertainment led to the formation of the Playground Association of America in 1907. Under the leadership of Joseph Lee and Luther Gulick the association developed a philosophy of supervised play, based upon the works of the psychologist G. Stanley Hall. The growth of children into adults involved developmental phases during which individuals recapitulated the primordial instincts of their primitive ancestry. During each phase organized play, and especially team games, served as "syphons" through which biosocial acquisitions might be isolated and then cultivated in a fashion that would render these instincts appropriate to the demands of modern urban life.[191] The association introduced a decidedly professional approach to the use of playgrounds. Professional field secretaries of the association were described as "Play Efficiency Engineers"; their duties were to run a "play factory" on a schedule and to produce the maximum amount of happiness. Under these circumstances the connection between progressive proposals and older ideas about the natural and spontaneous bases of community was completely severed.

Although the justifications of planning stressed the coordination of environmental and community issues, the design of neighborhoods increasingly became a technical response to the need for pedestrian access to local facilities under conditions of low-density housing. A community

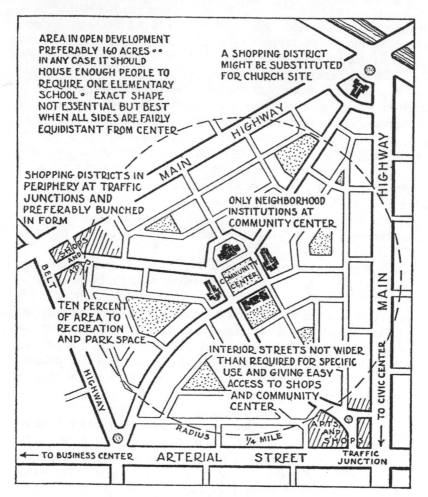

Figure 4.13 The neighborhood unit formula

Source: Regional Survey, vol. 7, *Neighborhood and Community Planning* (New York: Regional Plan of New York and Its Environs, 1927–31).

was defined as including those areas enclosed by a half-mile radius from a school and social center with higher-order facilities strategically located at points of maximum accessibility for appropriate groupings of neighborhoods (Figure 4.13).[192] These plans assumed a painless relocation of those replaced by improvements and neglected the issue of housing conditions. Robinson had assumed that decentralization would eliminate congestion and that housing improvement would result from "wise ordinances so enforced that there are no rookeries, that there is nothing worse than this to which the poor can go." The slum was simply a consequence of "the failure of the city to protect itself from gross evils and known perils, all of which should be corrected by the enforcement of simple principles of sanitation that are recognized to be just, equitable and necessary." For these reasons, the slum was described as "a condition, not a place, and will crop up in the most unexpected places, wherever vigilance is relaxed. The foundation of the slum rests in the social and economic relations of society, and can be effectually attacked only through them. The slum can never be eradicated by erecting model dwellings, however well planned, nor by any other superficial method alone."[193]

Between 1907 and 1917 numerous comprehensive plans were prepared, including those for the fifty most populous cities in the country. In New York the Bureau of Municipal Research under the leadership of William Allen, a former agent of the AICP, became a pioneering agency dedicated to research based policy analysis.[194] By 1920 there were twenty-five cities with similar agencies, and in 1922 these researchers formed the National Institute of Public Administration; despite the less receptive attitudes of the 1920s, no fewer than sixty-two cities had established municipal research agencies. The scale and ambition of city plans in the United States were unmatched in the rest of the urbanized world, but their physical implementation was actually partial and often nonexistent. Many plans were propaganda exercises that avoided confronting the adequacy of urban government to meet such ambitious visions.[195] Because of his commitment to comprehensive regional planning, Clarence Stein was one of the few experts who recognized: "The standard that the public has required for its own protection has gradually risen. The ability of the individual to pay for that standard has diminished. Thus there has steadily grown this divergence – this ominous parting of the ways – between the standard of house set by the community – the adequate house – and the inadequate incomes of those that cannot dwell in that house."[196] Apart from the activities of Stein and his associates, who organized the Regional Planning Association of America (RPAA), the need to provide appropriate credit facilities or public subsidies for housing construction was rarely confronted in ambitious proposals for the planned decentralization of urban society.[197]

The formation of the National Bureau of Economic Research at the federal level represented a similar approach to economic planning. This agency sought to organize and educate business people rather than civic executives and was based on the assumption that informed decisions at the managerial level would enhance the efficient outcome of the invisible hand of the market. In short, planning was to be achieved not by more government but by the creation of autonomous advisory agencies staffed by experts.[198] Urban society was too complex to be based entirely on face-to-face contacts, and the new American democracy would need the help of specialists and a more sensitive local polity. The conflicts between experts and interests were anticipated: "While it is true that the execution of radical measures must result inevitably in greater restrictions upon individuals and corporations, and thus interferes with that liberty which is the essence of American institutions[,] . . . in this matter the interests of the citizens collectively are identical with and supersede those of the individual." They were, however, confident that "the mere establishment of a comprehensive general proposition for improvements will result in voluntary conformity to it in many cases where such conformation will be simpler and more economical than to do otherwise."[199]

For these reasons, reevaluations of progressive social thought have argued that many reformers retained conservative and moralistic views of social problems. They also greatly exaggerated the indifference of public authorities to social needs during the second half of the nineteenth century, and especially the contrasts between Victorian individualism and progressive collectivism. The bulk of progressive reforms were intended to release the poor from circumstances that made it impossible for them to help themselves. The state was regarded as an acceptable instrument of moral improvement, and individualist means were abrogated in the higher interest of individualist ends.[200] The precise means and the specific ends never attracted the kind of agreement necessary to create a broad commitment to implementation. The limited impact of these visions of an orderly and efficient urban society did not provoke a reexamination of the prevailing interpretations of social problems but rather a growing conviction that the expertise of science might achieve a more orderly and desirable society if it was unencumbered by an ill-informed popular will.

Those skeptical of the educational approach to reform admired the results of the new laboratory-based preventive medicine "which should be universally applied for the defense of society against the evils which afflict it – such, for example, as alchoholism, prostitution and war. All the beneficent forces of society should combine to prevent these evils. . . . Medical research and preventive medicine are teaching the civilized world how to deal effectively with moral, as well as physical disease."[201] The issues of sanitary reform had been broadened into a public health movement that was highly dependent upon the sciences of engineering, chemistry and biology. The expertise of these sciences was often exempted from the critical debates about popular or legislative control of intervention. Indeed, in some matters of public health individuals might need to be forcefully protected from self-injury because of personal negligence. These claims were more narrowly defined once the medical profession was confronted with the fact that social causes were as critical as microbic influences in matters of public health.[202]

Frustrations about the impact of social reform were also expressed in relation to the effects of foreign immigration on the cultural unity of the United States. Some degree of cultural homogeneity was judged to be necessary for the survival of American democracy. Despite draconian measures to accelerate assimilation during and after World War I, the attainment of a cultural unity based upon adaptations to an Anglo-American host society or upon the fusion of specified immigrant strains was threatened by the continued arrival of incompatible immigrants. Since most immigrants were concentrated in the slums, their "ethnic" character became inextricably linked to social problems of the city. Whether they were viewed as undesirable aliens who ought to be excluded from the United States or as exotic newcomers facing the painful early adaptations to American life, the immigrant predicament was identified with the environmental limitations and social isolation of the slums. These more sensitive views of the immigrant poor did have the altruistic purpose of arousing sympathy for reform, and they were often tempered by a belief in the assimilative capacity of American society.

Those most committed to an open immigration policy were confident about the process of assimilation, but increasingly they saw the necessity for paternalistic educational measures to ensure the process.[203] This confidence remained rooted in conceptions of American society that presumed a high level of cultural homogeneity, although restrictionists expressed concern about the damaging effects of assimilation upon the racial character of the United States. Even those who, like Edward Ross, rejected "both the environmentalist position that belittles race differences and the racist fallacy that regards the actual differences of people as fixed and hereditary," were convinced that without restriction, the undesirable ethnic traits of the new immigrants would threaten the agenda for the reform of American society.[204] Since progressive reform was based upon the scientifically grounded proposals of specialists, the appeal of restriction was enormously increased by a growing confidence in the "science" of eugenics. Several leading restrictionists were committed to a eugenic interpretation of culture and insisted that although the new immigration "still included many strong elements from the north of Europe, [it also] contained a large and increasing number of the weak, the broken, and the mentally crippled of all races drawn from the lowest stratum of the Mediterranean basin and the Balkans, together with hordes of the wretched, submerged population of the Polish ghettos."[205]

Joseph Lee, pioneer of the playground movement, also organized the Immigration Restriction League, and Edward Devine, the radical editor of *Charities and Commons,* believed that "unselective" immigration threatened the established American heritage.[206] Some leaders of the settlement movement, including Robert Woods, eventually looked upon newly arrived immigrants "as an inferior breed of peasants in whom the human light had all but gone out. In time the residents would propose restricting immigration, and the gentlemen's burden would become, like the White Man's burden, an oppressive racism."[207] The compatibility of different races was now discussed within the framework of a "scientific" debate, the conclusions of which implied the imperative need to restrict immigration.

Growing anxieties about the feasibility of assimilation did not go unanswered. Grace Abbott, as director of the Immigrant's Protective League, encouraged newcomers to use their previous experience as a means of coping with American society and envisaged a society in which several "nationalities" might flourish within the fabric of American democracy.[208] Randolph Bourne, apprehensive about the aridity of the emerging mass culture of the host society, elaborated ideas projected by the melting pot. He envisaged a more cosmopolitan or "trans-national" culture that made more explicit recognition of the contributions of divergent immigrant cultures. His ideas were rooted in the works of the philosopher Josiah Royce, who had also confronted his fears about the "incomprehensible monster" of the nation-state, "in whose presence the individual loses his right, his self consciousness and his dignity." To Royce the solution was the preservation of provincial cultures that might serve as an intermediate loyalty, and Bourne recognized that ethnic groups might serve the same purpose.[209] Since the majority of immigrants from southern and eastern Europe had stronger loyalties to the villages and parishes of their homelands than they did to the remote empires or nations to which they formally belonged, these ideas were especially appropriate, if of limited influence, in describing the social world of most immigrants.

These efforts to recognize the contribution of ethnic cultures and to confront the cultural meaning of Americanization were most forcefully expressed by another philosopher, Horace Kallen, who was provoked to respond to the works of his academic colleague at that time, E. A. Ross.[210] In many respects his arguments were consistent with those of restrictionists who believed that ethnic cultures were not capable of assimilation, but Kallen saw no reason to exclude groups for this reason. There was no justification for either the exclusion or the forced assimilation of long-established cultures into a society that itself lacked the coherence of a highly developed national culture. Kallen envisaged a "symphonic harmony" of diverse tones that would enrich each other. To Kallen the nation's future was in the hands of dynamic cultures that set the fates of individuals. In a critique of Kallen, Isaac Berkson questioned the weight given to heritage in a federation of nationalities and argued that many immigrants, as individuals, sought to move beyond the limitations of their ethnic cultures.[211] Neo-Lamarckian ideas about heredity had influenced most discussion of immigration, and although an awareness of environmental influences modified these assumptions, their demise depended upon the growing influence of ideas that stressed the experiences of individuals as well as that of groups in the process of adaptation.[212] Precisely because of these hereditarian influences, the terms *race, ethnicity,* and *culture* were rarely used with precision, and as long as there were anxieties about the racial basis of ethnic cultures, the appeal of restriction was enhanced.

At the same time the debate about cultural and racial unity, which had been primarily confined to those areas of the country directly threatened by immigration, expanded to include the South and Southwest, and on the basis of this extended political base, discriminatory restriction was finally the law of the land.[213] Initially, the melting pot was a powerful symbol that aroused positive sentiments about assimilation.[214] Eugenic considerations, however, drew attention to the implications of miscegenation or hybridization, especially in regions that had not faced the issue of assimilation, and the image of a cauldron became a source of fear. In the words of John Highham, "The progressive spirit tended to weaken the late-nineteenth century connection between restriction and reform but did not generate an adequate countervailing philosophy of ethnic democracy. Consequently, the revival of a tolerant attitude toward immigration in the early twentieth century delayed the coming of restriction without revising its purpose and direction."[215] The residents of the slums were no longer simply the poor; they had become the unassimilated poor. Discussions of the slums were now inextricably connected with the racial and ethnic identity of their residents.

For almost a century the slums had evoked anxieties about the stability and quality of urban life. As an image, the slums projected the problems of environmental disabilities, social isolation, casual labor, and deviant behavior into a tidy, comprehensible object of reform. Initially the elaboration of these relationships amongst environment, space, and social problems softened the impact of changing interpretations of poverty. During the course of industrialization, social policies increasingly viewed the poor as morally delinquent rather than as the victims of providential misfortune. This indictment did, however, assume that delinquency would be responsive to reform, whereas the older patterns of paternalistic relief had assumed that poverty was endemic. Older social policies had also been based upon sedentary communities in which the beneficiaries of relief were friends and neighbors, but in the rapidly growing cities the migrant poor not only lacked any local patrons but also were judged to lack survival skills. Hereditary disabilities or ethnic limitations were reinforced in the adverse environment of the inner city, and since the poor were isolated from the elevating influences of the host society, the most depraved represented a contagious threat to those around them who strove to improve themselves. The slums were a symbol of these threatening conditions.

Despite the pessimism of hereditarian and cultural interpretations of poverty, for the vast majority of the poor, the environmental disabilities and social isolation of the slums were viewed as the main obstacles to self-improvement. Despite major efforts to confront these obstacles, social policies not only attempted to establish principles of moral eligibility for relief but also assumed that those who were morally ineligible were a residual minority. Under these circumstances the continued arrival of migrants from successively more exotic sources became a threat to the effectiveness of social policies and explained their modest impact. On the one hand, the limitations of the slums obstructed the self-improvement of their residents, but on the other, the hereditarian and cultural disabilities of residents inhibited their capacity for self-improvement. Towards the turn of the nineteenth century this paradox provoked explorations of the structural setting of poverty, and especially the degree to which unemployment was the most critical obstacle to self-improvement. During periodic economic depressions, the downward mobility of those who had earlier overcome the environmental obstacles of the slums led to a growing recognition that the slums were a consequence rather than a cause of poverty. The sociogeographic boundary between the slum and the remainder of urban society was a precipitous slope that had become too steep for the poor to climb.

Progressive public policies had attempted to lower the gradient and facilitate advancement, but increasingly the ethnic and racial identities of the poor were judged to be obstacles to their advancement and, more critically, a threat to the culture of the host society. The successful implementation of immigration restriction ironically exacerbated anxieties about the assimilation of the residents of the slums, for the reduction in the volume of immigration from southern and eastern Europe was offset by an increase in the movement of southern blacks to northern cities. The term *ghetto* was not used with any consistency until after World War I, but prior to the war it expressed a redefinition of the relationship between the slums and the remainder of urban society. Whereas "slum" had described the isolation of the poor from the moral order of a unified civic society, "ghetto" described an exclusion from a more complex, segmented world defined by varied patterns of consumption. This redefinition occurred at a time when another powerful symbol, the suburb, came to represent a natural solution to urban congestion. To a greater degree than in any other rapidly urbanizing country, American middle-income suburbs served by extensive systems of local transportation had attained unparalleled dimensions. This new urban vision deflected attention not only from the economic issues that had dominated the initial progressive response to the slums but also from adaptations to change that were occurring without the patronage of experts.

It was assumed that lower land costs on the edge of the city would yield housing costs within reach of all but the destitute, and although suburban neighborhoods did develop their own social order, it was based upon the new levels of consumption of a mass society. Increasingly the suburban movement was viewed as a natural process of social mobility in which public policies were of minor consequence. By about 1920 many reformers realized that government policies did not necessarily yield their intended results, and consequently the nature of urban society and especially the condition of the slums were examined as the product of broader social processes rather than as objects of reform. Although reformers were committed to removing obstructions to progress by means of social engineering, social theorists were developing generalizations that described a social transformation that, despite its disruptive character, was creating a new social order. These ideas undermined the hereditarian and eugenic assumptions upon which immigration restriction had been based. The ghetto was interpreted in relation to a growing body of generalizations that viewed migration from a genetic perspective. The social disruptions and adaptations that migrants encountered once they abandoned their more traditional rural world were identified with the ghetto, but the ghetto was also identified with adaptations that made possible the assimilation and advancement of their temporary residents.

PART II

The relationships reformulated

5
Ethnicity and assimilation

During the first two decades of the twentieth century, interpretations of the slums became embedded in efforts to confront the complex interdependencies of the modern city. These efforts were associated with trained professionals who staffed public agencies designed to alleviate and remove those social and environmental problems that obstructed self-improvement and the efficient conduct of urban life. Initially some progressive diagnoses of the social and environmental problems of the slums included an awareness of the structural obstacles to social mobility, but eventually solutions were linked to the zoned decentralization of people and activities. By the turn of the nineteenth century there was broad support for some degree of public intervention as a means to remove obstacles to social mobility, but increasingly the frustrations involved in the implementation of public policies raised questions about the degree to which the state could and did direct social change. The expanding role of the state was regarded as only one aspect of a broader social transformation, which had become the leading object of contemporary social theory. Modern society was the outcome of the disruption of traditional communities and the emergence of a more complex and highly differentiated social order. The old regime was based on primary relationships and local solidarities of family and ethnicity, whereas the new order was organized around the secondary relationships of occupational and interest groups. These generalizations also took the form of moral judgments about the respective merits of tradition and modernity. The growing dependence on the bureaucratic state and the degraded recreational purposes of many secondary associations provoked anxieties about a "mass society" in which culture would decline to the level of the lowest common denominator.

Since these changes were assumed to have been initiated in cities, modern society was judged to be generically urban, whereas the diminishing traditional world was identified with remote rural areas. The diffusion of modern social changes from cities had gradually transformed the countryside, and the cityward migration of rural people had compressed their experience of this transformation into weeks or months rather than decades. American cities were the leading recipients of rural migrants, not only from North America but from Europe, Central and South America, and South and East Asia as well. Most northeastern and midwestern and some western cities received substantial and diverse inflows of migrants; Chicago in particular became the symbol of the destiny of modern urban life. Chicago was a leading focus not only of the ideas and practice of progressivism but also of another influential generation of observers dedicated to extending scientific understanding of the city rather than to the immediate goals of reform. Their intensive investigations of this prototypical modern city yielded an interpretation of urban society described as the "Chicago School."[1]

Their loosely connected and occasionally inconsistent generalizations about urban society were based upon a concept of assimilation that described the migrants' experience of urbanization. They rejected the idea that social organization developed from the like-mindedness of individuals and stressed instead the frequencies and kinds of their social interactions. In the past, migrations and conquests had thrown different groups into contact. These encounters were initially a source of conflict, but eventually competing groups reached accommodations with each other. The modern nation-state represented the consequences of these fusions. These relationships between migrants and their host society had often taken the form of subjugation, but initial conflicts were also the basis of interactions upon which mutual accommodations between groups were constructed. As the most likely source of interactions between groups, conflict rather than like-mindedness sustained social organization. These ideas were derived from the works of Gustav Ratzenhofer, Georg Simmel, and other leading German sociologists, and Sarah Simons provided American audiences with an initial summary of this debate as part of a lengthy examination of social assimilation.[2] Through the writings and lectures of Albion Small, founder of the Chicago School, ideas about conflict and interaction reached a wider audience, but it was William Thomas who adapted this interpretation of social change to the experiences of European migrants in the United States.[3] Just as their ancestral cultures were based upon the common experiences of prolonged residence in their European homelands, their common experiences of migration and settlement in American cities would be the source of a new social world based upon their participation as individuals in the democratic polity of the United States. In contrast to the pessimistic and eugenic reactions of immigration restrictionists, the Chicago School offered an optimistic interpretation of assimilation as conflict, interaction, and participation.

With the departure of Thomas from Chicago, Robert Park became the key figure of the Chicago School. The majority of his collaborators and students elaborated his ideas in the context of rich local studies of Chicago, but several of his colleagues also made their own independent contributions to generalizations about urban society.[4] They shifted the focus of generalizations about the city from the diagnoses of social problems to the analysis of social processes. To Park the city epitomized modernity: "In the freedom of the city every individual, no matter how eccentric, finds somewhere an environment in which he can expand and bring what is peculiar in his nature to some sort of expression. A smaller community sometimes tolerates eccentricity, but the city often rewards it."[5] In the city traditions and customs no longer restrained individuals, and the challenge of urban society was the need to reconcile or balance the requirements of human collaboration with the goal of individual freedom.[6] Social change was interpreted in relation to an organic view of urban society that implied that interventions would be most successful when they were consistent with the direction of natural social processes.[7] These arguments implied that a level of public intervention more restrained than that proposed by progressive reformers might be prudent. This position was not held with any unanimity, and Louis Wirth, possibly the most influential of Park's students, considered planning to be a struggle against ecological processes. In the city, he argued, these processes created conditions that "weaken our capacity to act rationally, to determine consensual values and to make these values the basis of a planned moral and political order."[8]

The Chicago School felt that it had identified social processes of which its progressive predecessors were unaware. For these reasons, Park argued that the slum districts ought to be "studied not merely for their own sake, but for what they can reveal to us of human behavior and human nature generally."[9] Ernest Burgess distinguished the numerous social surveys designed to define a reform agenda from scientific social research, which was "not concerned with factors, but with forces. The distinction is not always drawn between a factor and a force. According to Park factors are elements that cooperate to make a given situation. Forces are type-factors operative in typical situations."[10] Most progressives were committed to policies based upon a scientific understanding of social problems, but in the opinion of the Chicago School, they retained many of the moral judgments of older reform traditions and proposed unrealistic modifications of the social order. Thomas concluded that the urban condition was "much more serious than the moralist conceives it, but much less limited and determined than it appears to the economic determinist."[11]

Like their own critics, participants of the Chicago School often exaggerated their differences with the progressive reform tradition and many of their local surveys and participant observations owed much to the experiential sensitivities of muckraking journalists and settlement house workers.[12] The Chicago School did stress social processes that had proceeded without the patronage of regulatory policies. For these reasons, its research was sensitive to the adaptations of migrants to their new urban environment. For over a century reformers had identified the deficiencies of family life as a critical defect in the social environment of the slums. They had, however, struggled to define the degree to which disruptions of the larger community setting rather than the family itself were a source of social problems. At a time when the treatment of social problems was increasingly based upon psychiatric principles, the Chicago School also stressed the ways in which local communities exerted a profound influence on individual behavior. Social problems were directly linked to circumstances that inhibited the development of those adaptations and to relationships that were replacing the once dominant influences of the family. Delinquency was, therefore, in Park's words, "the measure of the failure of our community organizations to function."[13]

The slums were those parts of the city where old forms of social control were losing their effectiveness and where new forms of association had failed to develop. This absence of either old or new forms of social organization was not necessarily found throughout the slums, and in the immigrant quarters ancestral patterns of life continued to guide the adaptations of the migrant generation. These adaptations revealed the continuing influence of traditional patterns of life, and although they assisted the migrant generation, they could also obstruct or delay the assimilation of their native-born children. The second generation was often marginal to both the modified world of their ancestors and the host society that demanded but resisted its assimilation. This marginality resulted in social disorganization. The discomforts of migration and urbanization and the confrontations with the different values of American society were judged to be the causes of short-term social problems. These negative interpretations of the immigrant experience did, however, assume that over the longer term, the descendants of most migrants would be assimilated into the mainstream of American society. In short, the disorganized social conditions of the inner city were temporary consequences of conflicts between the disrupted traditional world of the migrant generation and the pressures for and obstacles to rapid assimilation encountered by their native-born descendants.

The residents defined: temporary social disorganization

The extraordinary and excessive cityward movement of people greatly strained the adaptive capacities of modern society and was judged to be the primary reason why urbanization was associated with temporary social disorganization. As the outcome of natural social processes, the interpretation of urban society was presented in the form of an organic analogy. Park proposed "a conception of the city, the community and the region, not as a geographical phenomenon merely, but as a kind of social organism."[14] Burgess elaborated this viewpoint when he described urban growth as "a process of organization and disorganization analogous to the anabolic and katabolic processes of the body. While city growth based on natural growth might be thought of as normal, the excessive growth based upon migration was viewed as a disturbance of the normal metabolic system." He then developed an interpretation of the relationship between migration and social disorganization: "If the phenomena of expansion and metabolism indicate that a moderate degree of disorganization may and does facilitate social organization, they indicate as well that rapid urban expansion is accompanied by excessive increases in disease, crime, disorder, vice, insanity and suicide, rough indexes of social disorganization. But what are the indexes of the causes, rather than the effects, of the disordered metabolism of the city? The excess of the actual over the natural increase of the population has already been suggested as a criterion."[15]

Immigrants were not only the primary cause of this disturbing or excessive population growth of cities; as the predominant residents of the inner-city slums, immigrants were also likely to be the main victims of social disorganization. Uprooted from their rural homelands, immigrants were assumed to be ill prepared for the demands of an unfamiliar urban world. They shared the slums with those rootless individuals who sought freedom and anonymity in the city and those who had been unable to move on to improved quarters. Harvey Zorbaugh's classic study of the heterogeneous populations of the slums identified at least three distinct kinds of immigrants there: "birds of passage," who intended to return to their homeland with the savings made possible by their endurance of low living standards in America; newly arrived, impoverished immigrants who had not had time to accumulate any resources; and minority groups, such as blacks and Asians, who were excluded from more desirable areas.[16] These interpetations of the slums shifted attention from the eugenic speculations that had provided much of the impetus for immigration restriction. Assertions about ethnic predispositions and hereditary susceptibilities to delinquency were questioned, since "extremes of poverty, disease and behavioral troubles found everywhere in slum populations are products of social disorganization; rather than of low quality of the populations."[17]

Despite the association of the slums with social disorganization, most contributors to the Chicago School were aware of the degree to which many immigrant groups had transplanted or adapted their ancestral institutions and patterns of life to cope with the demands of American urban life. These developments protected the migrant generation from social disorganization, but they also presented barriers to the assimilation of later generations. These conflicts between the foreign-born and native-born generations were viewed as causes of social disorganization. Thomas and Znaniecki explored this conflict in their monumental examination of the Polish peasant in Europe and America. Although Polish peasants reestablished fragments of their village social order in American cities and thereby provided a familiar milieu for many newly arrived migrants, the necessity for employment usually involved direct confrontation with the values and expectations of American society. Polish peasants were therefore marginal to the social worlds of both their homelands and their adopted country. No longer subject to the restraints of the traditional culture, they were unable to cope with the uncertainties of modern life. Return migration and the continued arrival of newcomers maintained contacts between the homeland and the colonies in the United States, but emigration had also become indispensable to survival in rural Poland. The ancestral Polish village was no longer a stable and authentic cultural reference.[18]

On the basis of this detailed study of a major migrant group, Thomas prepared a broad survey of the immigrant experience that was published under the authorship of Park and Miller.[19] In this work greater emphasis was placed on the success of institutional adaptations to life in the American city. These developments were closer to a process of social reorganization than to the anticipated disorganization of migrant life. Jewish and Asian immigrants were identified as groups that had arrived in America with their social organization intact; they were therefore protected against the rapid dissolution of their ancestral culture. Similarly, Zorbaugh, in a study that emphasized social disorganization, recognized: "In the slum the immigrant finds quarters that he can afford and no opposition to his settlement. They created a social world of familiar institutions from which they derive respect, sympathy and encouragement." For these reasons immigrants often resisted efforts to relocate them in improved quarters, but it was not until a generation later that this issue became a critical part of the debate about the social damage of urban renewal.[20]

Notwithstanding the varying degrees to which different groups reestablished an ethnic social order in the slums, it was assumed that although the children of immigrants rejected their parents' pattern of life, they were not yet fully assimilated into American society. This marginality was judged to be the leading cause of juvenile delinquency amongst the native-born adolescents of immigrant groups. Interpretations of delinquency were, however, sensitive to the problems of adolescents who were unwilling or unable to gain access to the secondary associations of American sociey. In Park's judgment the culpability for delinquency lay in part with "[t]he older social agencies, the church, the school, and the courts, [which] have not always been able to meet the problems which new conditions of life have created. The school, the church, and the courts have come down to us with their aims and methods defined under the influence of an older tradition."[21] He had higher expectations of agencies like the juvenile courts, parent–teacher associations, the Boy Scouts, and playground associations, which had "taken over to some extent the work which neither the home, the neighborhood, nor the other older communal institutions were able to carry on adequately." These associations "are frankly experimental and are trying to work out a rational technique for dealing with social problems, based not on sentiment and tradition, but on science."[22] Park was apprehensive about these new institutions, particularly after his experience as president of the National Community Center Association from 1922 to 1924. He encountered firsthand the narrow perspectives of many new associations and was disillusioned with the limitations of their communal goals. For these reasons he was especially sensitive to the surviving sense of community in the presumably temporary immigrant subcultures of the inner city.[23]

Park stressed the ways in which new primary relationships based upon a defined turf or locality were more critical to the social organization of the slums than to most new secondary associations. He believed that this territorial organization could be the basis of social reconstruction since the urban political system of ward bosses was built upon broadly similar relationships.[24] The manipulation of elections, the extensive use of bribery, and the criminal diversion of public funds and resources under the direction of an ethnic "boss" had for long been viewed as direct threats dents of the ghetto failed to share the values of the host society. Of course, corruption was not unknown amongst established American politicians, and one Irish-American commentator was provoked to contrast the "dishonest" graft of individual greed from the "honest" graft of ethnic paternalism.[25] In the absence of organized public welfare, highly personal favors and services organized at public expense by local immigrant politicians have been judged, in retrospect, to have been indispensable supplements to the subsistence of many immigrant families. Clearly the fiscal and moral implications of this kind of social accounting are extremely controversial, but like many other negative indexes of life in the ghetto, "boss" politics was in fact an organized effort to obtain power and influence.

Although much attention was devoted to social disorganization, the Chicago School did not approach this process "so much from the standpoint of social pathology but as an aspect of interaction and adjustment process that eventually leads into social reorganization."[26] Burgess explicitly connected the processes of disorganization and organization, which, he argued, "may be thought of as in reciprocal relationship to each other, and as cooperating in a moving equilibrium of social order toward an end vaguely or definitively regarded as progressive. So far as disorganization points to reorganization and makes for more efficient adjustment, disorganization must be considered not as pathological, but as normal."[27]

The environment defined: ecological settings

Rather than defining the structural conditions that contributed to disorganization and reorganization, the Chicago School emphasized the relationships between social problems and the ecological processes of urbanization. Burgess described their agenda as an effort "to describe urban expansion in terms of extension, succession, and concentration; to determine how expansion disturbs metabolism when disorganization is in excess of organization; and finally, to define mobility and to propose it as a measure both of expansion and metabolism, susceptible to precise quantitative formulation, so that it might be regarded literally as the pulse of the community."[28] On the one hand, the outcomes of these ecological processes were natural areas or neighborhood communities, but on the other hand, in the modern city these same processes were leading to the dissolution of localized communities. Roderick McKenzie initially confronted these issues in a pioneering study of neighborhoods as local communities in Columbus, Ohio. He concluded that high rates of turnover disrupted the neighborhood principle and that this mobility was for many residents a source of emancipation from the narrow confines of a locality. Under conditions of turnover and mobility, the neighborhood principle was an obsolete or at least a questionable foundation of social reform.[29] Burgess was convinced that the social forces of city life were destroying the neighborhood and that social workers should turn their attention to the relationships between neighborhoods and the city at large, since many once local activities were increasingly becoming concentrated in specialized quarters.[30] The neighborhood as a natural area was itself threatened with dissolution as changes in urban society altered the territorial basis of social organization.[31]

Although their theory of social change predicted the diminution of primary relationships of neighborhoods, the persistence of these relationships in the natural areas of the inner city was a major focus of the Chicago School. Park described urban society as "a mosaic of minor communities, many of them strikingly different from one another, but all more or less typical. . . . Every American city has its slums; its ghettos; its immigrant colonies, regions which maintain more or less alien and exotic cultures. . . . These are the so called natural areas of the city. . . . They are natural," he added, "because they are not planned, and because the order that they display is not the result of design, but rather a manifestation of tendencies inherent in the urban situation; tendencies that city plans seek – though not always successfully – to control and correct. In short, the structure of the city, as we find it, is clearly just as much the product of the struggle and efforts of its people to live and work together collectively as are its local customs, traditions, social ritual, laws, public opinion and the prevailing moral order."[32] Natural areas "do not derive their features merely from the sum of the traits of the people who inhabit them; rather they attract populations appropriate to their character. Nor are they the result of the expressions of public will through governments, city planners, or community leaders."[33]

As "natural areas" immigrant quarters resembled the rural communities from which many residents had emigrated, but according to Thomas and Znaniecki, it was not a simple transplantation: "The evolution of the Polish community in this country is . . . the reverse of the evolution of the primary peasant communities in Poland. Whereas territorial vicinity is there the original foundation of community life and all social organization is built upon this basis, here reflective social organization becomes the main factor in territorial concentration. When, however, the latter has been in a considerable measure achieved the process is reversed again and social organization, just as in Poland, begins to depend on territorial neighborhood."[34] Park generalized about these developments and concluded that "partly as a result of selection and segregation, and partly in view of the contagious character of cultural patterns, that people living in the natural areas of the same general type and subject to the same social conditions will display, on the whole, the same characteristics." Consequently, "[p]roximity and neighborly contact are the basis for the simplest and most elementary form of association . . . in the organization of city life. Local interests and associations breed local sentiment, and, under a system which makes residence the basis for participation in government, the neighborhood becomes the basis of political control. . . . The neighborhood exists without formal organization. The local improvement society is a structure erected on the basis of spontaneous neighborhood organization and exists for the purpose of giving expression to the local sentiment in regard to matters of local interest."[35]

Wirth's interpretation of the Jewish ghetto of the near West Side of Chicago argued that the most remarkable aspect of the concentration of immigrant groups "is not where each shall locate, but the fact that each seems to find its own separate location without the apparent design of anyone. . . . [O]nce in the area, each group tends to reproduce the culture to which it was accustomed in its old habitat as nearly as the new conditions permit[,] . . . a patchwork of little ghettos that constitute the great immigrant quarters of our large cities. . . . Each seeks his own habitat much like plants and animals in the world of nature, each has its own kind of food, of family life and of amusement."[36] In his prefatory remarks to Wirth's study, Park defined the ghetto as a natural area because it "meets a need and performs a social function" and extended the term to include any segregated racial or cultural group. In addition to Jewish immigrants, "[o]ther alien people have come among us who have sought, or had imposed upon them the same sort of isolation. Our cities turn out, upon examination, to be a mosaic of segregated peoples – each seeking to preserve its peculiar cultural forms and to maintain its individuality and unique conception of life."[37] Zorbaugh was more certain about this broader American usage of the term when he argued: "Most of the foreign colonies in American cities are after the pattern of the medieval ghetto especially the Negro quarters or black belts, the Chinatowns and the Little Italies. They have their own traditions and customs and their own regulations and laws to which the Mafia and Tong wars bear evidence."[38]

The medieval ghetto was hardly a natural area, nor was the "black belt." The persistent segregation of blacks resulted from institutional racism and was therefore closer in genesis to the original medieval definition of the ghetto as a legally prescribed quarter within which Jews were forced to live. As natural areas, the social networks and associations of immigrant quarters were assumed to be based upon the principle of residential propinquity. Thomas and Znaniecki stressed this relationship between community and propinquity, but they also revealed discrete residential patterns of Polish immigrants. They acknowledged:

Simultaneously with this process of social organization of the Polish American group its territorial concentration goes on. There is of course a certain minimum of concentration preceding the establishment of the parish and resulting from the tendency of the immigrants to be sufficiently near one another for frequent social intercourse. But this tendency alone cannot completely counterbalance the desire to live near to the place of work or neighboring factories and shops. In large cities the obstacle of distance is only partially overcome and if the colony grows fast each separate neighborhood tends to become the nucleus of a separate parish. (eg. Chicago) If the colony remains small, relative to the size of the city, it may not form any territorially concentrated communities even after parishes have been established.[39]

On the northwest side of Chicago, the substantial Polish-born population settled in several well-defined clusters that became the foci of ethnic parishes, whereas in New York the Polish settlements were smaller and well separated from each other and did not form the basis of an elaborate territorial parochial arrangement.

The ecological principles underlying the spatial order of urban society did not create a random mosaic of natural areas but rather a mosaic design that approximated a zonal arrangement of residential land uses. This graphic representation of ecological processes described in organic terms the dynamics of urban residential differentiation.[40] The poor lived in an innermost zone adjacent to the central business district. The spasmodic expansion of business blighted the adjacent residential properties and was therefore described as a zone in transition from housing to business. By a process of invasion and succession the residents displaced from this zone moved into a zone of workingmen's housing from which the previous residents had moved to suburban zones. Accordingly, the outermost zone housed the most affluent stratum of urban society (Figure 5.1). Organic metaphors were not new to interpretations of urban society, but McKenzie in particular adapted the more precise language of plant ecology to describe the territorial patterns of human groups.[41] Park emphasized the impact of these ecological processes on "immigrant colonies and racial ghettos," where

... other processes of selection inevitably take place which bring about segregation based upon vocational interests, upon intelligence, and personal ambition. The result is that the keener, the more energetic, and the more ambitious very soon emerge from their ghettos and immigrant colonies and move into an area of second immigrant settlement, or perhaps into a cosmopolitan area in which the members of several immigrant and racial groups meet and live side by side. More and more, as the ties of race, of language, and of culture are weakened, successful individuals move out and eventually find their places in business and in the professions, among the older population group which has ceased to be identified with any language or racial group.[42]

As a natural area the ghetto was the temporary abode of the migrant generation unless there were institutional obstacles to assimilation.

The suburbs of American cities were symbols of modernity, and inferences about assimilation were confidently drawn from the changing levels of residential concentration amongst immigrant groups. Cressey explicitly connected assimilation to suburban dispersal and concluded:

The distribution of these various groups [in Chicago] reflects a definite process of succession. Immigrant stocks follow a regular sequence of settlement in successive areas of increasing stability and status. This pattern of distribution represents the ecological setting within which the assimilation of the foreign population takes place. An immigrant group on its arrival settles in a compact colony in a low-rent industrial area usually located in the transitional zone near the center of the city. If the group is of a large size several different areas may develop in various industrial sections. These congested areas of first settlement are characterized by the perpetuation of many European cultural traits. After some years of residence in such an area, the group, as it improves its economic and social condition, moves outwards to some more desirable residential district, creating an area of second

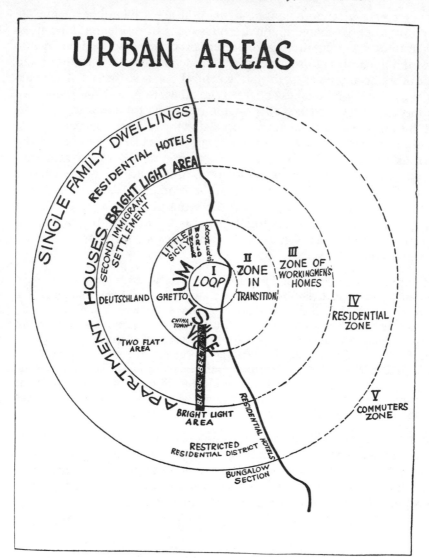

Figure 5.1 The zonal social geography of the city

Source: Ernest W. Burgess, "The Growth of the City: An Introduction to a Research Project," in Robert E. Park et al., eds., *The City* (Chicago: University of Chicago Press, 1925), 55.

settlement. In such an area the group is not so closely concentrated physically, there is less cultural solidarity, and more American standards of living are adopted. Subsequent areas of settlement may develop in some cases, but the last stage in a series of movements is one of gradual dispersion through cosmopolitan residential districts. This diffusion marks the disintegration of the group and the absorption of the individual into the general American population. The relative concentration and dispersion of various immigrant groups furnished an excellent indication of the length of residence in the city and the general degree of assimilation which has taken place.[43]

This ecological framework was especially influential in directing the work of Clifford R. Shaw and Henry D. McKay on delinquency. Their research was one of the most ambitious ventures of the Chicago School. On the basis of case records of the juvenile court system, they linked delinquency to the environmental conditions of the zone of blight. They established that "areas of low and high rates of delinquents assume a typical configuration with regard to the center of the city and also that this configuration ... has remained relatively unchanged over a long period of time."[44] This typical pattern reflected the inverse relationship between rates of truancy, delinquency, and adult crime and distance from the city center and major industrial concentrations. This relationship had persisted over three decades despite the turnover of populations in the areas with a high incidence of social problems.[45] The deterioration of property under circumstances of threatened invasion by business was combined with high rates of turnover; eventually, population decline created conditions leading to delinquency. Although most investigators subscribed to the association of delinquency with the inner city, several studies did indicate that within this blighted zone delinquency was higher in areas of ethnic heterogeneity or in "socially interstitial areas" (Figure 5.2). Despite blighted residential conditions, delinquency was not a major problem in those sections in which an immigrant group predominated and formed a well-defined colony or quarter.[46]

Wirth was sensitive to the limitations of an ecological approach to delinquency: "We may be able to determine statistically that certain regions in the city have more delinquency than others, but we will not be able to interpret the localization of crime adequately until we see that in each area we may be dealing with a different community and that in each community we may find a different set of conflicting strains of cultural influences and mutually referring groups."[47] He was, however, equally skeptical of the more dominant clinical approach to delinquency, which stressed individual causes and personal therapy. Using the analogy of "social therapy," he argued that changes in the institutional environment and efforts to raise the group consciousness of delinquents might reduce or redefine their conflicts with society at large. In response, Floyd Allport reiterated prevailing ideas about the need to release individuals from the confines of their group consciousness and thereby to remove the damaging stereotypical associations of minority identities.[48] Wirth, like Park, was seeking a means to recognize the continuing influences of heritage or

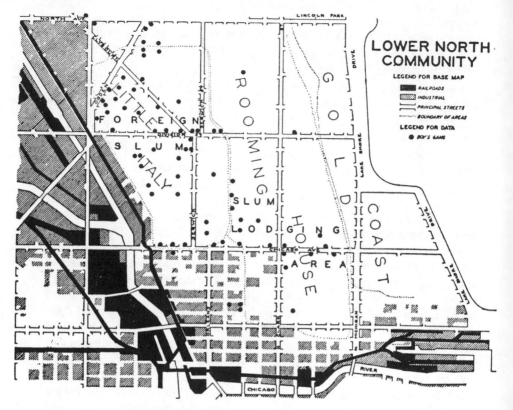

Figure 5.2 The ecology of delinquency, Chicago

Source: Harvey W. Zorbaugh, *The Gold Coast and the Slum* (Chicago: University of Chicago Press, 1929), 178.

culture on personality, but their critics viewed these relationships as vague and unscientific. Increasingly, racial and ethnic affiliations were viewed as dangerous illusions from which individuals ought to be rapidly released.

In response to these debates, Shaw and McKay introduced a sensitivity to the social environment of the slums into their ecological approach to delinquency. In particular, they relied upon Park's suggestion that the changing patterns of delinquency amongst the second generation actually revealed a process of assimilation.[49] The forms of corruption, crime, and delinquency of the second generation were, unlike those of the migrant generation, similar to those of native-born delinquents. These inferences did not, of course, celebrate the virtues of corrupt politics or adolescent gangs, but they did argue that reform would initially have to build on the primary relationships of a slum locality. In these areas exotic secondary associations were rarely successful. Shaw concluded: "While such formal indices as increasing and decreasing population, percentage of families owning their homes, percentage of foreign born, rate of dependency, and rate of adult crime, may serve as a basis for making rough distinctions between areas of the city, they do not disclose the more subtle and intangible processes which constitute the very essence of the social and moral life in the community."[50]

The inner city was, on the one hand, the location with the highest concentrations of those social problems that indicated social disorganization, but on the other hand, it possessed an indigenous if temporary social world that could modify the disruptive effects of invasion and succession. In short: "The delinquent gang may reflect a disorganized community life or a community whose life is organized around delinquent patterns."[51] In his experimental program known as the Chicago Areas Projects, Shaw explicitly worked through the indigenous social relationships of the locality rather than through external agencies, which he judged to be totally isolated from their clients. These localities did, however, vary in the degree to which their indigenous resources were able to respond to the projects. Established ethnic quarters in which associations and institutions could be identified scarcely needed the help of the projects, whereas those devoid of these resources were unable to respond.[52] The elaboration of these tentative explorations of the social environment of the slums awaited William Whyte's participant observer study of the dominantly Italian North End of Boston, which was published in 1943. Whyte documented this indigenous world of the immigrant slum and argued that delinquency itself was an organized part of the fabric of the migrant community. The "Street Corner Society" of Italian-American adolescents did not "lack organization but failed to mesh with the society around it"; however, "society at large puts a premium on disloyalty to 'Cornerville' and penalizes those who are best adjusted to the life of the district." These disjunctions between the slums and society at large resulted in misinterpretations of adolescent behavior that Whyte attributed to the moralistic inheritance of reformers.[53]

Whyte did, however, distinguish this organized world of the immigrant slum from the rooming house districts, which lacked social organization: "These two areas resemble each other in congestion of population, poor quality of housing, and low income of the inhabitants, but such physical and economic indices do not provide us with the discriminations needed for sociological analysis."[54] These findings were amplified in a study of another section of Boston's inner city that described the highly organized social life of Boston's West End as an "urban village." At a time when assumptions about the disorganized and deviant patterns of life in the slums were among the justifications of urban redevelopment, Herbert Gans stressed the adaptations of the local residents to their low status and economic deprivation. His use of the metaphor of the village implied that this social world was closer to traditional patterns of life than to those of the modern city. Gans, like Whyte, clearly distinguished a working-class subculture that was a "generally satisfactory way of adapting to opportunities which society has made available" from a lower-class subculture of those "who find it increasingly difficult to survive in modern society" and their lives are "not merely culturally different ... but ... in fact pathological."[55] In their case studies contributors to the Chicago School were aware of social variations within the zone of blight. Zorbaugh emphasized, in the title of his work, the presence of the affluent Gold Coast of Chicago, within a zone that was susceptible to the blighting effects of adjacent business expansion.[56] Affluent quarters within the inner city, in Chicago as elsewhere, were related to unique site characteristics that delayed or disrupted the patterns of invasion and succession. Similarly, under the special conditions of racial segregation the so-called black belt extended across several zones.[57] In a study dedicated to Park, St. Clair Drake and Horace Cayton revealed the complex internal social differentiation within the castelike world of blacks in urban America (Figure 5.3).[58] In their survey of the segregated world of black Chicago they distinguished the "disorganized segment of the lower class" and a criminal underworld from a pattern of life organized around churches and clubs. They also demonstrated the way in which levels of social club participation increased towards the suburban frontier of the black ghetto (Figure 5.4).

Other observers questioned the validity of the zonal model itself and argued that residential differentiation was based upon sectoral expansion from a diversified inner city. The inner city had for long been associated with the two extremes of poverty and affluence, and the contiguous sectoral expansion of these groups was the basis of an alternative pattern of urban residential differentiation.[59] Walter Firey avoided this debate about the precise geometric approximation of residential patterns and directly confronted this diversity of social worlds in his analysis of the complex land-use patterns of central Boston. He identified immigrant neighborhoods in the North and West Ends, a rooming house district in the South End, and an affluent segment extending from Beacon Hill into Back Bay (Figure 5.5).[60] Although at the time of Firey's study the capacity of the affluent residents of Beacon Hill and Back Bay to resist the threat of blight was in doubt, the persistence of the prestigious status of these quarters was based upon their symbolic association with families identified with New England's past.

This elaboration of the symbolic meaning of prestigious affluent quar-

THE STRENGTH OF CLASS CONTROLS

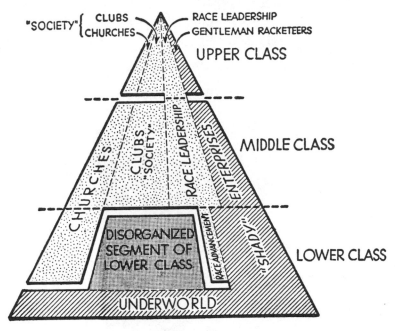

Figure 5.3 The internal stratification of urban blacks

Source: St. Clair Drake and Horace R. Cayton, *Black Metropolis: A Study of Negro Life in a Northern City* (New York: Harcourt Brace, 1945), 525.

ters was not new, but his extension of the same argument to explain the selective resistance of low-income residents to the blighting impact of adjacent business was a critical insight. The South End housed a heterogeneous population of immigrants in tenements along with many single native-born migrants in rooming houses, and the district came to symbolize the city wilderness, with a weak institutional structure and high rates of turnover. Consequently business and industry were often found in close proximity to dilapidated residential quarters in the classic fashion of a blighted area. In contrast, the North End, which had for long been regarded as a notorious slum, was actually a district that symbolized Italian ethnicity within Boston. The identification of distinctive residential quarters on the edge of the central business district was familiar to the Chicago School, but Firey's penetrating interpretation directly contradicted their ecological assumptions, which predicted that the entire inner

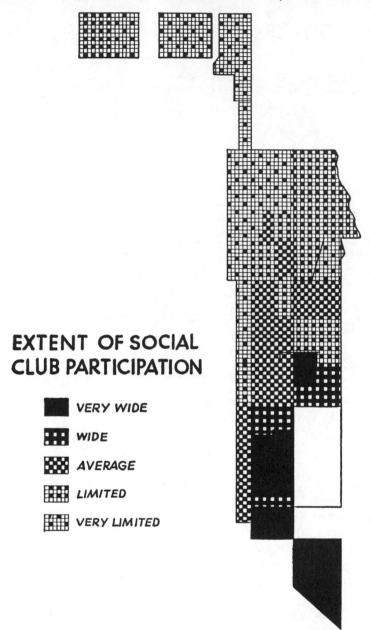

Figure 5.4 Social networks among urban blacks

Source: St. Clair Drake and Horace R. Cayton, *Black Metropolis: A Study of Negro Life in a Northern City* (New York: Harcourt Brace, 1945), 703.

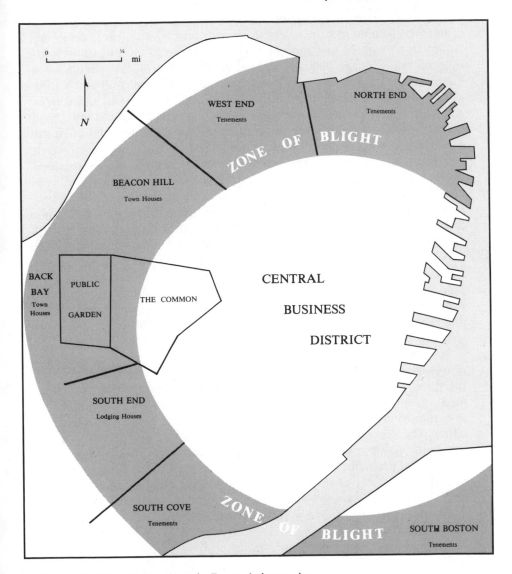

Figure 5.5 Variable land use in Boston's inner city

Source: After Walter I. Firey, *Land Use in Central Boston* (Cambridge, Mass.: Harvard University Press, 1948).

city was destined to lose its population to suburbanization and its dilapidated housing to the expanding needs of business.

The ghetto had once been viewed as a threat to American culture because it housed immigrants from southern and eastern Europe, who were unlikely or undesirable candidates for assimilation. The ghetto was also a threat to American democracy since the immigrant poor seemed unlikely to be able to gain access to opportunities for self-improvement. Although elaborated and modified by later research, the ideas and findings of the Chicago School recognized the role of the ghetto as a "decompression chamber" for newly arrived immigrants and as a setting of relationships indicative of both social disorganization and social reorganization. In retrospect Burgess declared: "The discovery that the ethnic community was a gigantic social defense mechanism which facilitated the survival and adjustment of immigrants but which the second generation sought to modify and escape was a major research accomplishment of urban sociology during the 1920's and 1930's. It was analytical and concentrated on exploring the behavioral patterns and processes of adjustment and change and the immigrant adaptation to the new economic environment. Hostility and tension between ethnic groups were treated as objective phenomena to be explained, rather than a battle joined."[61] This claim is somewhat exaggerated, for many progressives were fully conscious of ethnic communities, but then, many evaluations of the Chicago School have underestimated their awareness of ethnic community. From the very inception of the American use of the term, sympathetic and sensitive observers of the ghetto have qualified and contested negative and often defamatory judgments.

In many respects the Chicago School constructed a relatively complex image of the social consequences of migration and urbanization, but in its efforts to generalize about the spatial consequences of these processes, their interpretation of the social life of the inner city became embedded in assumptions about the inevitability of a unilinear process of assimilation. The "social abyss" of reform thought housed a deprived stratum that, without state intervention, would become a permanent and menacing social problem. The blighted inner city zone of the Chicago model shared many of the environmental disabilities of the "social abyss," but its boundaries were more easily breached without the direct intervention of the state. The Chicago School, like the earlier reform tradition, connected social problems with the inner city, but it interpreted an identical sociogeographic condition from a more positive perspective. Their ecological perspective directed attention to the relationships between assimilation and suburbanization, rather than to the structural obstacles that defined the sociogeographic boundary between the slums and the remainder of urban society.

Assimilation decomposed

Assimilation was and is a notoriously elusive concept that describes either independently or collectively psychological, cultural, and structural changes in individual and social relationships. Often it is difficult to distinguish assimilation from the processes of socialization associated with the equally indeterminate concept of modernization. Both concepts addressed the degree to which a sense of group consciousness might moderate the individualistic identities indicative of modern urban society. Depending on prevailing assumptions about the rate and desirability of assimilation, public policies have been invoked either to accelerate or to constrain it. Most discussions have therefore confronted the anticipated outcomes of assimilation and reveal more about ideological preferences than they do about social processes. The Chicago School certainly presumed that assimilation was desirable, but Park in particular was aware that some social processes ran counter to this end and yet were not necessarily undesirable.

The early discussions of assimilation by the Chicago School were derived from Thomas's work on the experience of Polish migrants.[62] Park and Burgess elaborated these ideas in their definitive text on modern sociology.[63] They acknowledged the contributions of each divergent migrant group to the emerging American whole and argued that the process of assimilation should preferably be slow. Most immigrants arrived with local or provincial loyalties, and their awareness of their own nationality was paradoxically part of their American experience. Park viewed this experience as part of a complex process by which immigrants assumed broader loyalties that eventually included their adopted homeland. As early as 1921 he argued: "If it is true that the immigrant, who arrives here a provincial, takes his first step in Americanization when he becomes concerned about the reputation of his own country in America, it is equally true that the immigrant who remains a provincial remains at the same time farthest removed from American life."[64] At a time when the demand for immigration restriction was charged with eugenic and cultural judgments about the inferiority of new immigrants, the text that set the agenda of the Chicago School rejected these defamatory arguments and also criticized coercive efforts to accelerate Americanization.[65] The Chicago School did, however, assume that the rapid adoption of English would be necessary for the kind of participatory experiences involved in assimilation, and it also implied that the rate of immigration should not exceed the capacity of the public schools to meet these needs.

Advocates of cultural pluralism often simplified the views of the Chicago School on assimilation. Although devoted to a sensitive elaboration of the critical role of the immigrant community in the process of migration and assimilation, a key work identified with the Chicago School concluded that assimilation is "as inevitable as it is desirable; it is impossible for the immigrants we receive to remain in separate groups."[66] This assertion provoked Kallen's most forceful advocacy of cultural pluralism.[67] Since the offending book was published under the authorship of Park and Miller, Kallen was unaware of Thomas's dominant role in the preparation of the manuscript. In fact, Thomas believed that social processes were leading to a society based upon individual identities and new associations based upon occupation or personality. In contrast, Park was not convinced that older group loyalties would necessarily disappear. Although he regarded both blacks and immigrants as ethnic groups with a common experience of migration and urbanization, he was especially sensitive to the unusual difficulties that black Americans had encountered in their attempts to participate in and therefore to assimilate into American society.

Whenever dominant groups remained hostile to minorities, Park believed that the latter would necessarily develop a sense of nationality. He was therefore sympathetic to the efforts of minority groups to rediscover their own culture and experience, for only on the basis of this sense of identity could they develop relationships that might further assimilation. This argument troubled a prominent black student of Park's, E. Franklin Frazier, who argued that black American culture was not distinctive in the same sense as that of European immigrants. Since blacks had long since acculturated to American conditions, their social problems were derived from those external conditions that obstructed individual advancement and assimilation.[68] Although Park's knowledge of the black experience qualified his views of assimilation, his investigation of the Japanese-American experience on the West Coast tended to confirm his general ideas about the migrant encounter with American society.[69] He had proposed a cycle or series of phases that described a sequential process of assimilation that initially involved competition and conflict but eventually resulted in accommodation and assimilation.[70] The progressive character of the cycle was based upon an increasing level of interaction between groups, and the concept of social distance was developed to express the likelihood of this interaction.[71]

William Carlson Smith summarized the efforts to describe and interpret assimilation during the interwar decades. The Chicago School was the predominant contributor to this effort. Its confidence in the desirability and inevitability of assimilation was certainly not without qualifications, but it was critical in undermining the scientific pretensions of discriminatory arguments that had justified the restriction of immigration. Smith's work was in a series under the editorship of a former advocate of restriction, Edward Ross, who in 1939 saw "honest differences of opinion" in discussions of the desirable rate at which assimilation should occur. Smith included psychological, cultural, and structural changes in his consideration of assimilation, but ultimately interpretations of each or all of these changes were dependent upon the definitions of the anticipated or preferred host society. Consequently, he distinguished the sociological approach of the Chicago School from three alternative models, which he described as the melting pot, the Americanization theory, and the ethnic federation theory. The sociological approach was based upon considerations of the mutual interactions of immigrant and native and revealed the ways in which the immigrant subcultures facilitated assimilation.[72] The anticipated outcome was, however, always a matter of some doubt. On the basis of the index of social distance, Emory Bogardus proposed a seven-stage cycle that terminated not with assimilation but with the ambiguous or marginal position of the second generation. Later he described two possible outcomes of this marginality. Since the index described the reactions of the host society and not those of minority groups, these outcomes were succinctly described as, firstly, acceptance and amalgamation and, secondly, exclusion and segregation.[73]

By that time Park had also abandoned his unilinear approach to assimilation and proposed three possible outcomes of social interaction. Curiously, his examples of these outcomes did not include reference to the American experience. Complete assimilation was associated with China, a caste system with India, and a persistent minority with European Jews.[74] Park's growing pessimism about modern American society was clearly indicated in his deliberations about the distinctions between civilizations and cultures. The United States was the epitome of modern civilization: an aggregation of specialists and devoid of an integrated culture. During the depressed economic conditions of the 1930s many observers, like Park, questioned the meaning of assimilation, in part because of their doubts about the destiny of the host society itself.

For most migrants the host society was too remote and, during the thirties, too distressed itself to offer a coherent image of American society. Caroline Ware revealed that in Greenwich Village the Irish, not established Americans, had represented the most culturally coherent social group. Among the most distinctive Irish adaptations to the American city were institutional elaborations of their traditional religious affiliation and their diversion of the urban political system to respond to their own needs. Although the Roman Catholic Church assumed a more subtle place in the succeeding Italian communities, and although the political loyalties of the newcomers were often deliberately different from those of the Irish, the adaptations of the Italians to the American city owed more to Irish precedents than they did to some image of native Protestant America. In any event, immigrants were confronted with an American society that was not only foreign to their own experience, but so lacking in coherence as to offer little guide to their adaptation.[75]

During the early forties, the publication of the early volumes of W. Lloyd Warner's collaborative venture based on Newburyport, Massachusetts, came to similar conclusions. Immigrants "partly through frustration in not gaining easy acceptance in the common life of Americans and partly through clinging to the ways of their fathers, have constructed separate social worlds of their own. Each group, without conscious imitation of others, has fashioned an ethnic sub-system much like that of the others, and each system seems to undergo the same changes as the systems which preceded it." Each preceding ethnic system served as a filter through which later groups encountered American society. The Irish in particular were viewed as agents of "other ethnic groups because they are the oldest and have climbed the highest in status structure."[76] Changes in social status were explicitly connected to the processes of assimilation and suburbanization, but Warner concluded that the rates of social mobility were not only selective but for some groups extremely slow indeed. Warner assumed that nineteenth-century Newburyport had been a place of entrepreneurial self-advancement, but during the twentieth century new kinds of industrial organization were creating an increasingly rigid system of social stratification. His false assumptions about the changing rates of social mobility and the ambiguities of his principles of stratification made it impossible for him to develop further insights into the processes of mobility and assimilation.[77]

Ethnicity redefined

The initial deliberations of the Chicago School predicted the rapid suburbanization and assimilation of immigrant groups, but during the depressed economic conditions of the thirties these optimistic expectations had been qualified. Concerns about economic advancement diminished following the termination World War II, as many European immigrants, and especially their American-born descendants, moved rapidly into the expanding suburbs. These developments were associated with the rapid adoption of the language and content of American popular culture and appeared to confirm the original expectations of the Chicago School. Although clearly linked to social mobility, suburbanization was not necessarily associated with immediate residential dispersal or with the abandonment of a sense of ethnic identity.[78] Many of the native-born descendants of immigrants did disperse into suburbs with no well-defined ethnic identity, but others relocated as part of a spatially restricted suburban movement of institutions, neighbors, and relatives. Increased resources made possible the relocation and enhancement of institutional facilities that often redefined the content and experience of ethnic identities.

Although the migrant residents of the inner city had been more highly segregated than their affluent descendants from the remainder of urban society, suburbanization had resulted in new patterns of ethnic residential differentiation. The resulting residential patterns resembled a wedge, the original inner-city concentrations forming an apex, below which there was a broadening as lower densities and higher levels of heterogeneity prevailed. Less mobile groups clung tenaciously to their original neighborhoods; the position of the apex was therefore reversed, since relatively few of them moved into the suburbs. In contrast, highly mobile groups abandoned their original inner-city quarters, which no longer served as a focus of institutional activities. Consequently their new surburban neighborhoods became as closely identified with their ethnic heritage as their original inner-city clusters had been, and they have evoked the descriptive term "gilded ghetto."[79]

Studies of several metropolitan centers have revealed the ethnic clustering in suburban settings or at least a much slower and less dramatic reduction in the levels of ethnic residential differentiation than might have been expected. An investigation of ethnic residential patterns in the Greater New York area revealed the complexity of the relationship between segregation and suburbanization.[80] This study confirmed that levels of residential segregation amongst those of European heritage were lower than those of black or Hispanic ancestry, but many individual European groups were as highly segregated from each other as from blacks or Puerto Ricans. Norwegian-Americans were, for example, one of the most highly segregated groups, and although their separation from blacks was high, their segregation from Jewish-Americans was even greater. A ranking of the degrees of segregation of each group from all other groups did not conform to an expected order in which the longer-established northwestern Europeans were less segregated from each other than they were from the more recent arrivals from southern and eastern Europe. These findings have stimulated efforts to develop more precise indicators of residential differentiation that are more sensitive than the index of dissimilarity to contiguity and scale. These revised indicators of ethnic concentration reveal that while the levels of residential segregation amongst most of the descendants of European immigrant groups are lower than those amongst their migrant ancestors, the differences do not describe a simple trajectory of residential dispersal from an inner-city ghetto.[81]

In the suburbs of western cities, where there are relatively few existing ethnic institutions and there is limited intergenerational reinforcement of ethnicity, ethnic associations are still maintained.[82] These associations are capable of serving the needs of multiple clusters or dispersed populations and do not necessarily depend upon high levels of residential concentration amongst their participants. Some level of neighborhood concentration may have been necessary to sustain an initial set of institutional and informal networks, but the persistence of their contributions to an enduring sense of ethnic identity is not dependent upon the maintenance or reestablishment of an ethnic neighborhood. To the degree that ethnicity is based upon associational involvements and social networks that extend far beyond the limits of a specific neighborhood, a preoccupation with diminishing levels of residential concentration may be a misleading indicator of the changing but persisting influence of ethnicity in American society.

These sociogeographic findings are consistent with refinements of the concept of assimilation, which had described the rapid amalgamation of migrants and especially their descendants into the host society. Milton Gordon, for example, described assimilation as a compound social process.[83] Those of the migrant generation, and especially their American-born children, experienced rapid cultural assimilation as they adopted the language and forms of American life, but they experienced only limited structural assimilation. Their primary group relationships remained concentrated in the ethnic community that had been maintained despite the generational conflicts of the initial settlements and despite the pronounced levels of suburbanization. For long it was assumed that structural assimilation was dependent upon intermarriage and that American society was a "triple melting pot" within which Protestantism, Judaism, and Catholicism, as the three major religious affiliations of American society, set the boundaries of ethnic intermarriage.[84] The triple melting pot described a condition of religious pluralism that was maintained despite cultural assimilation.[85] Reexaminations of rates of intermarriage have, however, revealed only modest differences in rates of intermarriage amongst and between Protestants, Catholics, and Jews, and more recently rates of intermarriage have increased so dramatically that structural assimilation would appear to be imminent for most denominations.[86] Intermarriage does not necessarily result in the abandonment of ethnic identities, and it has been argued that ethnic identities may survive structural assimilation, that "contrary to Gordon's notion that acculturation precedes assimilation, considerable residues of ethnic culture can remain among socially assimilated individuals."[87]

Ethnic residues in suburban America may be no more than a matter of self-declaration grounded in some remote or fragmentary genealogy. Ethnicity is usually expressed as participation in associations and social networks that proclaim an ethnic affiliation. In a mass society ethnic identity may provide a sense of belonging at a scale that is "smaller than the State, larger than the family, something akin to familistic alliance."[88] This intermediate world between an ancestral culture and assimilated Americans has also attracted hostile commentary. To Herberg the religious pluralism of the United States is "a religiousness without religion, a religiousness without almost any kind of content or none, a way of sociability or 'belonging' rather than a way of re-orientating life to God. It is thus frequently a religiousness without serious commitment, without real inner conviction, without genuine existential decision."[89] The so-called new ethnicity is "a jumble of manifestations whose meanings remain unanalyzed and within which ritual (way of living) and belief (cosmologies) are confused." Ethnicity is, "like religion, a set of mediocre cosmologies. In the two areas of the world to which it purports to be relevant, the sociopolitical and interpersonal, it is at best a secondary cosmology, playing a limited and uncertain role."[90] To the degree that an identity with events in an ancestral homeland triggers a sense of ethnic loyalty, it has been described as symbolic ethnicity, and except in these special circumstances, ethnic beliefs are no more than secondary or trivial cosmologies that merely identify a group.[91]

For these reasons, some observers are skeptical of the connections between the ethnicity of the migrant generation and that of their affluent descendants.[92] These skeptics have linked the persistence or resurgence of ethnic identities to the efforts of assimilated groups to defend their economic interests and recently established status against the increasingly belligerent claims of deprived minorities. Other critics have demonstrated strong associations between ethnicity and status and have therefore concluded that ethnic identities are merely superficial expressions of an underlying social stratification.[93] In short, ethnic consciousness is a contrived identity that obscures an underlying economic interest.[94] Ethnicity is a label to describe the reactive responses of interest groups that have perceived detrimental alterations in the allocation principles of public policies. Their political loyalties do not, therefore, reflect their interests in ancestral foreign causes but rather their concern over threats to their well-being from competing interest groups.

These discussions about the persistence or redefinition of ethnicity within suburban America also raise questions about the ethnicity of the migrant generation. The Chicago School had viewed ethnicity as the fragmentary elements of the ancestral culture that were transplanted to the American city. This social order served as a decompression chamber but also complicated and obstructed the assimilation and advancement of the second generation. New interpretations of migrant ethnicity emphasize changes in traditional patterns of life prior to migration and the degree to which these changes served as a "ramp" from which economic advancement was launched. Most migrants were initially confined to the lowest stratum of the labor force but since this stratum often included several competing ethnic groups, it has been argued that the political loyalties of ethnic neighborhoods proved to be more decisive than those based upon the experience of work and class.[95] These diverted ethnic expressions of class interests have also been linked to a vague association of migrants and middle-class aspirations. The migrant generation was prepared to endure the lowest stratum of the labor force as a temporary strategy since they believed in the possibility of a generational process of advancement.[96]

Although opportunities for social mobility varied from industry to industry and from group to group, many immigrants, and especially their children, eventually laid claim to a modest rate of occupational advancement. From this perspective, young labor migrants in industrial cities, like young agricultural laborers on midwestern farms, envisaged their wage labor as a means to future mobility either in America or their homeland. *Ethnicity* may be a vague term and assimilation a loosely defined process, but the concepts represent an attempt to confront variations in the ways migrants and their descendants encountered American urban life. Different experiences of this encounter may be the basis of a distinctive sense of identity despite the converging consequences of these experiences. Under these circumstances the so-called new ethnicity represents a positive identity grounded in the saga and myths of the accommodations of migrant ancestors to their American experience. Conversely, migrants whose adaptations were obstructed or inadequate experienced a slower and more difficult course of upward mobility and, consequently, their American experience cannot sustain a positive identity. This interpretation of migration and assimilation, like that of the Chicago School, assumes that, despite initial difficulties, most immigrants, or at least their native-born children, were able to gain access to an escalator of economic advancement and to move on to progressively higher floors. This "escalator" model of the migrant experience implies that, in the absence of discrimination, each group takes its turn in the process of social mobility and suburbanization. The escalator has moved at varying speeds for different migrant groups; for some it has failed to start. It is therefore necessary to examine how the effectiveness of ethnic resources was contingent upon the opportunities for advancement.

The debate about the persistence and authenticity of American ethnic groups certainly coincided with a growing awareness of the degree to which some groups encountered obstacles to their advancement and residential mobility.[97] After World War II the term *ghetto* was primarily used to refer to the segregated inner-city concentrations of blacks, and the term *barrio* eventually entered popular currency to describe presumed similar concentrations of Chicanos. Examinations of the inner-city became more firmly connected to the problems of discrimination, deprivation, and low status. Lower-class slums were increasingly viewed as being not merely a subcultural variation of modern society but a distinctive culture of poverty that was itself a barrier to material advancement.[98] By 1960 the inner city was linked to levels of pathological behavior and relative deprivation judged to be unprecedented in American urban history. Inferences about the unprecedented incidence of social problems within the ghetto are a matter of a debate.[99] The prevalence of adolescent delinquency and the fragility of family life are among the most common indictments of the ghetto today, but these conditions of juvenile delinquency and social disorganization were also major components of descriptions of the immigrant slums. For over a century interpretations of poverty had been preoccupied with distinctions amongst the poor and especially those cultural, hereditary, or moral deficiencies that would limit their response to opportunities and reform. From time to time, this distinction was not simply an internal classification of the poor but rather a qualitative distinction based upon ethnic or racial origin. Discussions of the cultural distinctions of the working class and the lower class clearly retain some elements of earlier arguments about the poor and their urban environment.

Retrospective reevaluations of the migrant experience have questioned the validity of these arguments and explored the ways in which migrants used their ethnic resources to cope with the environmental disabilities of the slums. These explorations have also revealed the degree to which fluctuating economic conditions set limits to their subsistence and security. Unlike the authentic "cultural ethnicity" of their ancestors and the "redefined ethnicity" of their assimilated descendants, the migrant generation's experience of industrialization was often a critical if not definitive aspect of its "emergent" ethnicity.[100] Ethnicity is clearly redefined or diminished during the course of emigration and settlement, but what might be described as "migrant ethnicity" was an integral and generic part of the impact of industrialization on urban life in the United States.

6

Ethnicity and industrialization

Efforts to document the varying encounters of different ethnic groups in the inner city ignited the retrospective reinterpretation of the migrant experience. Until about 1960, discussions of assimilation and ethnicity were attempts to describe current processes that were assumed to be of considerable longevity. After about 1960 new assumptions about the persistence and redefinition of ethnicity necessitated a reexamination of the migrant experience itself.[1] Initially the findings of the Chicago School set the agenda for this venture, but eventually those findings became the symbol of a misinterpretation of the migrant experience. The Chicago School attempted to describe the migrant experience within the context of a broad social transformation that began with emigration and ended with assimilation. In particular, they recognized that the transplantation of older patterns of life in the adverse environment of the city served as a decompression chamber for the migrant generation. These migrant adaptations were assumed to be of short duration and as obstructions to assimilation were a source of conflict between the migrant and second generations. Overall, they emphasized the disjunctions rather than the continuities in migrant experience.

This kind of interpretation was elaborated in Oscar Handlin's moving saga of how European peasants encountered the American city.[2] Handlin assumed that most immigrants were uprooted from traditional village societies to be deposited like flotsam on the American shoreline. This tidal movement was governed by the impersonal forces that directed labor to industry with little concern for social costs. Migration was punctuated by "shocks": the shock of removal from a familiar world, the shock of a difficult voyage, the shock of exploitation and hostility upon arrival, and the shock of alienation and isolation from the host society. Handlin stressed the "shocks" of an involuntary removal from a stable traditional peasant society and "hostile encounters" with the American environment and society. Although he was sensitive to the ability of migrants to reconstruct their lives around their own ethnic institutions, he believed that these efforts lacked the authentic meanings of their ancestral forms. This view of migration emphasized periodic if not persistent disruptions to which only fragmentary and not necessarily desirable adaptations were made. In some respects Handlin provided an elaboration of the retrospective implications of the deliberations of the Chicago School. His interpretation of the migrant experience set the agenda for historical reevaluations of migration and assimilation.[3] Neither the Chicago School nor Handlin was insensitive to the formation of immigrant communities, but their interpretation of these communities was based upon assumptions about migration and assimilation that have subsequently been questioned.

Over a generation ago, first Marcus Lee Hansen and then Frank Thistlethwaite stressed the need to examine both the conditions of emigration and the circumstances of immigration.[4] Belatedly, their recommendations have been followed, and revisionist interpretations of migration have stressed how adaptations to social and economic changes long before emigration enabled many migrants to cope with the disruptive consequences of migration and the painful confrontations with assimilation. These adaptations provided a thread of continuity during the course of complex and multiple migrations that often preceded more permanent settlement in the United States. The causal inferences about the relationships between social isolation, environmental deficiencies, and pathological social conditions have been modified to account for the coping capacities of most migrant groups. The retrospective reexamination of the migrant experience moved beyond assumptions about assimilation and considered ethnic groups to be discrete entities within a plural society.[5] Elaborate social networks of family, neighbors, and associations and levels of religious and political organization reveal a complex and autonomous way of life quite different from that of the traditional world. Although elements of this social order may have assisted immigrants in coping with their new environment and may therefore be identified as adaptations to deprivation, most interpretations have stressed the way in which family, institutions, and neighborhood together created an environment that ameliorated generational conflicts about values and authority.

The experiences of the migrant generations of most European ethnic groups initially were measured in relation to an earlier traditional social order. The traditional world was often formulated as an idealized memory of a world that had been lost in the remote rather than the recent past. The ancestral cultures of most American immigrants were already substantially altered from their original forms before their trans-Atlantic migration, and consequently the direct contribution of ancestral cultural traditions to the ethnicity of the migrant generation in America was already diluted before emigration. The ethnic resources of migrant communities were not primarily derived from transplantations of traditional patterns of life but were rather adaptations or even examples of resistance to an increasingly commercialized homeland and to the industrialized world of the American city. Barton has identified at least three social changes that altered the relationships between families and their resources in regions of high emigration. Firstly, kinship became the foundation of much broader patterns of reciprocity in the sharing of resources; secondly, voluntary associations were developed to provide mutual aid, especially when sickness or death strained family resources; finally, many communal festivals were restructured as private celebrations of public events.[6] These recent changes in the regions of migration were the sources of the most definitive ethnic features of migrant communities in the United States. Household mobility from continent to continent, from region to region, and from city to city was embedded within a network of friends and relatives who provided not only initial aid but also information on employment. These networks were not necessarily dependent upon high levels of residential propinquity. The original formulation of the immigrant slum as a segregated enclave within the adverse environment of the inner city describes only a fragment of the more complex urban environment encountered and created by most migrant groups.

The residents defined: discrete communities

Handlin's interpretation of "uprooted" migrants owed much to his earlier documentation of the Irish experience in nineteenth-century Boston. This pioneering historical study of the urban immigrant emphasized the devastating social consequences of the famine emigration and of settlement in the slums of the North End and Fort Hill. Despite the savage and disruptive experiences of emigration and urbanization, the Irish developed a group consciousness based upon their own religious and secular institutions.[7] Since the most publicized concentrations of Irish immigrants were identified as notorious slums, their social world was presumed to be disorganized, but their precocious development of political and religious networks also revealed a determined and distinctive response to their deprived and discriminated status within American society. They organized Roman Catholic parishes and schools, fraternal lodges, trade unions, and political associations. By 1960 Handlin had recognized, in his own reappraisal of immigration history, the way in which these developments had eased the shock of America, if not the shock of emigration.[8] Somewhat earlier, in a pioneering study of the immigrant experience in antebellum New York, Robert Ernst had proposed a more positive view of the emerging ethnic communities. In the adverse environment of the tenements of lower Manhattan, impoverished immigrants had created their own social world: "Few elements contributed more to the cohesiveness of a group than the compactness of its settlement. Existing customs prevailed with little outside interference, religious beliefs were nurtured in comparative security, and national languages were perpetuated over a long period of time. The immigrant community, like a decompression chamber, represented a place and a time of adjustment from one atmosphere to another."[9]

Subsequent interpretations of not only the Irish but the immigrant experience as a whole have explored more fully the role of the ethnic community as a decompression chamber. The Irish were able to convert the disadvantages of social isolation into the advantages of residential concentration, but their institutional fabric was not necessarily dependent upon the support of a single highly concentrated constituency. In New York the advantages of concentration were apparently not essential to ethnic communities, for Ernst also revealed that "individuals and families of most nationalities established themselves in every part of the city," creating "a complex agglomeration of little communities, a few of which showed clearly defined nationality but most of which included an heterogeneous mixture of foreign elements."[10] In 1880 there were five Irish clusters and only one of Germans in Philadelphia, but only 20 percent of the Irish and less than 15 percent of the Germans lived in these ethnic quarters.[11] In most cities the Irish were dispersed about several distinct clusters, and although migrant communities were often based upon some level of residential propinquity, these natural areas were only one component of a more complex and discrete pattern of ethnic residential differentiation.[12]

In the seaports of antebellum America immigrants concentrated near the waterfront and warehouses of the emerging central business districts, but the rate at which established Americans vacated these areas was much too slow to afford accommodations for the newcomers, who quickly accounted for a third or more of a city's population. Immigrants were housed at increasing densities by the conversion of existing dwellings into tenements and the infilling of their grounds or rear yards with cheap new structures, but substantial numbers also lived on the edge of the city in shanty-towns or often on poorly drained filled land that had been avoided by more substantial housing developments.[13] Within this complex pattern of ethnic settlements, German immigrants were usually more highly concentrated in specific sections of the city and more highly clustered within those concentrations than were the Irish. The social advantages of residential concentration were most frequently identified with the *"Kleindeutschlands"* of American cities. In midwestern cities, where they were not only the largest foreign-born group but also exceeded the native-born populations, German immigrants dominated extensive sections of the city as a microcosm of urban society at large rather than as a socially disorganized slum of impoverished newcomers.[14] In any event, the degree to which pathological social conditions prevailed in the most notorious immigrant slums is subject to debate. For example, the relatively high proportions of female-headed households amongst Irish immigrants in the Five Points area of Manhattan were not indicative of family breakdown but rather part of a more complex household structure that had to cope with frequent migration, itinerant working conditions, and limited resources.[15]

The multiple foci of immigrant residential patterns were often based upon subnational or intraethnic local loyalties and identities. These provincial, and often more local, distinctions were especially apparent amongst new immigrants from southern and eastern Europe. Whyte described the predominantly Italian North End of Boston as "made up of little communities within a community, and even today we can mark out sections ... according to the town of origin of the immigrants, although these lines are fading with the growth of the younger generation" (Figure 6.1).[16] Similar patterns in Chicago provoked Rudolph Vecoli's critique of Handlin's original interpretation of the migrant experience, in which he questioned both the idealization of the premigration conditions and the degree to which the social order of family, kin, and neighbors was disrupted by emigration.[17] For many immigrants it was their experience in America that made them aware of or at least heightened their national identities. Most Italians arrived with stronger loyalties to village and province than to their new nation, and their sense of loyalty to a larger Italian identity was experienced as part of their emerging ethnic identity in the United States. They were never in the strict sense Italians.[18] A similar transition from a provincial European identity to an American ethnic identity occurred amongst the diverse migrant groups who came from the Austro-Hungarian Empire. Their local loyalties were often the basis of multiple small concentrations.

Village and regional origins were often a stronger influence than religious preference in the residential patterns of Slavic migrants, but because the majority of new immigrants came from predominantly Catholic areas, religious institutions were closely linked to their ethnic identity.[19] The parochial organization of the Roman Catholic Church was responsive to these discrete but clustered ethnic residential patterns. Most of the original territorial parishes included several ethnic groups, but because their priests and original congregants were predominantly Irish, some "national" parishes with no well-defined boundaries were established to serve specific ethnic groups. In Chicago sixteen territorial parishes were complemented by no fewer than nine national parishes as

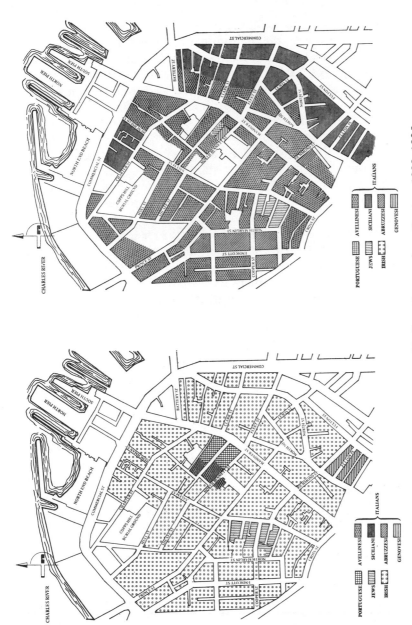

Figure 6.1 Residential patterns of Italians, by province, Boston, 1880–1925

Source: William M. De Marco, Ethnics and Enclaves: Boston's Italian North End (Ann Arbor, Mich.: UMI Research Press, 1981), 25, 29.

early as 1870. Thirty years later, there were sixty-three territiorial parishes usually identified with the predominant ethnic group of the locality and forty-seven national parishes that served the needs of smaller, more dispersed ethnic groups.[20] In Pittsburgh the first church to serve Slovaks was located centrally so that it might meet the needs of several neighborhoods that only later were able to support their own neighborhood church.[21] The fragmented if not dispersed patterns of southern and eastern European immigrants in Omaha were based upon well-defined clusters of ethnic institutions and of retail activities under the control of the same ethnic group. Under these circumstances, the district with the leading ethnic institutions and amenities was usually identified as the ghetto, but as a symbolic expression of an emerging ethnic identity rather than as a homogeneous immigrant concentration.[22]

At the turn of the nineteenth century, when the term *ghetto* was loosely used in combination with terms like *colony* and *quarter* to describe immigrant clusters, very few southern and eastern Europeans were exclusively confined to a single extensive inner-city neighborhood. The majority of European immigrants lived in several districts of varying extent; within these they were the dominant group, but the overlapping patterns of dominance also created areas of mixed ancestry. The mosaic-like patterns of specific immigrant groups were usually confined to a well-defined sector of the inner city, but there were also concentrations in the inner suburbs, which housed newcomers as well as established households.[23] The Italians of New York, for example, lived in no fewer than seventy-five distinct colonies in 1922, and at the same time, no fewer than seventeen distinct Italian quarters were identified in Chicago.[24] In Chicago, Thomas Philpott emphasized, the low proportions of specific immigrant groups were concentrated in districts where they were substantially overrepresented.[25] Only 2.9 percent of the Irish lived in such quarters, but with the exception of the Poles, less than half the new immigrants lived in districts in which they were predominant. These areas of dominance were far from homogeneous, for at least half their populations were made up of a variety of other groups, and together these clusters rarely housed more than one third of the ethnic group itself.

In his meticulous examination of the residential patterns of immigrants in Detroit, Olivier Zunz has captured the complexity of discrete patterns of different levels of ethnic dominance.[26] In 1880 the central sections of Detroit were the least differentiated on the basis of land use and the occupations and ethnicities of their residents. Many sections combined residential, industrial, and commerical uses, and although there were cells of impoverished residents, the native-born middle class formed the largest segment of the local population. In contrast, Germans dominated the east side of the city and the Irish prevailed in the west, but almost a quarter of the sampled residents lived in areas with no well-defined occupational or ethnic identity. Using high fertility as a means to distinguish immigrant from native patterns of life, Zunz concluded that while those Germans who lived in areas dominated by other groups exhibited no differences from those who lived in German-dominated areas, those who lived alongside the native born resembled their neighbors rather than their compatriots.

This pattern persisted until the turn of the century, but by 1920 the central city was overwhelmingly devoted to industrial and commercial activities, and the native middle class was now identified with the most desirable suburbs. Under conditions of rapid suburbanization, occupational status became as influential as ethnicity in the process of residential differentiation, but industrial decentralization did result in a pronounced ethnic suburban movement. Polish immigrants employed in newly established large-scale industrial enterprises were part of a suburban movement of a decidedly modest character. Unlike the Italians and the Russian Jews, who established some of their settlements on the edge of the business district, the Poles had moved directly to those sections of the urban fringe that had attracted neither public services nor the attentions of real estate promoters.[27] In many midwestern industrial cities, Slavic immigrants established neighborhoods with high levels of home ownership but, initially at least, devoid of the public infrastructure that was indispensable to the quality of life in middle-class suburbs. The ghetto was a focal point of ethnic institutions and social networks that served communities housed in several overlapping concentrations. Consequently the voluntary exclusivity of their social world rather than extremely high levels of residential segregation isolated them from the remainder of urban society. Rather than being dependent upon the reinforcement of concentration, institutional and associational networks made possible a more complex territorial arrangement of ethnic communities. Kinship rather than propinquity was the basis of a discrete ethnic community.[28]

In contrast to the highly segregated residential patterns of blacks and other minorities in contemporary American cities, most ethnic groups who had settled in American cities during the period of mass immigration established less exclusive and less contiguous residential quarters.[29] Prior to the massive increase in the cityward migration of blacks during World War I, blacks' residential patterns, like those of most immigrant groups, did not take the form of an extensive ghetto. Until about 1910 the black populations of northeastern and midwestern cities lived in the back alleys and rear lots of blocks inhabited by other groups, in a pattern similar to that of the much larger black populations of southern and border-state cities. Although they were highly segregated in interior blocks, blacks were also often found in small numbers in many sections of the city.[30] With the disruption of European migration during World War I, this highly dispersed supply of alley housing was insufficient to meet the needs of the corresponding increase in the volume of black migration.

Consequently more extensive supplies of housing were sought in districts somewhat removed from the already crowded immigrant districts of the inner city. The largest supply of housing was often found in those inner suburbs where the speculative overbuilding of middle-income houses had created a supply of structures that, once subdivided, could be rented at lower rates.[31] Harlem, Boston's Roxbury, and Chicago's South Side provide examples of a process by which blacks were excluded not only from the inner-city immigrant quarters but also from the expanding suburbs. In cities where the volume of black migration remained modest for another generation, the fragmented patterns of black residence persisted longer than in the major metropolitan centers. In Toledo, for example, as late as 1930, there was no well-defined central ghetto, and small clusters of blacks were found on "certain sections of certain streets on the fringes of all-white neighborhoods."[32] The continued migrations of southern blacks to northeastern and midwestern industrial cities during and after World War II consolidated the segregated residential patterns established during the earlier Great Migration. The institutional and associational lives of blacks in northern cities were also no less elaborate than those of their contemporaries from overseas. The level and longevity of their participation in primary and especially in secondary education actually exceeded that of most immigrant groups.[33] Prior to the turn of the century the predominant strategy of such black leaders as Booker T. Washington and W.E.B. DuBois involved self-help and economic advancement within the setting of the black community, but eventually the frustrations of economic and political discrimination provoked DuBois to adopt a more radical interpretation of the black predicament.[34]

The overrepresentation of particular household arrangements amongst the black poor in relation to the poor of other migrant groups is often the basis of arguments that imply that cultural predispositions of certain groups greatly diminish their chances of attaining economic security. At one time the predicament of the black family was attributed to the damage of two centuries of slavery followed by a century of segregation and discrimination. The pathologies of black America had been carried forward from an impoverished and racist rural world to an equally deprived and prejudiced urban setting.[35] Just as reinterpretations of the immigrant experience have stressed the adaptive capacities of family and kin, similar revisionist views have provided a more complete documentation of similar developments amongst black migrants. Rural black families, like those of the poor elsewhere, accommodated relatives as part of a system of mutual assistance, and these networks were sometimes connected to the growing black communities of large cities.[36] In any event the concern with female-headed families amongst the poor has a long ancestry, but in the past the issue was rarely phrased as a cultural problem of one group. Throughout the period of mass immigration, unmarried mothers, deserted wives, and indigent widows were a conspicuous part of any list of social problems, but because solutions were conceived exclusively within the framework of a male-headed nuclear family, the success of welfare was assumed to be dependent upon the reconstitution of a conventional household.[37]

In any event, most migrant groups encountered frustrations and obstacles in their search for material advancement. A preoccupation with the institutional and associational patterns of European immigrant groups has perhaps obscured the degree to which these groups, too, experienced social problems and expressed their frustrations and resentments by means of popular disturbances and labor unrest.[38] Although the inner city was one of the leading destinations of migrants, the migrant poor were not trapped in the inner-city slums of a single city but moved frequently between those of several cities. Research on premigration conditions and on return migration has complemented the findings about high population turnover in nineteenth-century America.[39] Spatial mobility was not merely an American behavior, and the ethnic residential quarters of American cities were the temporary abodes of households with extremely broad migratory fields. As temporary abodes they served as institutional nuclei of social networks that defined the routes within these fields. Their social networks were rarely confined to one destination, since each destination was also part of complex systems of circular and chain migration.[40] The regional economic differentiation of the American economy into an increasingly urbanized and industrialized core and a variety of dependent peripheries devoted to the supply of key raw materials and staple foods created a changing geographic setting of a complex pattern of migrations.[41] Although early efforts to connect the fluctuations in trans-Atlantic migration to the business cycle in the United States have been modified, they did provide insights into the macroeconomic environment with which migrants had to cope.[42]

The environment defined: migration fields

The growth of the American economy created a vast migration field, but the precise connections between origins and destinations changed during the course of the period of mass immigration. These changes in the volume and composition of migration revealed the selective diffusion of capitalism into the long-settled rural world of Europe, Latin America, and

East Asia and corresponding regional shifts in the expansion of the American economy. Some emigrants departed with experience of the market economy, but others encountered only the disruptive impact of the market economy on their traditional patterns of life. Although this distinction captures the extremes of premigration conditions, the vast majority of migrants were part of complex discrete households for whom spatial mobility had become an indispensable part of the strategy for subsistence or advancement. Specific regions, each with a distinctive set of livelihoods and different periodicities of growth and decline, defined both the structural environment and the spatial limits of each major phase of migration to the United States. This environment comprised the multiple destinations of most migrants during the course of mass immigration; the overlapping and superimposed migration fields resulted in striking variations in the ethnic composition of different regions and cities within the United States.

Migrants included those who left their homelands with every intention of becoming permanent settlers and those who departed in search of seasonal employment with every intention of eventually returning to their homelands. There were, of course, many intended settlers who returned to their homelands and many labor migrants who eventually settled in the United States. Permanent migrants or settlers were presumed to have left the most developed or modernized regions or sectors of their homelands because they perceived a higher ceiling for their material expectations in an economy unencumbered by legal restraints and social privilege. They came in families and occasionally in groups, and despite their commitment to economic individualism, they also sought a moral community grounded in religious congregationalism and voluntary associations. Immigrants or settlers were therefore fragments of the most "modern" or "entrepreneurial" segments of their homelands, and from the perspective of American immigration history they were in a sense "Americans" before their departure.[43]

In contrast, labor migration was a response to economic insecurity that was primarily dedicated to the preservation of the ancestral homestead. The increasing involvement of peasants in commodity markets coincided with the diminished availability of secondary subsistence supports in the form of paternalistic obligations of landowners and access to common lands. Consequently price fluctuations had a more direct impact on their security. Labor migration was one response to these changes; initially it involved spasmodic seasonal movements over relatively short distances, but later it developed into an intercontinental labor market involving lengthy sojourns and sometimes permanent settlement. Labor migrants were young single adults or married men without their families who were prepared to work in undesirable jobs in distant locations in the hope of raising funds that would permit them to advance their economic aspirations in their homelands.[44] The connections between labor migrants and their distant sources of employment were sometimes dependent upon professional agents who served as intermediaries between large-scale employers and a remote labor supply, but the informal social networks of kin and friends were the dominant sources of information. For some labor migrants this strategy was modified, and remittances from America made it possible for their families to become immigrants.

These contrasts in the circumstances of emigration recall some elements of the discriminatory distinctions made between the old and the new immigration, but they have been reformulated without the erroneous and judgmental cultural distinctions of the proponents of restriction. Labor migrants usually moved as individuals, but they remained part of a network of family, kin, and friends and relied upon information circulating through these networks to obtain employment. Settlers were not necessarily zealous entrepreneurs, and the way in which many of them participated in the market economy has been described as a distinctive household system of production. The primary motive of this kind of production was the security and independence of the family rather than the speculative optimization of individual profit.[45] Speculation in land and commodity prices certainly commercialized the settler economy, but small-scale proprietary production based primarily on family labor fulfilled the more immediate emigrant objectives. Although labor migrants were more vulnerable in the confrontation with industrial capitalism, they were also part of a household economy that possessed the resources to extend the seasonal movements of individuals into a lengthier and hopefully more remunerative sojourn in the United States.[46] Stereotypical contrasts of settlers and labor migrants reveal the range of emigrant conditions, but the vast majority of migrants, permanent and temporary, sought independence and security within the framework of a household economy. Settlement in the United States was not necessarily the only means of meeting these goals.

Relatively few migrants came from unchanged traditional societies, and although one of the leading causes of migration was the impact of industrial capitalism on peasant societies, the majority of emigrants was not drawn from the most destitute stratum of rural society nor from the most backward segments of local economies. For long the new immigrants were viewed as more traditional and backward than the old, and within the old the Irish were judged to be less prepared for the demands of American capitalism than were other groups from northwestern Europe. The collapse of a marginal subsistence agriculture culminating in famine conditions strongly influenced generalizations about the Irish and other peasant emigrations. A Malthusian crisis was assumed to evict the most impoverished stratum of rural society. For a generation before the famine, the disruptive impact of the English industrial revolution on rural life greatly increased the volume, the distances, and the longevity of migration from most parts of the British Isles, and the new republic was one of several destinations to which displaced artisans and farmers made their way. Irish migrants, both Protestant and Catholic, resembled those from other parts of Western Europe. Possessing modest resources and coming from the commercialized sections of Ireland, they were able to make their way to the American West or to find remunerative employment in rapidly growing cities of the Northeast.

This initial "push" was, however, compounded by extraordinary agricultural distress throughout Western Europe during the 1840s. The savage impact of crop failure and famine in parts of Ireland and the German states multiplied the volume of emigration. The agricultural distress of the forties is, however, no longer viewed as an abrupt Malthusian crisis in a traditional society; rather it is seen as the demographic consequences of the disruption of a subsistence system by market pressures. Although assisted emigration and remittances increased the flow of the destitute, the profile of the famine emigration was similar to that of the preceding decades. Small farmers and laborers departed from those areas of Ireland where the pressures to accumulate or preserve farms of a commercially viable size left many with the modest resources necessary to support emigration but not subsistence.[47] Although there was probably much unrecorded emigration to England and Scotland, rates of emigration to the United States from the more remote and impoverished sections of the south and west did not reach the national average until a generation after the famine.[48] Emigration from the west of Ireland became feasible as the margin of subsistence increased following the famine and thereby provided the modest resources for transportation when remittances were unavailable. Despite an ongoing decline in population, emigration continued as efforts to preserve economically viable family farms necessitated the "exile" of younger children of both sexes. Of course, not every eldest son was prepared to wait until his father's death, and the youngest sibling was often the most convenient inheritor.[49] Quite apart from these matters of inheritance, "No other society found itself obliged so remorselessly to rationalize the subversion of the family ideal inherent in the emigration solution to the problem of inheritance."[50]

Throughout the remainder of northwestern Europe the geography of emigration was also strongly influenced by the diffusion of the disruptive impacts of industrialization on farming and rural crafts. During the course of the second half of the nineteenth century, German emigration increasingly shifted from southwestern states to northeastern states, which were unified in 1871 as the German Empire.[51] Like most of the

Irish, German migrants came to America as individuals and families of modest means. They were no longer able to subsist under conditions of commercialization, but overall they were able to depart with somewhat larger capital resources than the Irish. Although smaller in volume, emigration from Scandinavia, Holland, and Switzerland was also initially confined to highly localized areas of recent commercialization but then spread rapidly in relation to the selective penetration and disruption of local economies by capitalist practices. As in Ireland and the British Isles more generally, the transoceanic movements from continental Europe were an extension of local and interregional movements that eventually included overseas movements.

By 1860 the destinations of those foreigners who had arrived in the first surge of mass immigration were clearly established and revealed striking regional variations amongst the predominant immigrant groups. Over a third of 4 million foreign born lived in the mid-Atlantic states, with an additional 11 percent concentrated in New England. The majority was clustered in the major seaports and manufacturing towns of the emerging industrial core region of the United States. Apart from several river ports, relatively few immigrants had settled in the southern states, whereas over a third of the newcomers had joined the substantial westward movement of the native born into the midwestern states, where immigrants from the German states and to a lesser degree the Low Countries and Scandinavia predominated. The Irish were underrepresented in the Midwest but were well represented in New England, where there were few Germans; in the mid-Atlantic states, both groups were highly represented. The English and Scots were relatively evenly distributed among the three major receiving regions, but the Welsh were highly concentrated in Pennsylvania, and the Dutch and Scandinavians in the Midwest.

After the Civil War, the midwestern states substantially increased their share of the foreign-born population. In 1860 approximately equal proportions of immigrants lived in the midwestern and mid-Atlantic states, but a generation later, in 1890, 45 percent lived in the Midwest and 30 percent in the latter region. German, Swiss, Dutch, and Scandinavian immigrants were found throughout the Midwest, but in the northern sections they were often the dominant element in the local population. These same groups expanded into the northern Plains and Pacific Northwest, where they also played a dominant role in the process of initial settlement. This direct movement of continental Europeans to the agricultural interior of the United States was made possible by improvements in both oceanic and land transportation. Steamships now plied the Atlantic in about one third the time of sailing ships, and railroad construction in the United States had been stimulated by huge government grants of land adjacent to railroad routes. In order to generate freight movements and to convert their land into liquid assets, the railroads had a vested interest in the rapid alienation of their holdings. The railroads were joined by state immigration agencies in efforts to recruit settlers, but the personal networks of the emigrants themselves were probably as influential as direct recruitment.[52]

Immigration from northwestern Europe continued at a relatively high level until the turn of the nineteenth century but thereafter decreased rapidly, accounting for less than 20 percent of the total. Diminishing rates of population growth combined with industrialization and the specialization of agriculture had greatly reduced the incentives for emigration from northwestern Europe and at the same time increased the demand for seasonal labor drawn from eastern and central Europe. By 1900, for example, Slavic migration into Germany had reached substantial proportions; at the same time the return flow of German migrants had also increased. Regions of highly commercialized agriculture from which Germans had once migrated in large numbers, as well as new centers of industry, experienced substantial inflows of Slavic migrants. During this later period of emigration, the distinctions once made between the Irish and other northwestern Europeans may have had some validity. In the absence of any compensating economic developments to offset the continued pressures for emigration, the Irish overseas perceived their migration as an enforced "exile," whereas emigration from continental Europe was viewed as wanderlust, a search for independence and security. From this perspective, "emigration from Imperial Germany emerges not as a phenomenon of crisis, but as an expression of its vigor and participation in a general European movement."[53]

Under these circumstances several new nationalities made their appearance in the ebb and flow of trans-Atlantic migration. Arrivals from southern, central, and eastern Europe began slowly in the 1880s, when over 750,000 came from these more remote sources and accounted for about 15 percent of the total; by the first decade of the twentieth century these new sources provided over two thirds of the newcomers (Figure 6.2). Political persecution in the form of pogroms greatly accelerated the emigration of Jews from the Russian Empire, and the removal of restraints on movement within the Austro-Hungarian Empire also facilitated emigration from Central Europe.[54] As in the case of earlier migrants, changes within Europe strongly influenced the initial foci of these new source areas, but it was the changing labor needs of the American economy that increased the volume and extended the range of trans-Atlantic migration. The changing composition of foreign immigration after about 1880 was associated with substantial increases in the return flow of labor migrants, and this ebb flow reduced the gross immigration by approximately one third.[55]

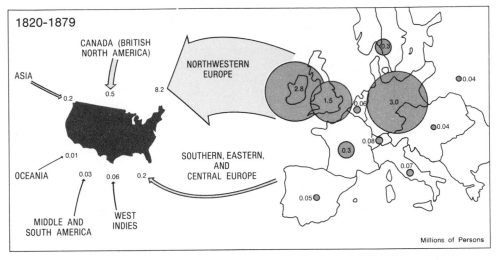

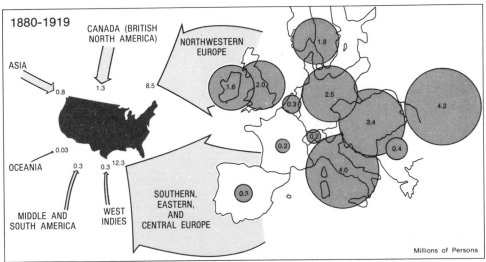

Figure 6.2 Sources of the "old" and the "new" immigration to the United States

Source: David Ward, *Cities and Immigrants* (New York: Oxford University Press, 1971), 54.

At the time of their arrival Slavic and Italian migrants were judged to be destitute peasants who, unlike their predecessors from northwestern Europe, were unlikely to make major contributions to American economic growth or to assimilate rapidly into the dominantly Anglo-American host society. The profiles of social origins of migrants from these new sources were not, however, radically different from those of their predecessors. The majority of migrants from southern and eastern Europe came from areas that had encountered a generation or more of seasonal interregional migration as a means of obtaining a livelihood in an agrarian world increasingly penetrated by capitalist practices. Many southern and eastern Europeans came from areas of petty proprietorship, where advancement for the majority of children was blocked by the need to establish a minimum land holding and the inability of artisan trades to compete with the new factory-made goods.[56] Social changes in these regions of emigration had already responded to commercial pressures; the networks of reciprocity amongst extended families had widened, voluntary associations had developed to provide mutual aid, and efforts were made to establish both basic education and adequate credit facilities.[57]

Although changes in the motives and circumstances of emigration during the course of the nineteenth century may have been exaggerated, the majority of migrants who arrived after 1890, with the exception of the Irish, had more localized and more urban American destinations than those of their predecessors. The leading destinations of the new arrivals from southern, central, and eastern Europe were the industrial cities of the Northeast and Midwest. Between 1890 and 1920 the mid-Atlantic states increased their share of the foreign born from a quarter to over a third; although the industrial cities of New England and the Midwest were also leading destinations of newcomers, their regional shares of immigrants remained stable between 1890 and 1920. Unfortunately, the census tabulations of the diverse ethnic groups coming from the Russian and Austro-Hungarian Empires were rarely consistent from decade to decade, but most Slavic immigrants were highly represented in the expanding centers of heavy industry in the mid-Atlantic states and the eastern Midwest. In contrast, Italians were well represented in New England, where they shared their predominance with Russian Jews and French Canadians; their more modest representation in the mid-Atlantic states and the Midwest was confined to major metropolitan cities rather than to specialized manufacturing centers.[58]

This selective superimposition of the more highly localized destinations of the new immigrants on the more extensive patterns of northwestern Europeans was clearly recorded in the variations in the ethnic profiles of American cities. These variations were largely based upon the temporal relationship between the regional patterns of economic growth and the changing geography of migration fields, but since each specialized regional economy also supported a diversified metropolitan center, functional differences among cities also influenced immigrant destinations.

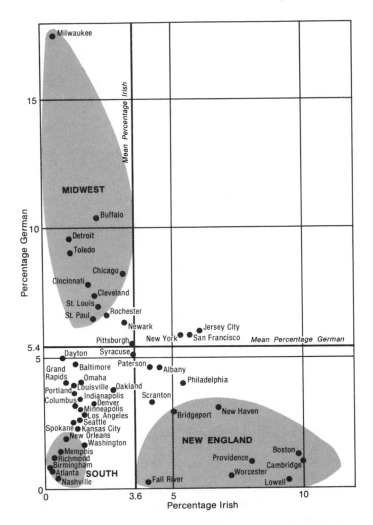

Figure 6.3 Regional clusters of "old" immigrants in U.S. cities, 1910

Source: David Ward, "Population Growth, Migration and Urbanization," in Robert D. Mitchell and Paul A. Groves, eds., *North America: The Historical Geography of a Changing Continent* (Totowa, N.J.: Rowman & Littlefield, 1987), 314.

The striking contrast between the predominantly German cities of the Midwest and the predominantly Irish cities of New England established during the middle decades of the nineteenth century persisted well into the twentieth century (Figure 6.3). Indeed, the cityward movement, not only of German born but also of other continental European immigrants

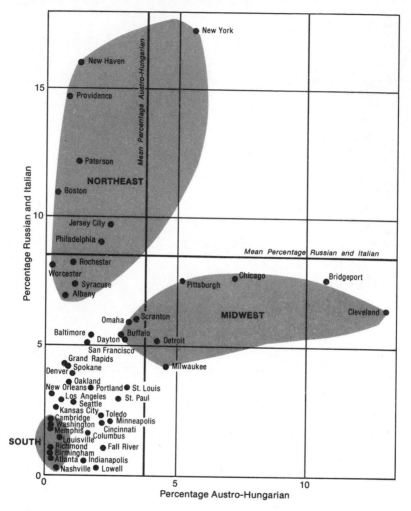

Figure 6.4 Regional clusters of "new" immigrants in U.S. cities, 1910

Source: David Ward, "Population Growth, Migration and Urbanization," in Robert D. Mitchell and Paul A. Groves, eds., *North America: The Historical Geography of a Changing Continent* (Totowa, N.J.: Rowman & Littlefield, 1987), 314.

who had originally settled on the land reinforced the distinctive ethnic populations of many midwestern cities. These regional distinctions were further amplified by the selectivity of the new immigration. Some but by no means all cities that had been dominated by German immigrants attracted relatively large numbers of Slavic newcomers, and those in which the Irish had predominated attracted the bulk of the Russians and Italians (Figure 6.4). Most new immigrants were highly represented in fewer of the most populous cities than were the old, but with the exception of the South, the ethnic profiles of most large cities included some representation of most nationalities.

The large cities of the industrial core region were also the primary destinations of black migrants from the American South. During the 1890s when emigration from Europe dropped in response to economically depressed conditions in the United States, blacks moved to the cities of the Northeast and Midwest, but it was the interruption of the flow of European immigrants during World War I that dramatically changed the dimensions of the black exodus from the South.[59] This exodus was further stimulated by immigration restriction. As late as 1890 over 90 percent of blacks lived in the South, but thirty years later this proportion had been reduced to two thirds and 10 percent were now established in the Northeast and eastern Midwest.

Although the Northeast and Midwest were the leading recipients of Europeans and southern blacks, a secondary arena of migration had also been established on the West Coast. East Asians and Mexicans rather than Europeans were the primary foreign-born contributors to the labor force of the western states. In 1890 over two thirds of the total Chinese born and over three quarters of the Japanese lived in California, and their presence provoked the first discriminatory measures to restrict foreign immigration, a generation before the more sweeping legislation of the early twenties. Although this trans-Pacific migration was designed to provide the unskilled, temporary, single-male labor necessary to construct railroads, East Asian immigrants were among the groups that were able to construct their economic advancement on the basis of familial networks. The Mexican presence was partly a consequence of annexation; almost 30 percent of the migrants from south of the border lived in California, with the remainder in the west south central states, where they became part of a system of seasonal migrations that has persisted, despite efforts at regulation, to the present.[60]

Household mobility from continent to continent, from region to region, and from city to city was embedded within a network of friends and relatives who not only provided initial aid but also information on employment. Despite the striking frequencies and vast distances of migration, lifetime social mobility was decidedly modest. These conclusions are primarily based upon the experiences of those who stayed long enough in one place to be recorded in consecutive directories or successive decennial census counts. It might be argued that those who moved most frequently, about whom we know the least, advanced the most, but the information on the most sedentary households suggests the opposite.

Prolonged residence in the same settlement was greatest amongst the affluent, influential members of a community, and the immigrant slums had extraordinarily high rates of population turnover.[61] Despite relatively high rates of return amongst late nineteenth- and early twentieth-century migrants, those who came as immigrants and those who became immigrants after arrival did gain access to the mainstream of the American economy and are viewed as later urban versions of sturdy rural pioneers. For some migrant groups, this process was both painful and prolonged, especially among those for whom return became impossible. The transition from labor migrant to immigrant was often spasmodic and slow. Primarily because structural changes in the organization of American capitalism altered the division of labor and the stratification of the labor force, the second and third generation of most but not all migrant groups did gain access to more secure strata of the labor force.

The ethnic division of labor

Although industrialization was often a source of new kinds of employment for those entering the labor force, technical and organizational changes also threatened the livelihoods and status of those whose skills and experience became redundant. These dislocations were also linked to assumptions about the impact of newly arrived immigrants on the wages and organization of the labor force. The idea of racial displacement was proposed during the period when the new immigration from southern and eastern Europe seemed to threaten the security of the native born and earlier immigrants from northwestern Europe. The term *racial* was used to describe both ethnic and racial differences and probably recorded the strength of ethnic prejudice at the time. These fears about displacement were especially prominent in the inquiries of the Dillingham Commission. In contrast, critics of the commission argued that the reorganization of industry intensified the recruitment of new sources of unskilled labor but these changes in employment also led to the corresponding elevation of the experienced and established segments of the labor force. Rather than "racial displacement," immigration led to "ethnic succession."[62]

In a survey that expressed concern about the degree to which racial factors placed obstacles to the employment and advancement of some groups in American industry, Herman Feldman repeated this more optimistic interpretation of the relationship between immigration and industrialization.[63] In a section entitled "Serving Their Turn at the Bottom" he concluded:

In one respect the vocational adjustment of the newcomer has tended to follow a certain pattern. The established tradition has been that newcomers start at the bottom with unskilled work, no matter what their qualifications for better jobs might be. Nearly every race thus pays the price of immigration by the suffering of the first generation. The second and the third descendants usually overcome the handicaps of language and education, and graduate out of their original lowly status. Then as a new group of immigrants or a new race descends upon the country, they too, are introduced into the American scheme by starting their cycle of adjustment. The history of American racial relations in industry may be read as a succession of attempted substitutions of one racial group for another.[64]

Despite his pessimism about the opportunities for continued mobility in American society, W. Lloyd Warner's study of Newburyport also concluded: "Each new ethnic group tended to repeat the occupational pattern of the preceding ones" in a process that appeared to have occurred without much friction.[65] These ideas resembled Robert Park's more general formulation of assimilation as a race-relations cycle, but precisely because conflict preceded accommodation in that cycle, ethnic succession was not assumed to be uncontested or inevitable.[66]

Historical examinations of social mobility have confronted these issues in their efforts to examine the varying rates and selectivity of advancement between native born and immigrants, between blacks and whites, and amongst the ethnoreligious groups who comprise the white population.[67] Documenting the ethnic variations in advancement has proved to be easier than explaining them. Efforts at explanation have generally linked slow or blocked mobility to discriminatory practices in both the labor and housing markets and rapid advancement to advantages derived from cultural orientation and premigration experiences. The determination of social mobility on the basis of the occupational categories of the Census Bureau presents many interpretative problems, especially since changes in the organization of capitalism altered the role and status of some occupations. Some basic occupational rankings have remained relatively stable over the past century, but during the course of mass immigration, proprietary opportunities diminished and a wide range of managerial and supervisory occupations replaced them. In any event, since lifetime rates of mobility were modest amongst the migrant generation, the key indicator of advancement is the degree to which their descendants were able to take advantage of those structural shifts in the organization of capitalism that created new and more remunerative strata in the labor force.

Variations in generational mobility clearly indicate that each major phase of immigration did not result in a queue on the lowest floor but rather in an ethnic stratification of the labor force that distinguished amongst newcomers as well as between newcomers and established immigrants.[68] Some groups had already made adjustments to the new capitalist order in their homelands and did not necessarily enter the lowest stratum of the labor force. High rates of mobility have been related to migrants who extend and specialize their entrepreneurial activities to serve markets beyond their ethnic groups. The scale and impact of these developments, especially the emergence of a stratum of small retailers or manufacturers, did vary from group to group.[69] Jewish, Asian, and to a lesser degree German and Italian entrepreneurs used their dominance in the business affairs and service needs of their own community as an initial base from which to extend their markets to include other immigrant groups and eventually the population at large. This sectoral specialization was attributed to premigration experiences of the market economy or to the selectivity of migration from within the region of origin. Consequently "human capital" provided an initial advantage in the establishment of small businesses.

This occupational overrepresentation included only a minority of the identified group, and the degree of that overrepresentation certainly fluctuated as opportunities for self-employment and petty entrepreneurship varied during the course of mass immigration. These "middlemen minorities" were most striking in the migrant generation, and although relatively high levels of entrepreneurial occupations persisted, occupational differentiation usually increased with each succeeding generation. The resulting ethnic stratification of the labor force within the American economy was reinforced as some groups moved rapidly into remunerative strata or became widely dispersed throughout the entire occupational profile and others remained in the lowest stratum for prolonged periods. The fluidity of this ethnic stratification varied, and some boundaries have still proved to be quite impermeable, but on the other hand, some groups have been the beneficiaries of the material improvements of the strata themselves. In contrast, discriminated groups have been trapped in the lowest stratum for generations, and although they might share that segment with other groups, it has been argued that they endure a "split" labor market in which they receive lower wages than others for identical services.[70]

Initially the impact of changes in industrialization was viewed as a threat to skilled workers and small proprietors, but some segments of these strata were able to take advantage of the technical and organizational changes associated with the initial phases of industrialization. The transformation of the scale of production of textiles and iron complemented the male-dominated artisanal system of manufacturing.[71] The large plants were initially established on new sites apart from existing urban centers and became the focus of specialized manufacturing towns. These new ventures relied upon new unskilled sources of labor, but they also created new kinds of skilled, semiskilled, and clerical employment and retained some elements of older forms of labor organization. The growth of nearby cities later engulfed some of these industrial centers as industrialization took the form of a new division of labor that multiplied but differentiated small-scale production.[72] The world of organized skilled labor had considerable discretion in the control of work routines, but the world of insecure and temporary employment in the sweated trades and the service industries was directly tied to the spasmodic and changing character of consumer demands. The semiskilled labor needs of textile factories, the workshops of needle trades, and a host of manufacturing that was put out into homes were initially met by women rather than by male immigrants.

As the demand for ready-made cheap clothing expanded, the artisanal workshop increasingly became the intermediary between merchant and domestic workers. Skilled processes were separated from those that could be accomplished by unskilled and often seasonal labor that was comprised largely of widows and single women in their own homes. Sometimes several pieceworkers together rented rooms in which both the unventilated environment and the pace of production brought forth the term "sweatshop."[73] Technical innovations like the sewing machine reinforced this sytem of production, which increasingly relied primarily on cheap immigrant labor. Some skilled German immigrants were able to take advantage of these organizational changes and become entrepreneurs; the unskilled outworkers were predominantly Irish women. Females accounted for 53 percent of the Irish immigrants, compared to only 41 percent of the Germans, and the predominance of women was one of the definitive attributes of emigration from Ireland. For the Irish, employment and emigration may have been an individual matter, but the economic returns in the form of remittances and mutual aid were certainly designed to support an extended household.[74] Although the majority of Irish immigrants were young single adults who married relatively late, they were usually attached to households comprised of relatives who also maintained contacts with kinfolk over great distances. Many Irish women were familiar with the domestic textile and needle trades in the United Kingdom, and they rapidly dominated the household production of clothing in American cities. Despite strong prejudices, the affluent middle class employed Irish women as resident domestic servants, and the less affluent relied upon Irish laundresses. The management of small boarding houses was another prominent source of female earnings in a society with a high proportion of female-headed households.[75]

Irish males were engaged in insecure, low-paid, itinerant employment and often in mortally dangerous construction trades. Although Irish laborers were involved in the construction of canals, railroads, and cities in the Midwest, proportionately few settled on the land, and the vast majority remained in the northeastern cities where, initially, they were confined to the lowest stratum of the labor market.[76] In some cities they competed with free blacks for the least remunerative strata of the labor market and from time to time engaged in open racial conflicts over sharing these jobs.[77] Their own religious identity also provoked the hostility of the predominantly Protestant native working class, especially when the subcontracting of artisanal production to unskilled immigrants threatened the security of native American craftsmen. Irish immigrants made possible a different organization of production that undermined the security of those craftsmen who were unable or unwilling to adopt the new forms of production. In contrast, German immigrants with appropriate skills entered trades that were not radically altered by the new forms of organization and successfully competed with the native born. The Germans quickly established themselves in several skilled crafts devoted to the production of consumer durables and in the preparation and retailing of food.

These striking contrasts in the occupational patterns of Irish and German immigrants were well established in New York before the Civil War. By 1855 relatively few immigrants had entered the professions and businesses, which remained firmly under the control of native-born Americans, but German immigrants were already well represented amongst small proprietors and actually dominated several of the artisanal trades requiring skills and experience. In contrast, over 60 percent of the Irish were confined to the least secure service-oriented occupations. Consequently, the selective entry of different immigrants into newly developed sectors and occupations had created a well-defined ethnic division of labor.[78] A similar ethnic division of labor had developed in Philadelphia, and although few Germans had settled in Boston, the Irish there were more strikingly limited to the lowest stratum of a labor market in which immigrants from rural New England and from the Maritime Provinces of British America dominated the middle strata.[79]

Unlike the Irish, who were overrepresented in the lowest strata of the cities in which they predominated, the Germans tended to become a microcosm of the occupational structure as a whole. Where they formed small minorities, as in New England or the South, they were primarily traders and dealers. In mid-Atlantic cities they were well represented in the middle range of occupations, but in the Midwest they were found across the entire range of occupations.[80] In the Midwest the Irish were often small minorities in cities in which the Germans rather than the native born were the largest segment of the population, and there they were able to establish themselves in a wider range of occupations than they had in eastern cities.[81] In the Far West the Irish were more broadly distributed throughout the various sectors of the regional economy and the different strata of the labor force. Indeed, in the West the Irish sensed that Asian immigration threatened their privileged position, and they were prominent in efforts to restrict or exclude newcomers from the Far East.[82]

Between 1890 and 1920 this ethnic division of labor was profoundly altered as emigrants from southern, central, and eastern Europe increasingly met the changing labor needs of the American economy. The United States was a pioneer in those technological and organizational innovations that marked the second stage of the industrial revolution and the transition from a predominantly entrepreneurial capitalism to one dominated by large corporations. Consequently, the new immigrants encountered not only the impact of a later and more highly industrialized capitalism but also a somewhat different and more complexly stratified labor market than had their predecessors. In addition to the expanding demand for unskilled labor, the new systems of production greatly expanded the clerical, supervisory, and managerial strata of the industrial labor force. Complex and hierachical job structures based upon prescribed rules created "internal" labor markets within large firms, which provided on-the-job training and well-defined routes of advancement to occupations that by any strict definition were not skilled.[83] The decisive boundaries in this labor market were between salaried managers and wage earners and also between the relatively secure, moderately paid unionized factory operatives and those with minimum wages and no security.

Long-established immigrants from northwestern Europe and especially their native-born children became the indispensable supervisors and managers of the new unskilled labor force recruited from southern and eastern Europe. The expansion of the public sector of urban employment and the growth of large-scale retail and service activities also contributed to the enlargement of occupations that increasingly became differentiated from the manual work of the working class and were described as being lower middle class. With the exception of New England, the Irish and their native-born children were especially prominent in this expanding stratum. By the turn of the century the occupational pattern of the population of Irish parentage was little different from that of the population of native white parentage. With the exception of relatively low representation in agriculture and a diminished but still high representation in services, the Irish were well represented in the growing lower middle class of managers and supervisors, as well as in the more secure skilled trades.[84] With the exception of carpentry, the Irish were prominent in the organization of most of the long-established building trades and in new activities based on structural steel and electricity. In the construction trades they moved into proprietary positions, where their experience with subcontracting and knowledge of local political arrangements proved advantageous. These advances in managerial and entrepreneurial strata were complemented by a major contribution to the leadership of several key unions and these divergent interests created some longstanding internal tensions and conflict within the broader Irish-American community.[85]

Under these circumstances the relationships amongst ethnic identity, class consciousness, union organization, and local politics varied from region to region, from city to city and within the same cities and regions in response to changes in the local economy and the ethnic composition of its labor force. In Denver, for example, as elsewhere, substantial numbers of the Irish were employed in unskilled occupations, but they were also well represented and influential in some professions and more broadly in business and the skilled trades. Initially, voluntary associations partly bridged these occupational distinctions within the Irish community and emphasized the sectarian divisions between Protestants and Catholics. Eventually, these divisions were diminished since both groups supported the Land Reform Movement in Ireland and explored its relevance to American social problems. During the eighties, however, the antipathies of the leadership of the Land League to the union movement, and to the Knights of Labor in particular, created new cleavages in the Irish community that reflected the degree to which the Irish had become a microcosm of American society.[86]

Although the Irish were numerically dominant in only a few trades and in only a few cities, they were influential in both unions and city politics. Assertions about the slow advancement of the Irish in relation to the Germans were usually based on the experience of the Irish in New England, where their economic advancement was more modest than elsewhere. Although about 11 percent of the Irish were recorded as being in unskilled occupations in the nation as a whole, in Massachusetts a quarter of the Irish labor force was unskilled, and the Irish accounted for 45 percent of the total employment in unskilled occupations. In New England the Irish shared their regional predominance with Canadians from the English-speaking sections of the Maritime Provinces and Newfoundland and also with French-speaking Canadians from Quebec. The latter often competed with the Irish for jobs in the textile industry, whereas English-speaking Canadians predominated in the skilled trades into which the Irish had advanced in the mid-Atlantic and midwestern cities. Indeed, in cities dominated by German immigrants and their descendants, the Irish population was invariably well represented in several strata in which it was scarcely present in New England.

At a time when a majority of the Irish were trapped in general laboring and the service trades, many Germans had been advantageously placed in small-scale production, but with the extension of mechanization and related-scale economies to an increasing range of industries, long-established German immigrants and certainly their American-born children had to adjust to the diminishing opportunities for self-employment. The Germans not only retained their established dominance in some highly skilled crafts that were unaffected by transformations of the production process but also moved into new industries, like electricity, where new skills were required.[87] Many newly arrived German migrants were, however, in a less advantageous position, since they were increasingly drawn from the agrarian northeast of the German Empire and competed with the growing mass of Slavic migrants in semiskilled and unskilled factory employment, and those with old artisanal skills found the market for their talents greatly diminished.[88] As with the Irish, the increasingly complex division of labor diversified the occupational range of the Germans; as a result, they were prominent both in the new lower middle class and in the relatively secure unionized trades. Although broader ethnic loyalties among the Irish and Germans often blurred the distinction between the new lower middle class and the upper stratum of the working class, ethnic differences between the old and the new immigration often amplified the contrasts between skilled unionized workers and the unorganized and unskilled lower stratum.

Access to the professions was increasingly regulated by educational attainment, and it has been argued that occupational mobility was greatest amongst those groups that placed emphasis on education as an avenue of mobility. The investment in education was, however, dependent upon the initial attainment of some degree of economic security, and for some groups this process could not be accomplished in one generation. Moreover, individual mobility may have been inconsistent with the broader aims of family security, and judgments about relative success and failure need to be qualified by considerations of motive.[89] Home ownership, for example, became an indicator and symbol of economic security, but it was often obtained at the expense of investments in the education of children. In any event, although the commitment to family security prevented children from gaining social advancement through extended education, the opportunities that existed in their communities provided them with an alternative if incomplete system of mobility.[90] The desire for security rather than mobility has been associated with the Irish and other groups amongst whom entrepreneurial self-employment was either rare or confined to a market that was comprised of their compatriots. This observation may apply to the migrant generation, but its applicability for subsequent generations is questionable.

Throughout the period of mass immigration the professions remained a preserve of the native born. Despite evidence from New England that indicates relatively slow rates of advancement, elsewhere the Irish were increasingly poised to breach these higher strata. By 1920, at a time when the national average for college attendance was 17 percent, the proportion amongst Irish Catholics was 25 percent.[91] A detailed survey of the relationship between ethnicity and occupational status in Buffalo revealed that the Irish had the highest representation in middle-class occupations.[92] These findings ought not to have been surprising, for it was only in New England that the Irish encountered a prolonged experience of occupying the lowest stratum of the labor market; elsewhere their role in the labor market was more favorable. In New England they encountered the competitive impact of Maritime Canadians, but in the Far West a different regional ethnic profile initially placed the Irish above the Chinese in the stratified labor market of that region. Consequently the ethnic mix and structural setting of each city and region actually redefined the relationship between migrant and employment.

As the primary sources and predominant destinations of foreign immigrants shifted during the last two decades of the nineteenth century, these regional differences in the occupational distributions of ethnic groups were amplified. Despite the restriction of most new immigrants to the lowest and least desirable jobs, many contemporary observers complained that southern and eastern Europeans were a threat to the livelihood of native-born Americans and long-established old immigrants. With the exception of Russian Jews, the majority of migrants from southern and eastern Europe were young males who, despite their low wages, provided remittances for absent families and struggled to accumulate savings to sustain an enterprise on their return. While substantial proportions of these groups returned to their homelands, others remained and were joined by their families. They were judged to be prepared to work for low wages and to assist in breaking strikes. In fact, the majority of new immigrants were not only employed in new kinds of jobs, but were also prepared to strike and resist abuses; however, they often found that the more privileged skilled workers resented their labor militancy. The degree to which an ethnically differentiated labor force divided the union movement varied from industry to industry, and for a brief period the packing industry of Chicago was able to forge an integrated union.[93]

The new ethnic division of labor was most clearly developed in the highly integrated large-scale production of steel. The huge plants, concentrated in Pennsylvania and Ohio but with major outliers on Lake Michigan, employed Slavic immigrants from eastern Europe who were trained to meet the highly repetitive and often strenuous tasks of a complexly divided work process.[94] Americans and established immigrants from the British Isles dominated the supervisory and residual skilled jobs; Slavic migrants were at first restricted to unskilled laboring, but eventually they were able to move into semiskilled machine-tending activities. Although corporate inducements and publicity, often directed by brokers or agents, facilitated the recruitment of this labor force, the vast majority of new immigrants found jobs by way of friends and family. For this reason ethnic subgroups drawn from highly localized sources dominated specific occupations or segments of the labor force. A similar ethnic stratification of the labor force developed in the textile industries of New England, where British immigrants predominated in the residual skilled jobs, French Canadians were machine tenders, and Portuguese and Polish newcomers dominated unskilled jobs.[95]

Slavic immigrants were the dominant components of the lower strata of the labor force of large-scale manufacturing, but the occupational patterns and predominant destinations of Italian and Jewish immigrants were quite different.[96] The bulk of Slavic immigrants found their way to specialized manufacturing cities, whereas the majority of Italians and Jews were concentrated in metropolitan cities with a more diverse employment profile. Southern Italians replaced the Irish in general laboring; like the Irish, their occupational structure varied from region to region. For long southern Italians and especially Sicilians were viewed as uprooted peasants or landless laborers who came to the United States as migrant laborers intending to return to their homelands. Accordingly they were presumed to be politically indifferent in the New World. In fact, southern Italians came from a region in the midst of economic disruptions and at the time of maximum emigration, these events provoked political responses in Italy that carried over to the United States. They were also drawn from a broad range of social strata, and the relationships between these strata varied in response to American conditions. In some northeastern cities and especially New York the majority of Sicilians, like the Irish before them, dominated unskilled occupations. In New York, Sicilians were part of a militant union movement, but elsewhere their communities included a wider range of more substantial occupations, and the success of their unions was contingent upon the leadership of skilled workers. In the absence of this leadership, socially prominent Sicilians established cohesive communities based upon voluntary associations, and these institutional developments often inhibited union organization.[97]

Although the changing structure of American capitalism redefined the division of labor and the organization of work, this transformation occurred in a fashion that left segments of the labor force employed in older forms of industrial practice. The expansion of many consumer-oriented industries continued to be based upon a complex system of subcontracting and small-scale production. Jewish immigrants found employment in the rapidly growing clothing industry, which had long been associated with the use of sweated labor, and they also became prominent in the rapidly changing retail sector of large cities. Although the exploitative aspects of small-scale production provoked conflicts and unionization, these trades also attracted large numbers of small entrepreneurs.[98] To a greater degree than any European ethnic group, Chinese and later Japanese immigrants developed a role as "middlemen minorities" within the context of the distinctive ethnic pluralism of the western states, where migrants from Mexico provided the labor for a highly capitalized agriculture and the service trades.

Throughout the period of mass immigration, there were spasmodic but intense resentments about the effects of the lower living standards of newly arrived immigrants upon the security of the established white labor force. The native white wage earners had been on the whole a privileged stratum of the labor force, and immigration certainly exacerbated their painful adjustments to mechanization and the reorganization of production. In contrast, the impact of immigration on the security and advancement of the native black wage earner was devastating.[99] The longevity of the black experience on the ground floor has been linked to unique levels of discrimination not only in their urban destinations but also in the rural South prior to their departure. Their economic predicament has also been attributed to the timing of their migration. They were presumed to be a third major immigrant stream, following those of the old and new immigration, and they were therefore last in the queue of advancement.[100] Free blacks had, in fact, formed a modest part of the antebellum urban labor market. The abolition of slavery exposed blacks to a competitive labor market, and many skills that had been nurtured and valued while they were slaves became a threat to free white labor after emancipation.

Although the bulk of black migrants to American cities did enter the labor market after those from abroad, most large cities had housed small black minorities before most new immigrants had arrived. In Philadelphia, for example, blacks accounted for almost 4 percent of the population in 1890. About a decade later, this community was the subject of one of very few investigations of urban blacks prior to the major migrations of the twentieth century. The pioneer black sociologist DuBois documented a world in which blacks were concentrated in several small clusters within which there were well-established professionals and successful businesses as well as a range of effective institutions. The arrival of large numbers of southern blacks in search of unskilled employment disturbed this world and created tensions between the established black community and the rapidly growing contingent of newcomers.[101] The newcomers made it possible for outsiders to redefine the black community as predominantly impoverished and unskilled at a time when many of the established residents faced the increasing competition of European immigrants in several trades.

By the turn of the century these established black communities had experienced a progressive constriction of their already narrow range of occupations. These problems of labor competition with newly arrived European immigrants had first occurred during the old immigration, when the Irish encroached upon the prior claims of blacks to an established preeminence in several waterfront occupations. Later the Irish used their political influence to restrict the access of blacks to unskilled public employment. Later in the century, blacks encountered a reduced range of employment options in small-scale consumer-oriented service trades. Italians, in particular, competed with them for these activities.[102] In most northern cities the range of occupations available to the small black populations was diminished as European labor migrants replaced blacks. In 1905 it was reported that "the Negro barber who once had such a grip in the North, . . . now, in Boston, as elsewhere, is being excluded by the wide-spreading anti-Negro feeling . . ." Another observer concluded: "In the matter of employment, the colored people of Chicago have lost in the last ten years every occupation of which they once had a monopoly. There is scarcely a negro barber left in the business district. Nearly all the janitor work in the large buildings has been taken away from them by the Swedes."[103]

They also failed to share in the structural mobility made possible by the reorganization of large-scale industrial production. Although blacks had established themselves in the iron-fabricating industries before the arrival of Slavic immigrants, the shift to large-scale steel production worked to their disadvantage. European ethnic groups were able to establish a predominance in key processes in large plants, whereas blacks were often widely dispersed in several segments of the production process, invariably as unskilled laborers. In 1910 blacks accounted for about two thirds of the unskilled labor in Pittsburgh's iron and steel industries, but a decade later this proportion had grown to almost 90 percent. These changes in the proportions of skilled workers affected all workers, but they proved to be especially severe for blacks, who were consistently paid less for the same work than were European immigrants. Blacks were, therefore, increasingly confined to the lowest stratum of the manufacturing labor force, and although the needs of the black community itself supported a small business and professional class, the modest resources of the community set limits to such ethnic enterprise.[104]

The most comprehensive documentation of the consequences of this restricted access to the full range of semiskilled occupations was presented in the monumental survey of black Chicago by St. Clair Drake and Horace Cayton.[105] They established the existence of a job ceiling that excluded blacks from access to growing sectors of the economy during the 1920s and condemned them to the highest rates of unemployment during the depressed 1930s. The occupational profile of blacks in Chicago clearly reveals the impact of both a "stratified" and a "split" labor market. These developments do not support arguments about a migrant queue. Long before the mass departure of rural blacks during and after World War I, and long before their enforced segregation in the extensive inner-city ghetto, blacks occupied an especially discriminated place in the ethnic division of labor, but under the conditions of mercantile and entrepreneurial capitalism, the spatial expression of that discrimination had been quite different from that expressed by the inner-city ghetto of the contemporary American city.

Ethnicity, employment, and residence

Reinterpretations of the migrant experience in American cities have stressed the degree to which migrants' elaborate social organizations made possible the establishment of complex, discrete residential patterns. These patterns were, however, embedded within even broader patterns of circular and chain migrations that were linked to the uneven regional development of the American economy. These constraints set the margins of migration fields, within which there was considerable interurban migration; the changing locations of employment within cities set limits to the often ephemeral residential choices in specific cities. In view of the prevalence of the pronounced ethnic stratification of the urban labor force, occupational status and ethnicity ought to have reinforced one another if either exerted a profound effect on patterns of residential differentiation. Under conditions of finance capitalism this assumption is plausible, but mercantile and entrepreneurial capitalism set different constraints on the patterns of land-use assignment and residential differentiation.[106]

During the transition from mercantile to industrial capitalism, employment opportunities were highly dispersed not only within cities but also between cities. The households of many general laborers were based in large cities, but their employment shifted frequently and was not necessarily confined to large cities. During the middle decades of the nineteenth century the embryonic inner city still housed substantial numbers of middle-class Americans, and consequently many immigrants were forced to live in shanties on the edge of the city, from which they might seek daily employment in many sections of the city or in construction activities far beyond the limits of the city itself. Some specialized artisan trades and many sweatshops were highly clustered in the rapidly expanding warehouse section of the emerging central business district. The other foci of skilled employment were satellite industrial suburbs based upon producer-goods industries, which required abundant water and space and, initially at least, constructed company housing on adjacent land. The rapid physical expansion of cities eventually outflanked these cellular developments, and their labor needs were met more broadly from adjacent sections of the city. Some skilled workers in those artisanal trades, which were protected from the sweatshop system, were able to move away from the deteriorating environment of the waterfront and warehouses. For most artisans, however, the journey to work was short and their homes were only rarely in exclusively residential quarters.[107]

In most cities newly constructed warehouses were the dominant sites of centrally located employment. These structures had expanded from the increasingly specialized waterfront and had necessitated the demolition of substantial houses. On their margins they created the first blighted residential zones into which immigrants crowded. Most warehouses were devoted to multiple uses, with commercial activities at street level and workshop manufacturing in the rear rooms and upper stories. The sweated trades in particular rented cheap space for limited terms and relied upon the immigrant labor force in nearby tenements. Since the bulk of urban employment was in small workshops or homes, many consumer goods and personal services were dispersed in most sections of the city. Only the most affluent neighborhoods were exclusively residential, but these neighborhoods also housed their share of immigrants acting as resident domestic servants.

To the degree that those migrants in an ethnic group dominated a particular service, they settled among groups in which that activity was underrepresented.[108] For example, some German purveyors of food who met the needs of other groups were interspersed with their customers, but much retailing also took the form of itinerant peddling. Under these circumstances urban employment, like ethnic residential quarters, was a complex hybrid of highly clustered and widely dispersed patterns. Those Irish and German immigrants who were employed in the warehouse and waterfront districts or more specialized concentrations of manufacturing activities lived in adjacent but separate tenements and thereby created the initial foci of what later became the vast expanses of inner-city slums. Neither the rate of abandonment of middle-class housing nor the concentration of employment provided the basis for the kind of extensive inner-city concentrations of immigrants that were to characterize the American city at the turn of the century.

During the transition from industrial to finance capitalism, the central business district became the dominant and most diverse source of urban employment. The multifunctional warehouse quarter became part of a more specialized and highly differentiated central district in which public and corporate administration and mass retailing became the predominant land uses. Some sections of the central business districts were devoted to activities with a labor force heavily derived from a specific ethnic group living in the nearby tenements. The close association of Italians with the wholesale markets for fresh food and of Russian Jews with the clothing sweatshops of the warehouse quarter created related concentrations of migrants and jobs. The reorganization of many industrial enterprises also involved the establishment of large industrial plants on the urban fringe, where they were connected to the facilities for interregional railroad transportation and where they might avoid the threatening labor problems of the inner city. These plants recruited an ethnic labor force that often clustered in adjacent residential quarters, but they also made efforts to "Americanize" or socialize the labor force to the regimen of mass production.[109]

The necessity for multiple employment within individual households, the frequency of job turnover, and the high rates of migration between jobs and among relatives diminished the direct impact on residential locations of any individual journey to work. In Detroit residence "near no particular factory but not too distant from any, was an asset in the context of the family economy when men, women, parents and children parted to work in different directions." Like many other cities that employed large numbers of migrants, "Detroit had become industrialized in such a way that the geography of work did not seriously interfere with the creation of autonomous neighborhoods."[110] While there were expanding suburbs that served the needs of the upwardly mobile, much residential mobility was also part of an elaborate system of labor migration. Contemporary observers were especially sensitive to this trade-off between ethnic facilities and place of work in the selection of residential locations. Thomas and Znaniecki, for example, indicated the degree to which the creation of Polish quarters was contingent upon access to employment.[111]

Work did not set any precise limits on the residential choices of highly mobile migrants, but the different patterns of employment in the inner city today reveal the degree to which the linkage between employment and residence was critical to past migrants.[112] The levels and extent of the residential segregation of black and Hispanic minorities are much higher than those of the migrant generation of most European ethnic groups, but this residential predicament is made even more critical by the decentralization of urban employment. The advantages to newly arrived migrants of proximity to the central business district have greatly diminished; there has been a loss of the kinds of jobs that once created the "ramp" of advancement. Under these circumstances the sociogeographic boundary between the inner city and the suburbs remains an object of anxiety and a focus of reform. The original progressive concerns about the fixity of the sociogeographic boundary between the growing mass of slums and the remainder of urban society had provoked anxious inquiries into the structural obstacles to self-improvement but had eventually stressed the advantages of decentralization as a solution to urban congestion. This process of decentralization has proceeded, but some groups were unable to gain access to the new industrial quarters at a time when the labor needs of activities that retained a central location were declining.[113]

Since this process of advancement has varied from group to group, some studies have implied that ethnically specific resources have been conducive to coping with the experience of migration. Despite variations in both the complexity and social impact of voluntary associations, most migrant groups, including blacks, established a wide range of organizations that initially served discrete communities similar to those of European immigrant groups. Indeed, some authorities have argued that too complete a set of ethnic institutions might also deprive a group of access to opportunities for assimilation and mobility.[114] Although ethnic institutions provided direct links with ancestral traditions and values, they did not necessarily delay cultural assimilation. These institutions, and especially religious organizations, responded to their demanding social role in immigrant communities by adopting the congregational patterns of American Protestantism. Some immigrants may indeed have intended to re-create in the New World authentic and traditional religious values that had long since been eclipsed in their homelands, but most religious institutions were preoccupied with adaptation and organization rather than orthodoxy and tradition.[115] Immigrant religious institutions may have symbolized ethnicity, but in their participatory arrangements they were agencies of cultural assimilation.

Under some circumstances voluntary associations were actually a source of divisive rivalries over competing strategies to confront discrimination and exclusion. These conflicts were muted when associational life was reinforced by ascriptive loyalties and a pride in a common ancestral culture.[116] Certainly, the effectiveness of voluntary associations was to some degree dependent upon the solidarities of family and kin, and presumably their impact was impaired under conditions of family disorganization. When migration is frequent and sexually selective, households are obviously subjected to unusual stress, but that stress is rooted in the insecurity of employment that is to some degree alleviated by a reliance on the dispersed resources of family and kin. Under extreme and prolonged conditions of economic insecurity social adaptations may become impossible, and a process of individuation results in anomic conditions.[117] The social implications of delayed or blocked advancement on the longevity of the coping capacities of a migrant group remain unclear, but to a greater degree than their predecessors, the deprived minorities of the inner city today have tested those limits. The presumed poverty of institutional resources and related limitations in the organization of family life are often integral, if controversial, parts of the definition of deprived minorities. Under these circumstances conventional welfare policies are assumed to exacerbate rather than to solve the problems of poverty.[118]

The implied contrasts in the capacities of different migrant groups to cope with the inner-city environment are not unlike equally discriminatory observations about cultural differences between the old and new immigrations that found expression in the explicit quotas of the immigration restriction legislation of the early twenties. At that time both actual and imagined levels of social problems among migrant groups were related to their slow rates of economic advancement. If ethnic communities served as a critical resource in coping with the disruptions of migration and the obstructions of discrimination and also served as a "ramp" for social and economic advancement, then by implication failure to advance was a matter of cultural disability. This kind of argument is perilously close to the concepts of the unworthy poor and the residuum upon which the nineteenth-century views of the slums were based! At that time moral, hereditarian, and cultural interpretations of the poor were tempered by deep concerns about the adverse environment of the inner city. This environmental focus did deflect attention from the coping capacities of the immigrant poor, but elaborations of these coping capacities have sometimes lost sight of the degree to which the urban environment severely constrained the lives of the poor.

Concepts like adaptation, accommodation, or coping capture the varying responses of different migrant groups to the urban environment, but the varying character of that environment from time to time, from group to group, and from place to place should receive more emphasis. The lack of balance is in part a consequence of the particular way the environment was formulated in the original definitions of the slums. These definitions stressed the secondary consequences of poverty and discrimination and retained assumptions about the inevitability of a residual impoverished stratum that for moral, hereditarian, or cultural reasons have been unresponsive to reform or opportunity. The term *ghetto* evocatively expresses the predicament of the inner city, but because attention was drawn to the deficiencies of the immediate environment and the social costs of residential segregation, the environs of the inner city became the sole object of attention.[119]

The reinterpretation of the experiences of European and East Asian immigrants has been contrasted with those of the residents of the inner city today. In particular, the extent, homogeneity, and overt segregation of black residential quarters form a striking contrast with the more complex patterns of overlapping dominance that characterized the residential quarters of most European immigrant groups. As long as it was assumed that the initial experience of migrant groups was concentration in the adverse environment of the inner city, the black experience was viewed as a replication of the earlier immigrant experience and it was expected that patience would eventually bring its rewards. These assumptions have been rejected, and some observers have argued that the ghetto experience is specific to the minorities of the modern American city.[120] Recent research has explored the degree to which the specificity of this ghetto experience combines the disadvantages of racial discrimination and economic deprivation.[121]

For these reasons the uniformly negative interpretation of the ghetto in the original American definition appears to have had a prophetic validity. Since the validity of that earlier definition has been questioned, skepticism concerning its current validity might be prudent, too. In attempting to confront the degree to which migrants coped with that environment, some of the sensibilities about environmental constraints that were embedded in the original formulation were lost. While neither deprivation nor minorities are confined to segregated inner-city quarters, the ghetto describes precisely those extreme circumstances where a limited access to resources is decisively compounded by environmental disabilities and ethnic or racial discrimination. These compound effects have created an inner-city predicament that is often viewed as unprecedented in American urban history, but this judgment retains many assumptions about culture and environment, about people and place, and about residence and work that have a long and complex ancestry.

Notes

1. The slum, the ghetto, and the inner city

1 John Higham, "Integrating America: The Problem of Assimilation in the Nineteenth Century," *Journal of American Ethnic History* 1 (1981): 7–25; John Higham, "Current Trends in the Study of Ethnicity in the United States, *Journal of American Ethnic History* 2 (1982): 5–15.

2 Manuel Castells, *The Urban Question* (London: Arnold, 1977); Peter Saunders, *Social Theory and the Urban Question* (London: Holmes and Meier, 1981).

3 Richard Walker, "A Theory of Suburbanization: Capitalism and the Construction of Urban Space in the United States," in Michael Dear and Alan Scott, eds., *Urbanization and Urban Planning in Capitalist Society* (London: Methuen, 1981), 383–430.

4 Mary Jo Deegan, *Jane Addams and the Men of the Chicago School, 1892–1918* (New Brunswick, N.J.: Transaction Books, 1988).

5 Stow Persons, *Ethnic Studies at Chicago: 1905–45* (Urbana and Champaign, Ill.: University of Illinois Press, 1987); Peter Jackson and Susan Smith, *Exploring Social Geography* (London: Allen & Unwin, 1984), 65–97.

6 Kathleen Neils Conzen, "Immigrants, Immigrant Neighborhoods and Ethnic Identity: Historical Issues," *Journal of American History* 66 (1979): 603–15.

7 Ira Katznelson, *City Trenches: Urban Politics and the Patterning of Class in the United States* (New York: Pantheon, 1981), 25–44.

8 Timothy L. Smith, "Religion and Ethnicity in America," *American Historical Review* 83 (1978): 1155–85.

9 David Montgomery, "To Study the People: The American Working Class," *Labor History* 21 (1980): 485–512.

10 David Harvey, "Class Structure and the Theory of Residential Differentiation," in David Harvey, ed., *The Urbanization of Capital: Studies in the History and Theory of Capital Urbanization* (Baltimore: The Johns Hopkins University Press, 1985), 109–24.

11 John Bodnar, *The Transplanted: A History of Immigrants in Urban America* (Bloomington: Indiana University Press, 1985), 206–16; Ewa Morawska, *For*

218

Bread with Butter: Life Worlds of East Central Europeans in Johnstown, Pennsylvania, 1890–1940 (Cambridge: Cambridge University Press, 1985), 1–11.

12 W. L. Yancey, E. P. Ericksen, and R. N. Juliani, "Emergent Ethnicity: A Review and Synthesis," *American Sociological Review* 41 (1975): 391–403.

2. The slums discovered: 1840–1875

1 David Ward, "The Early Victorian City in England and America: On the Parallel Development of an Urban Image, European Settlement and Development in North America," in James R. Gibson, ed., *Essays on Geographical Change in Honour and Memory of Andrew Hill Clark* (Toronto: University of Toronto Press, 1978), 170–89.

2 Francis Wayland, *The Elements of Political Economy* (New York: Leavitt, Lord, 1837), 431–9.

3 Joseph Tuckerman, *On the Elevation of the Poor*, ed. Edward Everett Hale (Boston: Roberts Bros., 1874), 103.

4 Paul S. Boyer, *Urban Masses and Moral Order in America, 1820–1920* (Cambridge, Mass.: Harvard University Press, 1978), 56; David Ward, "The Victorian Slum: An Enduring Myth?" *Annals of the Association of American Geographers* 66 (1976): 323–36; Carroll S. Rosenberg, *Religion and the Rise of the American City: The New York City Mission Movement, 1812–1870* (Ithaca, N.Y.: Cornell University Press, 1971), 31–3.

5 Charles L. Brace, *Second Annual Report of the Children's Aid Society* (New York: Wynkoop, 1855), 3.

6 Archibald Allinson, *The Principles of Population and the Connection with Human Happiness* (Edinburgh: Blackwood, 1840), 11.

7 Boston City Document, No. 42, *Report of the Committee on the Expediency of Providing Better Tenements for the Poor* (1846), 31.

8 Charles L. Sanford, *The Quest for Paradise: Europe and the American Moral Imagination* (Urbana: University of Illinois Press, 1961), 155–75; Thomas Bender, *Toward an Urban Vision: Ideas and Institutions in Nineteenth Century America* (Lexington: University of Kentucky Press, 1975).

9 Amy Bridges, *A City in the Republic: Antebellum New York and the Origin of Machine Politics* (Cambridge: Cambridge University Press, 1984), 12.

10 Barbara Solomon, *Ancestors and Immigrants, A Changing New England Tradition* (Chicago: University of Chicago Press, 1956); John Higham, *Strangers in the Land: Patterns of American Nativism 1860–1925* (New Brunswick, N.J.: Rutgers University Press, 1955).

11 Reginald Horsman, *Race and Manifest Destiny: The Origins of American Racial Anglo-Saxonism* (Cambridge, Mass.: Harvard University Press, 1981).

12 Dale T. Knobel, *Paddy and the Republic: Ethnicity and Nationality in Antebellum America* (Middletown, Conn.: Wesleyan University Press, 1986).

13 Ibid.

14 Robert Ernst, *Immigrant Life in New York City, 1825–1863* (New York:

Columbia University Press, 1949), 16–17, 52–59; Edward K. Spann, *The New Metropolis: New York City 1840–1857* (New York: Columbia University Press, 1981), 23–44.

15 Charles L. Brace, *The Dangerous Classes of New York* (New York: Wynkoop & Hallenbeck, 1872), 90–3.

16 Ibid.

17 Roy Lubove, "The New York Association for Improving the Condition of the Poor: The Formative Years," *New York Historical Society Quarterly* 43 (1959): 301–27; Allan S. Horlick, *Country Boys and Merchant Princes: The Social Control of Young Men in New York* (Lewisburg, Pa.: Bucknell University Press, 1975), 48–59; Boyer, *Urban Masses and Moral Order,* 56–75.

18 George G. Foster, *New York in Slices by an Experienced Carver* (New York: Graham, 1849), 5; Ned Buntline (E. Z. C. Judson), *The Mysteries and Miseries of New York: The Story of Real Life* (New York: Berford, 1848).

19 Stuart M. Blumin, "Explaining the New Metropolis: Perception, Depiction, and Analysis in Mid-Nineteenth Century New York City," *Journal of Urban History* 11 (1984): 9–38.

20 Boyer, *Urban Masses and Moral Order,* 5–9; Horlick, *Country Boys and Merchant Princes,* 12–19; David J. Rothman, *The Discovery of the Asylum: Social Order and Disorder in the New Republic* (Boston: Little, Brown, 1971), 73.

21 Robert N. Bellah, "Religion and Legitimacy in the American Republic," *Society* 15 (1978): 35–50.

22 Christine Stansell, *City of Women: Sex and Class in New York, 1789–1860* (New York: Knopf, 1986), 74.

23 Raymond A. Mohl, *Poverty in New York 1783–1825* (New York: Oxford University Press, 1971), 159–62; Rosenberg, *Religion and the Rise of the American City,* 37–9; Rothman, *The Discovery of the Asylum,* 3–56.

24 Robert M. Mennel, *Thorns and Thistles: Juvenile Delinquency in the United States, 1825–1940* (Hanover, N.H.: University Press of New England, 1973), 3–31; Mohl, *Poverty in New York,* 222; Rothman, *The Discovery of the Asylum,* 155–79.

25 New York Society for the Reformation of Juvenile Delinquents, *Annual Report* (1826), 3–4.

26 Ex parte Crouse, 4, Wharton, Penna., 9, 1838.

27 Charles I. Foster, *An Errand of Mercy: The Evangelical United Front: 1790–1837* (Chapel Hill: University of North Carolina Press, 1960), 90; Rosenberg, *Religion and the Rise of the American City,* 5–7; Boyer, *Urban Masses and Moral Order,* 9–45.

28 Rosenberg, *Religion and the Rise of the American City,* 152–3.

29 Mohl, *Poverty in New York,* 166; Rosenberg, *Religion and the Rise of the American City,* 49–51.

30 Thomas Chalmers, *The Christian and Civic Economy of Large Towns.* 3 vols. (Glasgow: Starke, 1821–6).

31 Daniel T. McColgan, *Joseph Tuckerman: Pioneer in American Social Work* (Washington, D.C.: Catholic University of America Press, 1940), 93–133; Walter D. Kring, *Liberals Among the Orthodox: Unitarian Beginnings in New York City, 1829–1839* (Boston: Beacon Press, 1974).

32 Horatio Wood, Jr., "Memoir of Horatio Wood, by His Son," *Contributions of the Old Residents' Historical Association* 4 (1891): 385.

33 Chalmers, *The Christian and Civic Economy,* vol. 1, 53–5.

34 McColgan, *Joseph Tuckerman,* 105.

35 Tuckerman, *On the Elevation of the Poor,* 155.

36 Lubove, "The New York Association for Improving the Conditions of the Poor," 322–5; Foster, *An Errand of Mercy,* 251; and Rosenberg, *Religion and the Rise of the American City,* 95.

37 Stansell, *City of Women,* 203.

38 M. J. Heale, "From City Fathers to Social Critics: Humanitarianism and Government in New York, 1790–1860," *Journal of American History* 63, (1976): 21–41.

39 Lubove, "The New York Association for Improving the Conditions of the Poor," 307–27; Rosenberg, *Religion and the Rise of the American City,* 245–73; Boyer, *Urban Masses and Moral Order,* 85–90.

40 Frank D. Watson, *The Charity Organization Movement in the United States: A Study in American Philanthropy* (New York: Macmillan, 1922), 79; Lubove, "The New York Association for Improving the Conditions of the Poor," 307–11.

41 Isaac Smithson Hartley, ed., *Memorial of Robert Molham Hartley* (Utica, N.Y.: Curtiss & Child, 1882), 147.

42 Stansell, *City of Women,* 203.

43 Bender, *Toward an Urban Vision,* 127–36; Rothman, *The Discovery of the Asylum,* 237–64; Boyer, *Urban Masses and Moral Order,* 96.

44 New York Association for Improving the Condition of the Poor (hereafter NYAICP), *Twenty-fifth Annual Report* (1868), 87.

45 Charles L. Brace, *Short Sermons to Newsboys* (New York: Scribner's, 1866), 9.

46 Brace, *The Dangerous Classes of New York,* 91–3.

47 Horlick, *Country Boys and Merchant Princes,* 179–209.

48 Henry W. Bellows, "Cities and Parks: With Special Reference to the New York Central Park," *Atlantic Monthly* 7 (1861): 419; Henry W. Bellows, "City and Country," *The Nation* 5 (1867): 256–7.

49 NYAICP, *Eighth Annual Report* (1851), 16.

50 NYAICP, *Ninth Annual Report* (1852), 33.

51 Charles E. Rosenburg, *The Cholera Years* (Chicago: University of Chicago Press, 1962), 37–8.

52 Lemuel Shattuck, Massachusetts Special Commission, *Report of a General Plan for the Promotion of Public and Personal Health* (Boston: Dutton & Wentworth, 1850), 200–6.

53 NYAICP, *Fifteenth Annual Report* (1858), 36.

54 Timothy L. Smith, *Revivalism and Social Reform in Mid-Nineteenth Century America* (New York: Abingdon Press, 1957); Robert T. Handy, *A Christian America: Protestant Hopes and Historical Realities* (New York: Oxford University Press, 1971), 27–64; Ira M. Leonard and Robert D. Parmet, *American Nativism, 1830–1860* (New York: Van Nostrand Reinhold, 1971), 35–47; Ray A. Billington, *The Protestant Crusade: 1800–1860; A Study in the Origins of American Nativism* (New York: Macmillan, 1938), 322–44.

55 New York Assembly Document, No. 205, *Report of the Select Committee Appointed to Examine into the Condition of Tenant Houses in New York and Brooklyn* (1857), 1–15.

56 Anonymous, "Model Lodging Houses in Boston," *Atlantic Monthly* 5 (1860): 673.

57 Spann, *The New Metropolis,* 268–70.

58 Gertrude Himmelfarb, *The Idea of Poverty: England in the Early Industrial Age* (New York: Knopf, 1983), 360–6.

59 John H. Griscom, *The Sanitary Condition of the Laboring Population of New York* (New York: Harper & Brothers, 1845); Isaac Parrish, "Report on the Sanitary Condition of Philadelphia," *Transactions, American Medical Association* 2 (1849): 460–7; Boston City Document, No. 66, *Report on the Asiatic Cholera, Together with the Report of the City Physician on the Cholera Hospital* (1849), 7–10.

60 Rosenburg, *The Cholera Years,* 40–3.

61 Charles-Edward A. Winslow, *The Conquest of Epidemic Disease: A Chapter in the History of Ideas* (Princeton, N.J.: Princeton University Press, 1944), 249–55.

62 Boston City Document, No. 66, 165.

63 Ibid., 9.

64 Gert H. Brieger, "Sanitary Reform in New York City: Stephen Smith and the Passage of the Metropolitan Health Bill," *Bulletin of the History of Medicine* (40): 1966, 407–29; Harold M. Cavins, "The National Quarantine and Sanitary Conventions of 1857 to 1860 and the Beginnings of the American Public Health Association," *Bulletin of the History of Medicine* 13 (1944): 404–26.

65 James H. Cassedy, *American Medicine and Statistical Thinking, 1800–1860* (Cambridge, Mass.: Harvard University Press, 1984), 188.

66 Griscom, *Sanitary Condition,* 2; *Memorial Relating to a Sanitary Survey of the State,* Massachusetts House Document, No. 16 (1848), 18.

67 Roy Lubove, *The Progressives and the Slums: Tenement House Reform in New York City, 1890–1891* (Pittsburgh: University of Pittsburgh Press, 1962), 6–8.

68 Stephen Smith, *The City That Was* (New York: Allaben, 1911), 59, 124.

69 Griscom, *Sanitary Condition,* 25–38; Boston City Document, No. 69, *Report of the Joint Special Committee of the Census of Boston, May 1, 1855, with Analytical and Sanitary Observations by Josiah Curtis* (1855), 64–83. The quotation is from Josiah Curtis, "Public Hygiene of Massachusetts; but More Particularly of the Cities of Boston and Lowell," *Transactions, American Medical Association* 2 (1849): 523.

70 Edwin H. Chapin, *Moral Aspects of City Life* (New York: Lyon, 1856), 19–20.

71 NYAICP, *Ninth Annual Report* (1853), 4.

72 New York Assembly Document, No. 205, 3.

73 Smith, *The City That Was,* 100–1.

74 John H. Griscom, *Sanitary Legislation, Past and Future* (New York: Jones, 1861), 10.

75 Shattuck et al., *Report of a General Plan,* 176–7.
76 New York Assembly Document, No. 205, 10–15; New York Senate Document, No. 49, *Report of the Select Committee Appointed to Investigate the Health Department of New York City* (1859), 1–13.
77 Heale, "From City Fathers to Social Critics."
78 Bridges, *A City in the Republic.*
79 David Grimstead, "Rioting in Its Jacksonian Setting," *American Historical Review* 77 (1972): 361–97; Boyer, *Urban Masses and Moral Order,* 69; John Schneider, *Detroit and the Problem of Order, 1830–1880* (Lincoln: University of Nebraska Press, 1980), 1–14.
80 James C. Mohr, *The Radical Republicans and Reform in New York During Reconstruction* (Ithaca, N.Y.: Cornell University Press, 1973), 35; Steven J. Ross, *Workers on the Edge: Work, Leisure, and Politics in Industrializing Cincinnati, 1788–1890* (New York: Columbia University Press, 1985), 20; Gary L. Browne, *Baltimore in the Nation, 1789–1861* (Chapel Hill: University of North Carolina Press, 1980), 139–58; Howard Gillette, Jr., "The Emergence of the Modern Metropolis: Philadelphia in the Age of Consolidation," in William W. Cutler III and Howard Gillette, Jr., eds., *The Divided Metropolis: Social and Spatial Dimensions of Philadelphia, 1800–1897* (Westport, Ct.: Greenwood, 1980), 3–25.
81 Michael B. Katz, Michael J. Doucet, and Mark J. Stern, *The Social Organization of Early Industrial Capitalism* (Cambridge, Mass.: Harvard University Press, 1982).
82 Gary B. Nash, "Urban Wealth and Poverty in Pre-Revolutionary America," *Journal of Interdisciplinary History* 6 (1971): 545–84; James A. Henretta, "Economic Development and Social Structure in Colonial Boston," *William and Mary Quarterly* 22 (1965): 75–92; and Sam Bass Warner, Jr., *The Private City: Philadelphia in Three Periods of Its Growth* (Philadelphia: University of Pennsylvania Press, 1968), 3–22.
83 Edward Pessen, *Riches, Class, and Power Before the Civil War* (Lexington: University of Kentucky Press, 1973); Bruce Laurie, *Working People of Philadelphia, 1800–1850* (Philadelphia: Temple University Press, 1980), 85–104; Sean Wilentz, *Chants Democratic: New York City and the Rise of the American Working Class, 1788–1850* (New York: Oxford University Press, 1984).
84 Schneider, *Detroit and the Problem of Order.*
85 Seymour J. Mandelbaum, *Boss Tweed's New York* (New York: Wiley, 1965), 1–39.
86 Brieger, "Sanitary Reform in New York City," 407–29.
87 Council of Hygiene and Public Health of the Citizen's Association of New York, *Report upon the Sanitary Condition of the City* (New York: Appleton, 1865), 184–6.
88 N. P. Willis, quoted in Smith, *The City That Was,* 99–100.
89 Adrian Cook, *The Armies of the Streets: The New York Draft Riots of 1863* (Lexington: University of Kentucky Press, 1974), 193–209.
90 New York Assembly Document, No. 122, *Second Annual Report of the Metropolitan Board of Health, 1867* (1868), 79–116.

91 New York Assembly Document, No. 205, 11.
92 Griscom, *Sanitary Legislation,* 6; Boston City Document, No. 66, 14; NYAICP, *Eighth Annual Report,* 56; Council of Hygiene and Public Health of the Citizen's Association of New York, *Report,* 56.
93 Lubove, *The Progressives and the Slums,* 8–9.
94 Massachusetts Senate Document, No. 120, *Bureau of Statistics of Labor, First Annual Report* (1870), 182.
95 James D. McCabe, Jr., *Lights and Shadows of New York Life; or, The Sights and Sensations of the Great City* (Philadelphia: National, 1872), 686, 697.
96 Massachusetts Board of State Charities, *Second Annual Report* (1866), xlv.
97 E. L. Godkin, "The Labor Crisis," *North American Review* 105 (1867): 178; William E. Nelson, *The Roots of American Bureaucracy, 1830–1900* (Cambridge, Mass.: Harvard University Press, 1982), 89–90.
98 Rosenburg, *The Cholera Years.*
99 George M. Frederickson, *The Inner Civil War: Northern Intellectuals and the Crisis of the Union* (New York: Harper & Row, 1965), 98–112; Clifford E. Clark, "Religious Beliefs and Social Reform in the Gilded Age: The Case of Henry Whitney Bellows," *New England Quarterly* 43 (1970): 59–78.
100 Harold Schwartz, *Samuel Gridley Howe: Social Reformer 1801–1876* (Cambridge Mass.: Harvard University Press, 1956), 253–6; Frederickson, *The Inner Civil War,* 98–112.
101 Mary O. Furner, *Advocacy and Objectivity: A Crisis in the Professionalization of American Social Science, 1865–1905* (Lexington: University of Kentucky Press, 1975), 10–34; James Leiby, *A History of Social Welfare and Social Work in the United States* (New York: Columbia University Press, 1978), 90–106.
102 E. L. Godkin, "The Prospects of the Political Act," *North American Review* 110 (1870): 417.
103 Quoted in Cavins, "The National Quarantine and Sanitary Conventions," 411.
104 William R. Brock, *Investigation and Responsibility: Public Responsibility in the United States 1865–1900* (Cambridge: Cambridge University Press, 1984), 226; James Leiby, *Carroll Wright and Labor Reform: The Origin of Labor Statistics* (Cambridge, Mass.: Harvard University Press, 1960), 20; Gerald N. Grob, *Mental Institutions in American Social Policy to 1875* (New York: The Free Press, 1973), 257–302.
105 Massachusetts Senate Document, No. 2, *First Annual Report of the State Board of Health* (1870), 2.
106 Henry I. Bowditch, "Preventive Medicine and the Physician of the Future," *Massachusetts State Board of Health, Fifth Annual Report, 1874,* 32.
107 Cavins, "The National Quarantine and Sanitary Conventions," 416; Barbara G. Rosencrantz, *Public Health and the State: Changing Views in Massachusetts, 1842–1936* (Cambridge, Mass.: Harvard University Press, 1972), 71–3.
108 Rosencrantz, *Public Health and the State,* 7.
109 Michael H. Frisch, *Town into City: Springfield, Massachusetts, and the Meaning of Community, 1840–1880* (Cambridge, Mass.: Harvard University Press, 1972), 175.

110 Ibid., 174; Mohr, *The Radical Republicans,* 1–20.
111 Nelson, *The Roots of American Bureaucracy,* 1–6.
112 Massachusetts Board of State Charities, *Fourth Annual Report, 1868,* xcvii, xci–xciii.
113 Bender, *Toward an Urban Vision,* 189–94; John Tomisch, *A Genteel Endeavor: American Culture and Politics in the Gilded Age* (Stanford, Calif.: Stanford University Press, 1971).
114 Frisch, *Town into City,* 174.
115 William E. Forbath, "The Ambiguities of Free Labor: Labor and Law in the Gilded Age," *Wisconsin Law Review* 4 (1985): 787–9.
116 Blumin, "Explaining the New Metropolis."
117 NYAICP, Twenty-fourth Annual Report (1867), 42–3.
118 Matthew H. Smith, *Sunshine and Shadow in New York* (Hartford, Conn.: Burr, 1869), 144–5, 688.
119 Steven Schlossman, "The Culture of Poverty in Antebellum America," *Science and Society* 38 (1974): 150–66.
120 Grob, *Mental Institutions,* 257–302; Mohr, *The Radical Republicans,* 271–80; Brock, *Investigation and Responsibility,* 220–6.
121 John Higham, *From Boundlessness to Consolidation: The Transformation of American Culture, 1848–1860* (Ann Arbor, Mich.: William L. Clements Library, 1969).

3. The slums defined: 1875–1900

1 Ira Steward, "Poverty," *Massachusetts Bureau of the Statistics of Labor, Fourth Annual Report,* Massachusetts House Document, No. 173 (1873), 414.
2 James C. Mohr, *The Radical Republicans and Reform in New York During Reconstruction* (Ithaca, N.Y.: Cornell University Press, 1973); Mary O. Furner, *Advocacy and Objectivity: A Crisis in the Professionalization of American Social Science, 1865–1905* (Lexington: University of Kentucky Press, 1975), 10–34; Michael B. Katz, *Poverty and Policy in American History* (New York: Academic Press, 1983).
3 Stephen Smith, *Movements and Conditions of the Tenement House Population, with Suggestions for Relief* (New York: Gildersleve, 1873), 12–16; Dwight Porter, *Report on the Sanitary Inspection of Certain Tenement House Districts of Boston* (Boston: Rockwell & Church, 1889).
4 Helen Campbell, *The Problem of the Poor: A Record of Quiet Work in Unquiet Places* (New York: Fords, Howard, and Hulbert, 1882), 117.
5 Nathan I. Huggins, *Protestants Against Poverty: Boston's Charities, 1870–1900* (Westport, Conn.: Greenwood Press, 1971).
6 Josiah Strong, *Our Country: Its Possible Future and Its Present Crisis* (New York: Baker & Taylor, 1885), 45.
7 F. B. Sanborn, "Migration and Immigration," *Proceedings, National Conference of Charities and Correction* 13 (1886): 256–7.

8 Van Wyck Brooks, *The Times of Melville and Whitman* (New York: Dutton, 1947), 466.

9 Samuel L. Loomis, *Modern Cities and Their Religious Problems* (New York: Baker and Taylor, 1887), 61–81.

10 David J. Hogan, *Class and Reform: School and Society in Chicago, 1880–1930* (Philadelphia: University of Pennsylvania Press, 1985), 1–25.

11 Strong, *Our Country,* 40.

12 Daniel T. Rodgers, *The Work Ethic in Industrial America, 1850–1920* (Chicago: University of Chicago Press, 1974), 69.

13 Campbell, *The Problem of the Poor,* 215.

14 Terence V. Powderly, "A Menacing Eruption," *North American Review* 147 (1888): 165–6.

15 Richmond Mayo-Smith, *Emigration and Immigration: A Study in Social Science* (New York: Scribner's, 1890), 77.

16 John Higham, *Strangers in the Land: Patterns of American Nativism, 1860–1925* (New Brunswick, N.J.: Rutgers University Press, 1955); Robert T. Handy, *A Christian America: Protestant Hopes and Historical Realities* (New York: Oxford University Press, 1971), 95–116; Barbara Solomon, *Ancestors and Immigrants: A Changing New England Tradition* (Chicago: University of Chicago Press, 1956); John Tomisch, *A Genteel Endeavor: American Culture and Politics in the Gilded Age* (Stanford, Calif.: Stanford University Press, 1971), 73–93.

17 John S. Haller, *Outcasts from Evolution: Scientific Attitudes of Racial Inferiority, 1859–1900* (Urbana: University of Illinois Press, 1971), 166–87.

18 Steward, "Poverty," 415.

19 Solomon, *Ancestors and Immigrants;* Higham, *Strangers in the Land.*

20 Carroll D. Wright, "Introduction," *Massachusetts Bureau of the Statistics of Labor, Eighth Annual Report* (1877), vi–vii.

21 Daniel Horowitz, "Genteel Observers: New England Economic Writers and Industrialization," *New England Quarterly* 48 (1975): 74.

22 New York Association for Improving the Condition of the Poor, *Thirty-second Annual Report* (1875), 33.

23 Boston Overseers of the Poor, *Tenth Annual Report* (1874), 6.

24 Robert T. Davis, "Pauperism in the City of New York," *Journal of Social Science* 6 (1874): 77.

25 Katz, *Poverty and Policy in American History,* 157–81; Paul T. Ringenbach, *Tramps and Reformers, 1873–1916: The Discovery of Unemployment in New York* (Westport, Conn.: Greenwood Press, 1973), 18–20.

26 Katz, *Poverty and Policy in American History,* 134–56.

27 Ibid., 90–156; Charles S. Rosenberg, "The Bitter Fruit: Heredity, Disease, and Social Thought in Nineteenth Century America," *Perspectives in American History* 8 (1974): 189–235.

28 Hamilton Cravens, *The Triumph of Evolution: American Scientists and the Heredity-Environment Controversy, 1900–1941* (Philadelphia: University of Pennsylvania Press, 1978).

29 Massachusetts Board of State Charities, *Second Annual Report* (1866), xxviii–xxxii.

30 Katz, *Poverty and Policy in American History,* 90–156.

31 Charles S. Hoyt, "The Causes of Pauperism," *Tenth Annual Report of the State Board of Charities, New York* (1877), 287–8.
32 Robert C. Bannister, *Social Darwinism: Science and Myth in Anglo-American Social Thought* (Philadelphia: Temple University Press, 1979); J. A. Campbell and D. N. Livingstone, "Neo-Lamarckism and the Development of Geography in the United States and Great Britain," *Transactions, Institute of British Geographers,* n.s. 8 (1983): 267–94.
33 William R. Brock, *Investigation and Responsibility: Public Responsibility in the United States, 1865–1900* (Cambridge: Cambridge University Press, 1984).
34 Frank D. Watson, *The Charity Organization Movement in the United States: A Study in American Philanthropy* (New York: Macmillan, 1922), 186–90.
35 Olivier Zunz, *The Changing Face of Inequality: Urbanization, Industrial Development and Immigration in Detroit, 1880–1920* (Chicago: University of Chicago Press, 1982), 263–79.
36 Charles R. Henderson, "Public Outdoor Relief," *Proceedings, National Conference of Charities and Corrections* (1891): 18, 40.
37 Alexander Johnson, *Adventures in Social Welfare; Being Reminiscences of Things, Thoughts and Folks During Forty Years of Social Work* (Fort Wayne, Ind.: The author, 1923), 21–22.
38 Watson, *The Charity Organization Movement,* 177–217.
39 In Edward T. Devine, *When Social Work Was Young* (New York: Macmillan, 1939), 35.
40 George M. Frederickson, *The Inner Civil War: Northern Intellectuals and the Crisis of the Union* (New York: Harper & Row, 1965), 215.
41 Katz, *Poverty and Policy in American History,* 183–200.
42 Watson, *The Charity Organization Movement,* 214.
43 Ibid., 177–89; Johnson, *Adventures in Social Welfare,* 21–5; Leah H. Feder, *Unemployment Relief in Periods of Depression* (New York: Russell Sage Foundation, 1936), 59.
44 Lilian Brandt, *Growth and Development of the Association for Improving the Condition of the Poor and the Charity Organization Society,* Report to the Committee on the Institute of Welfare Research, New York Community Service Society, 1942, 74.
45 Ibid., 75.
46 S. Humphrey Gurteen, *A Handbook of Charity Organization* (Buffalo, N.Y.: The author, 1882), 30–2, 120–9.
47 Johnson, *Adventures in Social Welfare,* 52.
48 Daniel Horowitz, *The Morality of Spending: Attitudes Toward the Consumer Society in America, 1875–1940* (Baltimore: Johns Hopkins University Press, 1985), 13–29.
49 Amos Warner, *American Charities,* rev. ed. (New York, Crowell, 1908), 43.
50 Ibid., 44.
51 "A Tenement House Census of Boston," 435.
52 Horace G. Wadlin, "Unemployment," *Massachusetts Bureau of Statistics of Labor, Twenty-fourth Annual Report* (1894), 248.
53 Warner, *American Charities,* 40.

54 Ibid., Fig. X, 41.
55 George B. Buzelle, "Individuality in the Work of Charity," *Proceedings, National Conference of Charities and Corrections* 13 (1886): 187.
56 Mark H. Haller, *Eugenics: Hereditarian Attitudes in American Thought* (New Brunswick, N.J.: Rutgers University Press, 1963).
57 Albert O. Wright, "The New Philanthropy," *Proceedings, National Conference of Charities and Corrections* 23 (1896): 4.
58 M. Christine Boyer, *Dreaming the Rational City: The Myth of American City Planning* (Cambridge, Mass.: MIT Press, 1983), 9–32.
59 Campbell, *The Problem of the Poor,* 215.
60 Helen Campbell, Thomas W. Knox, and Thomas Byrnes, *Darkness and Daylight; or, Lights and Shadows of New York Life* (Hartford, Conn.: Worthington, 1892), 38.
61 L. S. Rowe, "The Social Consequences of Urban Growth," *Yale Review* 10 (1901): 298–310.
62 Anonymous, "Black Holes in New York," *Harper's Weekly,* March 22, 1879, 223; William H. Tolman, "The Tenement House Curse: Evils of the System," *Arena* 9 (1894): 659–62; J. F. Harder, "The City's Plan," *Municipal Affairs* 2 (1898): 25–43.
63 Robert G. Barrows, "Beyond the Tenement: Patterns of American Urban Housing, 1870–1930," *Journal of Urban History* 9 (1983): 395–420.
64 Ohio Bureau of Statistics of Labor, *First Annual Report* (1877), 310; *Fifth Annual Report* (1881), 38–41; *Seventh Annual Report* (1883), 145–7.
65 Jane Addams, *Twenty Years at Hull House* (New York: Macmillan, 1910), 200.
66 Anonymous, "Tenement Houses in Summer," *Harper's Weekly,* July 28, 1883, 475.
67 F. W. Draper, "The Homes of the Poor in Our Cities," Massachusetts State Board of Health, *Fourth Annual Report* (1873), 399.
68 Charles E. Buckingham, *The Sanitary Conditions of Boston; The Report of a Medical Committee Appointed by the Board of Health of the City of Boston* (Boston: Rockwell & Churchill, 1875), 23, 158.
69 Charles F. Wingate, "The Health of American Cities," *Journal of Social Science* 21 (1886): 92.
70 Charlotte Adams, "Italian Life in New York," *Harper's* 62 (1881): 682.
71 Henry D. Chapin, "Preventable Causes of Poverty," *Forum* 7 (1889): 415–23.
72 Clifford E. Clark, Jr., "Religious Beliefs and Social Reform in the Gilded Age: The Case of Henry Whitney Bellows," *New England Quarterly* 43 (1970): 59–78.
73 New York Association for Improving the Condition of the Poor, *Forty-fifth Annual Report* (1888), 21.
74 Roy Lubove, *The Progressives and the Slums: Tenement House Reform in New York City, 1890 to 1917* (Pittsburgh: University of Pittsburgh Press, 1962), 34–9, 100–6; Anthony Jackson, *A Place Called Home: A History of Low-Cost Housing in Manhattan* (Cambridge, Mass.: MIT Press, 1976), 41–3, 106–10.

75 Draper, "The Homes of the Poor," 433.
76 Charles F. Wingate, "The Moral Side of the Tenement House Problem," *The Catholic World* 41 (1885): 160; Frederick D. Huntington, "Education and Lawlessness," *Forum* 4 (1887): 133–42.
77 Lubove, *The Progressives and the Slum*, 34–40.
78 Alfred T. White, *Improved Dwellings for the Laboring Classes: The Need and the Way to Meet It on Strict Commercial Principles, in New York and Other Cities* (New York: Putnam's, 1879), 41.
79 Ibid., 2.
80 Robert T. Paine, "Homes for the People," *Journal of Social Science* 15 (February 1882): 115–16, 119–20.
81 Campbell, *The Problem of the Poor*, 117.
82 E. R. L. Gould, "The Housing Problem in Great Cities," *Quarterly Journal of Economics* 14 (1900): 391.
83 Ibid., 378.
84 Jackson, *A Place Called Home*, 110.
85 James C. Bayles, New York City Health Department, *Tenement House Problem in New York* (New York: Mitchell, 1887), 13–20.
86 Jackson, *A Placed Called Home*, 30–44; Lubove, *The Progressives and the Slums*, 25–48.
87 Anonymous, (no title), *American Architect and Building News* 5 (1879): 97.
88 Edwin R. A. Seligman, *The Tenement Houses of New York* (New York Tenement House Building Commission, 1888), 26.
89 Jacob Riis, *How the Other Half Lives* (New York: Scribner's, 1892); Lubove, *The Progressives and the Slums*, 49–79; Jackson, *A Place Called Home*, 76–90.
90 Peter B. Hales, *Silver Cities: The Photography of American Urbanization, 1839–1915* (Philadelphia: Temple University Press, 1983).
91 Riis, *How the Other Half Lives*, 226.
92 Ibid., 120–1.
93 Jacob Riis, *The Peril and the Preservation of the Home* (Philadelphia: Jacobs, 1903), 15, 17.
94 Ibid., 78.
95 Lubove, *The Progressives and the Slums*, 81–94.
96 Jacob Riis, "The Battle with the Slum," *Atlantic Monthly* 83 (1899): 634.
97 Michael G. Kammen, "Richard Watson Gilder and the New York Tenement House Commission of 1894," *Bulletin of the New York Public Library* 66 (1962): 364–82; Gerald W. McFarland, *Mugwumps, Morals, and Politics, 1884–1920* (Amherst: University of Massachusetts Press, 1975), 81–123.
98 Jackson, *A Place Called Home*, 116–17.
99 Robert W. DeForest and Lawrence Veiller, eds., *The Tenement House Problem* (New York: Macmillan, 1903).
100 Lawrence M. Friedman, *Government and Slum Housing: A Century of Frustration* (Chicago: Rand McNally, 1968), 33–6.
101 Lawrence Veiller, *Housing Reform* (New York: Charities Publication Committee, 1911), 6–7.
102 Lubove, *The Progressives and the Slums*, 174–84.

103 Veiller, *Housing Reform*, 45.
104 Robert W. DeForest, "Tenement House Regulation," *Annals of the American Academy of Political and Social Science* 20 (1902): 83–95.
105 Richard W. Gilder, "The Wage-Earner's Interest in Improved Housing," *The Century* 30 (1896): 794.
106 Henry George, "Tenement House Reform," *Leslie's Weekly* 80 (1895): 201.
107 Marcus T. Reynolds, "The Housing of the Poor in American Cities," *American Economic Association* 8 (1893): 139–262; A. S. Daniel, "The City's Health – Living Conditions," *Municipal Affairs* 2 (1898): 247–61.
108 Elgin R. L. Gould, *The Housing of the Working People*, Eighth Special Report of the U.S. Commissioner of Labor, 53d Cong., 3d Sess., House Executive Document No. 354, Serial 3325, 442, 1895.
109 Addams, *Twenty Years at Hull House;* Anthony Sutcliffe, *Towards the Planned City: Germany, Britain, and France, 1780–1914* (New York: St. Martin's, 1981), 289–91.
110 Charles-Edward A. Winslow, *The Conquest of Epidemic Disease: A Chapter in the History of Ideas* (Princeton, N.J.: Princeton University Press, 1944), 266.
111 Stuart Galishoff, "Drainage, Disease, Comfort and Class: A History of Newark's Sewers," *Societas* 6 (1976): 121–38.
112 Gordon Atkins, *Health, Housing, and Poverty in New York City, 1865–1898* (Ann Arbor, Mich.: Edwards Bros., 1947), 230.
113 Jon A. Peterson, "The Impact of Sanitary Reform upon American Urban Planning, 1840–1890," *Journal of Social History* 13 (1979): 83–103.
114 John S. Billings, *Social Statistics of Cities, Eleventh Census of the United States,* vol. 20 (Washington, D.C.: Government Printing Office, 1895); John S. Billings, "Municipal Sanitation in New York and Brooklyn," *Forum* 16 (1893), 346–54.
115 United States Commission of Labor, *Seventh Special Report: The Slums of Baltimore, Chicago, New York and Philadelphia* (1894), 19.
116 Billings, *Municipal Sanitation,* 348.
117 New York Assembly Document, No. 37, *Report of the Tenement House Committee of 1894* (1895), 20–1.
118 Hull-House Maps and Papers (New York: Crowell, 1895), 95–6.
119 New York Senate Document, No. 36, *Report of the Tenement House Commission* (1885).
120 Massachusetts Bureau of Statistics of Labor, *Twenty-third Annual Report* (1893): "A Tenement House Census of Boston: Section III: Place of Birth, Occupations, etc., of Residents," Massachusetts Public Document, No. 15 (1892), 207, 435, 58–61, 206.
121 Carroll D. Wright, *The Slums of Baltimore, New York, and Philadelphia,* Seventh Special Report of the U.S. Commissioner of Labor, 53d Cong., 2d Sess., House Executive Document No. 257, Serial 3228, 1894, 12–13.
122 Clare de Graffenried, "Need of Better Homes for Wage-Earners," *Forum* 21 (1896): 302–3.
123 William T. Elsing, "Life in New York as Seen by a City Missionary," in Rob-

ert A. Woods, ed., *The Poor in Great Cities* (New York: Scribner's, 1895), 42–85.

124 Alvan F. Sanborn, "The Anatomy of a Tenement Street," *Forum* 18 (1895), 559–69.

125 Kate H. Claghorn, "Foreign Immigration and the Tenement House in New York City," in Robert W. DeForest and Lawrence Veiller, eds., *The Tenement House Problem,* vol. 11 (New York: Macmillan, 1903), 85.

126 Anonymous, "Italian Immigrants," *Harper's Weekly* 33 (1889): 940.

127 Alzina P. Stevens, "Some Chicago Tenement Houses," *Arena* 9 (1894): 667; Robert A. Woods, ed., *The City Wilderness* (Boston: Houghton Mifflin, 1898).

128 House Executive Document No. 2309, serial 3140, Testimony of A. S. Daniel, *Report on the Committee on Manufactures on the Sweating System* (1893), 199, 210.

129 Ida M. Van Etten, "Russian Jews as Desirable Immigrants," *Forum* 15 (1893): 172–82.

130 M. J. McKenna, *Our Brethren of the Tenements and the Ghetto* (New York: Ogilvie, 1899), 1–28.

131 *Hull-House Maps and Papers,* 103.

132 New York Assembly Document, No. 37, 81.

133 Charles Booth, ed., *Life and Labour of the People of London,* 9 vols. (London: Macmillan, 1892–7).

134 E. Idell Zeisloft, ed., *The New Metropolis* (New York: Appleton, 1899), 273, 287.

135 Warner, *American Charities,* 164.

136 Alexander Johnson, *Methods and Machinery of the Organization of Charity* (Chicago, 1887), 1.

137 Warner, *American Charities,* 164, 190.

138 Zeisloft, *The New Metropolis,* iv.

139 Watson, *The Charity Organization Movement,* 63.

140 Warner, *American Charities,* 19.

141 Ernest P. Bicknell, "Problems of Philanthropy in Chicago," *Annals of the American Academy of Political and Social Science* 21 (1903): 382.

142 William Tolman, New York Association for the Improvement of the Condition of the Poor, *Notes,* vol. 1 (February 1898), 20.

143 *Journal of the General Conference of the Methodist Episcopal Church* (1900): 63–4.

144 Johnson, *Adventures in Social Welfare,* 380.

145 William T. Stead, *If Christ Came to Chicago: A Plea for the Union of All Who Love in the Service of All Who Suffer* (Chicago: Laird & Lee, 1894), 410.

146 David Montgomery, "Labor and the Republic in Industrial America, 1869–1920," *Mouvement Social* 111 (1980): 211.

147 Benjamin O. Flower, *Civilization's Inferno; or, Studies in the Social Cellar* (Boston: Arena, 1893); Louis A. Bands, *White Slaves; or, the Oppression of the Worthy Poor* (Boston: Lee & Shepard, 1892).

148 Stead, *If Christ Came to Chicago,* 113.

149 John L. Thomas, "Utopia for an Urban Age: Henry George, Henry Demarest Lloyd, Edward Bellamy," *Perspectives in American History* 6 (1972): 135–63.

150 William J. Tucker, *My Generation: An Autobiographical Interpretation* (Boston: Houghton Mifflin, 1919), 96–7.

151 William J. Tucker, "The Authority of the Pulpit in a Time of Critical Research and Social Confusion," *Andover Review* 16 (1891): 399.

152 Graham Taylor, *A Religious Census of the City of Hartford Made in the Year 1889,* Hartford Seminary Publication 10 (Hartford, Conn.: Hartford Seminary, 1890), 40.

153 William E. Nelson, *The Roots of American Bureacracy, 1830–1900* (Cambridge, Mass.: Harvard University Press, 1982), 11.

154 Frederick C. Jaher, *Doubters and Dissenters* (Glencoe; Free Press, 1964).

155 Cf. Thomas Haskell, *The Emergence of Professional Social Science: The American Social Science Association and the Nineteenth Century Crisis of Authority* (Urbana: University of Illinois Press, 1977); Katz, *Poverty and Policy in American History,* 157–81.

156 David Hammack, *Power and Society: Greater New York at the Turn of the Century* (New York: Russell Sage Foundation, 1982), 303–26.

4. From slum to ghetto: 1900–1925

1 James T. Kloppenberg, *Uncertain Victory: Social Democracy and Progressivism in European and American Thought, 1870–1920* (New York: Oxford University Press, 1986), 298–348; 381–94.

2 Roy Lubove, "The Twentieth Century City: The Progressive as a Municipal Reformer," *Mid-America* 41 (1959): 195–209; Augustus Cerillo, Jr., "The Reform of Municipal Government in New York City," *New York Historical Society Quarterly* 57 (1973): 51–71.

3 Don S. Kirschner, *The Paradox of Professionalism: Reform and Public Service in Urban America, 1900–1940* (Westport, Conn.: Greenwood Press, 1986), 1–26.

4 Kellogg Durland and Louis Sessa, "Italian Invasion of the Ghetto," *University Settlement Studies* 1 (1906): 106–17.

5 Cost of Living in American Towns, Senate Document No. 22, 62d Congress, 1st Session, 1911, series 6082, 8; Immigration Commission, *Report: Immigrants in Cities,* United States Senate Document 338, serial 5665, 61st Congress, 2d session, vol. 66, 1911, *Immigrants in Cities,* 6–8.

6 Jacob Riis, *How the Other Half Lives* (New York: Scribner's, 1982), 18–19.

7 Thomas J. Jones, *The Sociology of a New York City Block,* Columbia University Studies in History, Economics, and Public Law, 21, no. 2 (New York: Columbia University Press, 1904), 24–5, 106–7.

8 Allen F. Davis, *Spearheads for Reform: The Social Settlements and the Progressive Movement, 1890–1914* (New York: Oxford University Press, 1967), 90–4.

9 Moses Rischin, "Introduction" to Hutchins Hapgood, *The Spirit of the Ghetto* (Cambridge, Mass.: Belknap, 1967), xxiii.

10 Horace M. Kallen, "Democracy Versus the Melting Pot: A Study of American Nationality, *The Nation* 100 (1915): 190–220; Isaac B. Berkson, *Theories of Americanization* (New York: Teachers College, Columbia University, 1920), 39–54.

11 Massachusetts House Document, No. 50, *Report of the Massachusetts Board to Investigate the Subject of the Unemployed,* vol. 5 (1895), xii.

12 Robert Hunter, "The Relation Between Social Settlements and Charity Organization," *Journal of Political Economy* 11 (1902): 75–88; Leah H. Feder, *Unemployment Relief in Periods of Depression* (New York: Russell Sage Foundation, 1936), 131–3.

13 Stanton Coit, "Necessity of State Aid to the Unemployed," *Forum* 17 (1894): 285.

14 Jane Addams, "The Subtle Problems of Charity," *Atlantic Monthly* 83 (1899): 163, 164.

15 Robert A. Woods and Albert J. Kennedy, *The Settlement Horizon* (New York: Russell Sage Foundation, 1922), 174–5.

16 Amos Warner, *American Charities,* rev. by Mary Coolidge (New York: Crowell, 1908), 133.

17 Mary Simkhovitch, *The City Worker's World in America* (New York: Macmillan, 1917), 3–4.

18 Clarke A. Chambers, *Paul U. Kellogg and the Survey: Voices for Social Welfare and Social Justice* (Minneapolis: University of Minnesota Press, 1971), 1–24.

19 Warner, *American Charities,* 168.

20 Ibid., 134.

21 Lilian Brandt, "The Causes of Poverty," *Political Science Quarterly* 23 (1908): 643.

22 Lee Frankel, "The Relation Between Standards of Living and Standards of Compensation," *Proceedings, New York State Conference of Charities and Correction* (1906): 30–1.

23 Quoted in Robert C. Chapin, *The Standard of Living Among Workingmen's Families in New York City* (New York: Charities Publication Committee, 1909), 253–4.

24 Lilian Brandt, *Growth and Development of the Association for Improving the Condition of the Poor and the Charity Organization Society: Report to the Committee on the Institute of Welfare Research* (New York: Community Service Society of New York, 1942), 225.

25 Edward T. Devine, *When Social Work Was Young* (New York: Macmillan, 1939), 4.

26 Quoted in Chapin, *The Standard of Living,* 254.

27 Daniel Horowitz, *The Morality of Spending: Attitudes Towards the Consumer Society in America, 1875–1940* (Baltimore: Johns Hopkins University Press, 1985).

28 Elsa G. Herzfeld, *Family Monographs* (New York: Kempster, 1905).

29 Warner, *American Charities,* 133–61.

30 Louise Bolard More, *Wage Earners' Budgets: A Study of Standards and Cost*

of Living in New York City (New York: Holy, 1907); Chapin, *The Standard of Living.*

31 Frederick Almy, "The Ethics of Too Low a Standard of Living," *Ninth New York State Conference of Charities and Corrections, Elmira* (1908): 40.

32 Devine, *When Social Work Was Young,* 114–15.

33 Edward Devine, quoted by William Tucker in Chapin, *The Standard of Living,* 253–4.

34 United States Commissioner of Labor, *18th Annual Report* (1903).

35 Frank H. Streighthoff, *The Standard of Living Among the Industrial People of America* (Boston: Houghton Mifflin, 1911), 24–30.

36 Second Mayor's Committee on Unemployment in New York, quoted in Feder, *Unemployment Relief in Periods of Depression,* 221

37 Hunter, "The Relationship Between Social Settlements and Charity Organization," 75–88; and Brandt, "The Causes of Poverty," 644–5.

38 Frederick C. Mills, *Contemporary Theories of Unemployment and Unemployment Relief,* Columbia University Studies in History, Economics, and Public Law, 79, no. 1 (New York: Columbia University Press, 1917), 13–17; Mary K. Simkhovitch, *The City Worker's World in America* (New York: Macmillan, 1917), 41.

39 Mills, *Contemporary Theories of Unemployment,* 146–56.

40 New York Senate Document, No. 29, *Report of the Commission of Immigration (1909),* 5–20; Massachusetts House Document, No. 2300, *Report of the Commission of Immigration on the Problem of Immigration in Massachusetts* (1914).

41 Immigration Commission, *Report,* 494–502.

42 Ibid., 39.

43 J. W. Jenks and W. J. Lauck, *The Immigration Problem* (New York, Funk and Wagnalls, 1913), 68; Isaac Hourwich, *Immigration and Labor* (New York: Putnam's), 228.

44 Lilian Brandt, "On the Verge of Dependence," *Charities and Commons* 15 (1905–6): 462–8.

45 William L. Lieserson, "The Problem of Unemployment Today," *Political Science Quarterly* 31 (1916): 1–24.

46 Jane Addams, "Charity and Social Justice," *Proceedings, National Conference on Charities and Corrections, St. Louis* (1910), 1–18.

47 Allen F. Davis, "The Campaign for the Industrial Relations Commission, 1911–1913," *Mid-America* 45 (1963): 211–28; Leiserson, "The Problem of Unemployment Today," 1–24; Mills, *Contemporary Theories of Unemployment,* 120.

48 Roy Lubove, "Workmen's Compensation and the Prerogatives of Voluntarism, *Labor History* 8 (1967): 259.

49 Eugene M. Tobin, *Organize or Perish: America's Independent Progressives, 1913–1933* (Westport, Conn.: Greenwood Press, 1986), 43–61.

50 Ibid., 144–74; Feder, *Unemployment Relief in Periods of Depression,* 219, 305.

51 Roy Lubove, *The Struggle for Social Security, 1900–1935* (Cambridge, Mass.: Harvard University Press, 1968), 25–44; 91–112.

52 Edward T. Devine, "Social Ideals Implied in Present American Programs of Voluntary Philanthropy," *American Journal of Sociology* 18 (1912–13): 784–95.

53 Brandt, *Growth and Development of the Association for Improving the Condition of the Poor,* 195–6.

54 Carol Aronovici, "The Cost of a Decent Home," *Forum* 51 (1914): 112.

55 Anthony Jackson, *A Place Called Home: A History of Low-Cost Housing in Manhattan* (Cambridge, Mass.: MIT Press, 1976).

56 John A. Ryan, "The Standard of Living and the Problem of Dependency," *Proceedings, National Conference of Charities and Corrections* (1907): 343–4.

57 Peter Roberts, *The New Immigration: A Study of the Industrial and Social Life of Southeast Europeans in America* (New York: Macmillan, 1912), 131–46.

58 H. L. Cargill, "Small Houses for Working Men," in Robert DeForest and Lawrence Veiller, eds., *The Tenement House Problem,* vol. 2 (New York: Macmillan, 1903), 331–2.

59 Roswell F. Phelps, *South End Factory Operatives: Employment and Residence* (Boston: South End Associates, 1903).

60 H. R. Seager, "Where People Live That Work in Congested Districts," *Charities and Commons* 20 (1908): 39–43.

61 "The Disease and Poverty Charts," *Charities and Commons* 4 (1900): 7.

62 Riis, *How the Other Half Lives,* 126.

63 Aronovici, "The Cost of a Decent Home," 112.

64 Gustavus Webber, "Congestion in Philadelphia," *Proceedings of the Second National Conference on City Planning and the Problems of the City, Rochester, New York* (1910): 58–60.

65 Ernest Poole, *The Lung Block and a Handbook for the Prevention of Tuberculosis* (New York: Charity Organization Society of New York, 1903).

66 Henry Morgenthau, "A National Constructive Programme for City Planning," First National Conference on City Planning, May 21 and 22, 1909, in *City Planning,* 61st Cong., 2d Sess., Senate Documents, vol. 59, no. 422, series 5659 (1909), 59–60.

67 Josiah Strong, *The Challenge of the City* (New York: Eaton & Mains, 1907), 103.

68 Benjamin C. Marsh, "The Public Health as Affected by Congestion of Population," *Tenth New York State Conference of Charities and Correction, Albany* (1909): 248.

69 Ibid., 249.

70 V. G. Simkhovitch, *Address on the Subject of City Planning,* Hearing before the Committee on the District of Columbia, 61st Cong., 2d Sess., Senate Document No. 422, series 5658 (1910), 102.

71 Mel Scott, *American City Planning Since 1890* (Berkeley: University of California Press, 1969), 99.

72 Bailey Burritt, "Comments on the Public Health as Affected by Congestion of Population by Benjamin C. Marsh," *Tenth New York State Conference of Charities and Corrections, Albany* (1909): 253–7.

73 Grosvenor Atterbury, "An Introductory Outline" [To the Prevention and Relief of the Congestion of Population], *Second National Conference on City Planning and the Problems of Congestion, Rochester, New York* (1910): 67–8.

74 *Report of the New York City Commission on Congestion of Population* (New York: Lecouver Press, 1911), 4.

75 Ibid., 13–14.

76 Charles S. Bernheimer, "Health and Sanitation in Philadelphia," in C. S. Bernheimer, ed., *The Russian Jew in the United States: Studies of Social Conditions in New York, Philadelphia, and Chicago* (Philadelphia: Winston, 1905); Burton Hendrick, "Great Jewish Invasion," *McClure's Magazine* 28 (1907): 307–21; Edward A. Steiner, *On the Trail of the Immigrant* (New York: Revell, 1906), 304; Ruth Crawford, "The Immigrant in St. Louis," *Studies in Social Economics (St. Louis School of Social Economy)* 1, no. 2 (1916): 23–4.

77 Maurice Fishberg, "Health and Sanitation of the Immigrant Jewish Population of New York," *Menorah* 33 (1902): 37–46.

78 Eliot Lord, John Trenor, and Samuel Barrows, *The Italian in America* (New York: Buck, 1905), 74.

79 *Cost of Living in American Towns*, 6.

80 Massachusetts Public Document, No. 15, "Living Conditions of the Wage-Earning Population in Certain Cities of Massachusetts," *Forty-First Annual Report of the Massachusetts Bureau of Statistics of Labor* (1911), 246.

81 Mary W. Ovington, "The Negro Home in New York," *Charities and Commons* 15 (1905–6): 25–30; and Fannie Williams, "Social Bonds in the 'Black Belt' of Chicago," *Charities and Commons* 15 (1905–6): 40–4.

82 Kate Claghorn, "Foreign Immigrants in New York City," *Report of the Industrial Commission*, House Document 78, No. 184, 57th Cong., 1st Sess., serial 4345, vol. 15 (1901–2), xx–xxii; New York Senate Document, No. 29, 19–20; Edith Abbott, *Report of the City Council Committee on Crime of the City of Chicago* (Chicago, 1915), 54–5.

83 Steiner, *On the Trail of the Immigrant*, 304–16.

84 Robert A. Woods (ed.), *The City Wilderness* (Boston: Houghton Mifflin, 1898), 39.

85 Ignatz L. Nascher, *The Wretches of Povertyville: A Sociological Study of the Bowery* (Chicago: Lanzit, 1909); Crawford, *The Immigrant in St. Louis*, 23–4.

86 Mary K. Simkhovitch, *Neighborhood: My Story of Greenwich House* (New York: Norton, 1938), 73.

87 Robert Hunter, *Tenement Conditions in Chicago, Report of the Investigating Committee of the City Homes Association* (Chicago: the Association, 1901), 189.

88 Robert A. Woods, ed., *Americans in Process* (Boston: Houghton Mifflin, 1902), 54.

89 Ibid., 192.

90 Kate H. Claghorn, "Foreign Immigration and the Tenement House in New

York City," in Robert DeForest and Lawrence Veiller, eds., *The Tenement House Problem*, vol. 2 (New York: Macmillan, 1903), 86.

91 Immigration Commission, *Report*, 3.

92 Ibid., 5.

93 Ibid., 36.

94 Jenks and Lauck, *The Immigration Problem*, 129.

95 Immigration Commission, *Report*, 208.

96 Lord, et al., *The Italian in America*, 74.

97 Claghorn, "Foreign Immigrants in New York City," 491.

98 Charlotte Rumbold, *Report of the Housing Committee of the Civic League of St. Louis: Housing Conditions in St. Louis* (1908), 7.

99 Emily Dinwiddie, *Housing Conditions in Philadelphia* (Philadelphia: Octavia Hill Association, 1904), 22.

100 F. A. Craig, *A Study of the Housing and Social Conditions in Selected Districts of Philadelphia* (Philadelphia: Henry Phipps Institute, 1915), 12, 17.

101 Ibid., 53.

102 E. A. Goldenweiser, "Immigrants in Cities," *The Survey* 25 (1911): 596–602.

103 Aronovici, "The Cost of a Decent Home," 112.

104 Edith E. Wood, *The Housing of the Unskilled Wage Earner: America's Next Problem* (New York: Macmillan, 1919), 12.

105 Warner, *American Charities*, 39.

106 E. R. A. Seligman, *Principles of Economics, with Special Reference to American Conditions*, 9th ed. (New York: Longmans, Green, 1921), 591.

107 Warner, *American Charities*, 135–6.

108 Feder, *Unemployment Relief in Periods of Depression*, 349.

109 Harold Finestone, *Victims of Change: Juvenile Delinquency in American Society* (Westport, Conn.: Greenwood, 1976), 49–52.

110 William Healy, *The Individual Delinquent* (Boston: Little, Brown, 1917), 4.

111 James T. Carey, *Sociology and Public Affairs: The Chicago School* (Beverly Hills, Calif.: Sage, 1975), 83–4.

112 Ibid., 85; David J. Rothman, *Conscience and Convenience: The Asylum and Its Alternatives in Progressive America* (Boston: Little, Brown, 1980), 43.

113 Warner, *American Charities*, 472–5.

114 Healy, *The Individual Delinquent*.

115 Mary E. Richmond, *Social Diagnosis* (New York: Russell Sage Foundation, 1917).

116 Mary E. Richmond, "Charitable Cooperation," *Twenty-Eighth National Conference of Charities and Corrections* (Washington, D.C.: 1901), 298.

117 Kathleen D. McCarthy, *Noblesse Oblige: Charity and Cultural Philanthropy in Chicago, 1849–1929* (Chicago: University of Chicago Press, 1982), 125; Robert H. Wiebe, *The Search for Order, 1877–1920* (New York: Hill and Wang, 1967), 169; Dominick Cavallo, *Muscles and Morals: Organized Playgrounds and Urban Reform, 1880–1920* (Philadelphia: University of Pennsylvania Press, 1981); Lubove, *The Struggle for Social Security*, 110–12.

118 Kirschner, *The Paradox of Professionalism*, 84.

119 Chambers, *Paul U. Kellogg and the Survey*, 22–9.

120 Mary Bacha, "The Pittsburgh Survey of the National Publication Committee of Charities and Commons," *The Survey* 19 (1908): 1665–70; Paul U. Kellogg, "Boston's Level Best – The 1915 Movement and the Work of Civic Organizing for Which It Stands," *The Survey* 22 (1910): 382–96.
121 Paul U. Kellogg, "Field Work of the Pittsburgh Survey," in P. Kellogg (ed.), *The Pittsburgh District: Civic Frontage*, vol. 6 of *The Pittsburgh Survey* (New York: Russell Sage Foundation, 1914), 494.
122 Shelby M. Harrison, *The Social Survey: The Idea Defined and Its Development Traced* (New York: Russell Sage Foundation, 1931), 14–15.
123 Ibid., 12–13.
124 Margaret Byington, "Fifty Annual Reports," *The Survey* 23 (1910), 972.
125 Peter B. Hales, *Silver Cities: The Photography of American Urbanization, 1839–1915* (Philadelphia: Pennsylvania University Press, 1983), 161–276.
126 John F. McClymer, "The Pittsburgh Survey, 1907–1914; Forging an Ideology in the Steel District," *Pennsylvania History* 41 (1974): 169–88.
127 Michael H. Frisch, "Urban Theorists, Urban Reform, and American Political Culture in the Progressive Period," *Political Science Quarterly* 97 (1982): 295–315.
128 Edward T. Devine, "Efficiency and Relief: A Program of Social Work," *Charities* 15 (1905–6): 145–51.
129 Shelby M. Harrison, *Community Action Through Surveys* (New York: Russell Sage Foundation, 1916), 27.
130 Ibid., 10.
131 Kirschner, *The Paradox of Professionalism*, 73.
132 Barbara Howe, "The Emergence of Scientific Philanthropy, 1900–1920: Origins, Issues and Outcomes," in Robert F. Arnove, ed., *Philanthropy and Cultural Imperialism: The Foundations at Home and Abroad* (Boston: Hall, 1980), 25–54.
133 Sheila Slaughter and Edward T. Silva, "Looking Backwards: How Foundations Formulated Ideology in the Progressive Period," in Arnove, ed., *Philanthropy and Cultural Imperialism*, 55–86.
134 Tobin, *Organize or Perish*, 55–9.
135 Brandt, *Growth and Development of the Association for Improving the Condition of the Poor*, 195.
136 Paul U. Kellogg, "The 1915 Boston Exposition," *The Survey* 23 (1909): 328–34.
137 Scott, *American City Planning*, 110–14.
138 *Report of the Homestead Commission*, Massachusetts House Document 2000, 1913, 37; and *First Annual Report of the Homestead Commission*, Massachusetts Public Document 103, 1913, 48–9, 75.
139 Andrew Lees, *Cities Perceived: Urban Society in European and American Thought 1820–1940* (New York: Columbia University Press, 1985), 230–5.
140 Robert A. Woods and Albert J. Kennedy, *The Settlement Horizon*, 59.
141 Graham Taylor, *Religion in Social Action* (New York: Dodd & Mead, 1913), 141.
142 Ibid., 166.
143 Jane Addams, quoted in Lees, *Cities Perceived*, 168.

144 John Collier, "What Shall We Substitute for the Saloon?" *American City* (February 1919): 163–5.
145 Jane Addams, in William D. P. Bliss, ed., *The New Encyclopedia of Social Reform* (New York: Funk & Wagnalls, 1910), 588.
146 Grace Abbott, *The Immigrant and the Community* (New York: Century, 1917), 277–97; George C. White, "Social Settlements and Immigrant Neighbors, 1886–1914," *Social Service Review* 33 (1959): 55–66.
147 Robert A. Woods and Albert J. Kennedy, *The Zone of Emergence: Observations of the Lower Middle and Upper Working Class Communities of Boston, 1905–1914* (Cambridge, Mass.: MIT Press, 1962).
148 Rivka Lissak, "Myth and Reality: The Pattern of Relationship Between the Hull House Circle and the 'New Immigrants' on Chicago's West Side, 1890–1919," *Journal of American Ethnic History* 2 (1983): 21–50.
149 Charles Cooley, *Human Nature and the Social Order*, rev. ed. (New York, Scribner's, 1922).
150 Paul S. Boyer, *Urban Masses and Moral Order in America, 1820–1920* (Cambridge, Mass.: Harvard University Press, 1978), 250–70; Kenneth L. Kusmer, "The Functions of Organized Charity in the Progressive Era: Chicago as a Case Study," *Journal of American History* 60 (1973): 657–78; and Lees, *Cities Perceived,* 230–2.
151 Boyer, *Urban Masses and Moral Order in America,* 255.
152 Dwight F. Davis, "The Neighborhood Center – A Moral and Educational Factor," *Charities and The Commons* 17 (1908): 1504–6.
153 Anthony Sutcliffe, *Towards the Planned City: Germany, Britain, the United States, and France, 1780–1914* (New York, St. Martin's, 1981), 122; Edward J. Ward, *The Social Center* (New York: Appleton, 1913); Scott, *American City Planning,* 73–4.
154 Lees, *Cities Perceived,* 108.
155 Edward J. Ward, *Rochester Social Centers and Civic Clubs* (Rochester, N.Y.: League of Civic Clubs, 1909), 12–13; Edward W. Stevens, Jr., "Social Centers, Politics, and Social Efficiency in the Progressive Era," *History of Education Quarterly* 12 (1972): 16–33.
156 George E. Hooker, "City Planning and Political Areas," *American City* (1917): 122–5.
157 Mary P. Follett, *The New State, Group Organization, the Solution of Popular Government* (New York: Longmans Green, 1923).
158 Frank Goodnow, "The Work of the American Political Science Association," *Proceedings of the American Political Science Association* (1906), 35–46; Lubove, "The Twentieth Century City," 195–209.
159 John Collier, "Community Councils: What Have They Done and What Is Their Future?" *Proceedings, National Conference on Social Work* (1919): 476–9.
160 Patricia Mooney Melvin, *The Organic City: Urban Definition and Neighborhood Organization, 1880–1920* (Lexington: University Press of Kentucky, 1987), 77–97.
161 Wilbur C. Phillips, "Health Centers as an Aid to Democracy," *The Survey* 36 (1916): 93.

162 Wilbur C. Phillips, *Adventuring for Democracy* (New York: Social Unit Press, 1940), 153–63.

163 Edward T. Devine, "The Social Unit in Cincinnati: An Experiment in Organization," *The Survey* 42 (1919): 869–70.

164 Hyman Kaplan, "Federating from the Bottom Up," *The Survey* (1924): 681–5.

165 William Healy, *Twenty Five Years of Child Guidance,* Studies from the Institute for Juvenile Research, Series C. 256 (Springfield: Illinois Department of Public Welfare, 1934), 14–16.

166 Mary E. Richmond, *What Is Social Casework?* (New York: Russell Sage Foundation, 1930), 249; Kathleen Woodroofe, *From Charity to Social Work in England and the United States* (London: Routledge and Kegan Paul, 1962), 115.

167 Woodroofe, *From Charity to Social Work,* 101–16; John Ehrenreich, *The Altruistic Imagination: A History of Social Work and Social Policy in the United States* (Ithaca, N.Y.: Cornell University Press, 1985).

168 Judith Ann Trolander, *Professionalism and Social Change: From the Settlement House Movement to Neighborhood Centers, 1886 to the Present* (New York: Columbia University Press, 1987).

169 Park Dixon Goist, *From Main Street to State Street: Town, City, and Community in America* (Port Washington, N.Y.: Kennikat Press, 1971); Jean B. Quandt, "Community in Urban America, 1890–1917: Reformers, City Planners, and Greenwich Village," *Societas* 6 (1976): 255–74; Fred H. Matthews, *Quest for an American Sociology: Robert E. Park and the Chicago School* (Montreal: McGill–Queens University Press, 1977).

170 Horowitz, *The Morality of Spending,* 136–7.

171 Scott, *American City Planning,* 47–65; Richard E. Fogelsong, *Planning the Capitalist City: The Colonial Era to the 1920s* (Princeton: Princeton University Press, 1986), 124–66.

172 M. Christine Boyer, *Dreaming the Rationale City: The Myth of American City Planning* (Cambridge, Mass.: MIT Press, 1983), 33–113; Leonardo Benevolo, *The History of the City* (Cambridge, Mass.: MIT Press, 1980), 756–840; Richard Wilson, *American Renaissance* (New York: Pantheon, 1979); Scott, *American City Planning,* 27–30.

173 J. F. Harder, "The City's Plan," *Municipal Affairs* 2 (1989): 30.

174 Charles M. Robinson, *Modern Civic Art; or, The City Made Beautiful* (New York: Putnam's, 1909), 29, 58, 271.

175 Scott, *American City Planning,* 69–71.

176 Marsh, "The Public Health," 248–58.

177 Cargill, "Small Houses for Working Men," 352; Immigration Commission, *Report,* 6–8.

178 Edward E. Pratt, "Relief [of Congestion] Through the Proper Distribution of Factories," *Proceedings of the Second National Conference on City Planning and the Problems of Congestion* (Rochester, N.Y.: 1910), 107–12.

179 Scott, *American City Planning,* 82–7.

180 Lawrence Veiller, "The Safe Load of Population on Land," *Proceedings of*

the *Second National Conference on City Planning and the Problems of Congestion* (Rochester, N.Y.: 1910), 73–8; "Reactions to Reports of Committee on Congestion," *Eleventh New York State Conference of Charities and Corrections* (Rochester, N.Y.: 1910), 139–43.

181 Harvey Kantor, "Benjamin C. Marsh and the Fight over Population Congestion," *Journal of the American Institute of Planners* 40 (1974): 422–9.

182 John Ihlder, "Private Houses and Public Health," *National Municipal Review* (1912): 54–60; John Bauman, "Disinfecting the Industrial City: The Philadelphia Housing Commission and Scientific Efficiency, 1909–1916," in Michael H. Ebner and Eugene M. Tobin, eds., *The Age of Reform: New Perspectives on the Progressive Era* (Port Washington, N.Y.: Kennikat, 1977), 117–30.

183 Stanley K. Schultz and Clay McShane, "To Engineer the Metropolis: Sewers, Sanitation and City Planning in Late Nineteenth Century America," *Journal of American History* 65 (1977): 389–411.

184 George B. Ford, "The City Scientific," *Proceedings, National Conference on Charities and Corrections* (1913): 31–41.

185 Robert W. DeForest and Lawrence Veiller, eds., *The Tenement House Problem*, vol. 1 (New York: Macmillan, 1903), xxvii.

186 Roy Lubove, *The Progressives and the Slums: Tenement House Reform in New York City, 1890–1917* (Pittsburgh: University of Pittsburgh Press, 1962), 238–45; Sutcliffe, *Towards the Planned City*, 116–17.

187 George E. Hooker, "A Plan for Chicago," *The Survey* 22 (1909): 778–90.

188 Atherton, "Urban Order and Moral Order," 165–82.

189 Scott, *American City Planning*, 106–10; Jon A. Peterson, "The City Beautiful Movement: Forgotten Origins and Lost Meanings," *Journal of Urban History* 2 (1976): 415–34; Sutcliffe, *Towards the Planned City*, 106–10; and Robinson, *Modern Civic Art*, 259.

190 Don S. Kirschner, "The Perils of Pleasure: Commercial Recreation, Social Disorder, and Moral Reform in the Progressive Era," *American Studies* 21 (1980): 27–42; John Atherton, "Urban Order and Moral Order: Burnham's Plan of Chicago (1909) and the Conceptualization of the City," in Mark Chenetier and Rob Kroes, eds., *Impressions of a Gilded Age: The American Fin de Siecle* (Amsterdam: Amerika Instituut, 1983), 165–82; Dom Cavallo, "Social Reform and the Movement to Organize Children's Play During the Progressive Era," *History of Childhood Quarterly* 3 (1976): 509–22; Robert Lewis, "Well-Directed Play: Urban Recreation and Progressive Reform," in Chenetier and Kroes, eds., *Impressions of a Gilded Age,* 183–202.

191 Cavallo, "Social Reform and the Movement to Organize Children's Play."

192 Clarence Perry, *The Neighborhood Unit: A Scheme of Arrangement for the Family-Life Community,* Regional Survey of New York and Its Environs, vol. 7 (New York: Russell Sage Foundation, 1929), 22–140.

193 Carl W. Condit, *Chicago 1910–1929: Building, Planning, and Urban Technology* (Chicago: University of Chicago Press, 1973), 76; Henry Fairchild, *Immigration: A World Movement and Its American Significance* (New York: Macmillan, 1914), 242.

194 John L. Hancock, "Planners in the Changing American City, 1900–1940," *Journal of the American Institute of Planners* 32 (1967): 290–304; Jane S. Dahlberg, *The New York Bureau of Municipal Research: Pioneer in Government Administration* (New York: New York University Press, 1966), 7–19.

195 James Leiby, *A History of Social Welfare and Social Work in the United States* (New York: Columbia University Press, 1978), 163–90; Sutcliffe, *Towards the Planned City,* 88.

196 Clarence Stein, "The New York Puzzle," *Journal of the American Institute of Planners and Architects* 12 (1924): 84.

197 Roy Lubove, *Community Planning in the 1920's: The Contribution of the Regional Plan Association of America* (Pittsburgh: University of Pittsburgh Press, 1963).

198 Guy Alchon, *The Invisible Hand of Planning: Capitalism, Social Science, and the State in the 1920s* (Princeton: Princeton University Press, 1985), 3–7.

199 Boyer, *Urban Masses and Moral Order,* 255.

200 Stephen Collini, *Liberalism and Sociology* (Cambridge: Cambridge University Press, 1979).

201 Charles W. Eliot, quoted in William T. Sedgewick, "American Achievements and American Failures in Public Health Work," *American Journal of Public Health* 5 (1915): 1108.

202 Barbara G. Rosencrantz, *Public Health and the State: Changing Views in Massachusetts, 1842–1936* (Cambridge, Mass.: Harvard University Press, 1972), 108, 149–79.

203 Edward G. Hartmann, *The Movement to Americanize the Immigrant* (New York: Columbia University Press, 1948), 55–94; Howard C. Hill, "The Americanization Movement," *American Journal of Sociology* 24 (1919): 609–42; Frances A. Kellor, *Immigrants and the Future* (New York: Doran, 1920), 236–8.

204 Edward A. Ross, *Foundations of Sociology* (New York: Macmillan, 1905), 353.

205 Madison Grant, *The Passing of the Great Race; or, The Racial Basis of European History* (New York: Scribner's, 1916), 80.

206 Joseph Lee, "Immigration," *Proceedings, National Conference on Charities and Corrections* (1906): 282–5; Edward T. Devine, "The Selection of Immigrants," *The Survey* (1911): 715–16.

207 Arthur Mann, *Yankee Reformers in the Urban Age* (Cambridge, Mass.: Belknap, 1954), 122.

208 Abbott, *The Immigrant and the Community,* 277–80.

209 Randolph Bourne, "Trans-National America," *Atlantic* 118 (1916): 86–97; Josiah Royce, *Race Questions and other American Problems* (New York: Macmillan, 1908), 57–96.

210 Horace M. Kallen, "Democracy Versus the Melting Pot."

211 Berkson, *Theories of Americanization.*

212 R. Fred Wacker, *Ethnicity, Pluralism and Race: Race Relations Theory in America Before Myrdal* (Westport, Conn.: Greenwood, 1983), 27–32.

213 John Higham, *Send These to Me: Immigrants in Urban America* (Baltimore:

Johns Hopkins University Press, 1984), 29–66; Don S. Kirschner, *City and Country: Rural Responses to Urbanization in the 1920's* (Westport, Conn.: Greenwood, 1970), 27–41.

214 Henry P. Fairchild, *The Melting Pot Mistake* (Boston: Little, Brown, 1926).
215 Higham, *Send These to Me.*

5. Ethnicity and assimilation

1 Robert E. L. Faris, *Chicago Sociology, 1920–1932* (Chicago: University of Chicago Press, 1970); James T. Carey, *Sociology and Public Affairs: The Chicago School* (Beverly Hills, Calif.: Sage, 1975); Fred H. Mathews, *Quest for American Sociology: Robert E. Park and the Chicago School of Sociology* (Montreal: McGill–Queen's University Press, 1977); Martin Bulmer, *The Chicago School of Sociology* (Chicago: University of Chicago Press, 1984); Stow Persons, *Ethnic Studies at Chicago: 1905–45* (Urbana and Champaign, Ill.: University of Illinois Press, 1987).

2 Sarah E. Simons, "Social Assimilation," *American Journal of Sociology* 6 (1901–2): 790–82; 7 (1902–3): 53–79, 234–48, 386–404, 539–56.

3 Persons, *Ethnic Studies at Chicago,* 28–59.

4 Maurice R. Stein, *The Eclipse of Community: An Interpretation of American Studies* (Princeton, N.J.: Princeton University Press, 1960), 13–46.

5 Robert E. Park, "The City: Suggestions for the Investigation of Human Behavior in the Urban Environment," in Robert E. Park and Ernest W. Burgess, eds., *The City* (Chicago: University of Chicago Press, 1925), 41.

6 Ralph Turner, "Introduction," in Ralph H. Turner, ed., *Robert E. Park: On Social Control and Collective Behavior* (Chicago: University of Chicago Press, 1967), xvii.

7 Harvey W. Zorbaugh, *The Gold Coast and the Slum* (Chicago: University of Chicago Press, 1929), 221.

8 Michael P. Smith, *The City and Social Theory* (Oxford: Blackwell, 1980), 1–48.

9 Park and Burgess, eds., *The City,* 9.

10 Ernest W. Burgess, "Can Neighborhood Work Have a Scientific Basis?" in Park and Burgess, eds., *The City,* 143.

11 William I. Thomas, *The Unadjusted Girl* (Boston: Little, Brown, 1931), 256–7.

12 Mary Jo Deegan, *Jane Addams and the Men of the Chicago School, 1892–1918* (New Brunswick, N.J.: Transaction Books, 1988).

13 Robert E. Park, "Community Organization and Juvenile Delinquency," in Park and Burgess, eds., *The City,* 106.

14 Robert E. Park, *Race and Culture* (Glencoe, Ill.: The Free Press, 1950), viii.

15 Ernest W. Burgess, "The Growth of the City: An Introduction to a Research Project," in Park and Burgess, eds., *The City,* 53–4, 57.

16 Zorbaugh, *The Gold Coast and the Slum,* 128.

17 Faris, *Chicago Sociology,* 5.

18 William I. Thomas and Florian Znaniecki, *The Polish Peasant in Europe and America* (New York: Dover, 1958), 1469–511.

19 Robert E. Park and Herbert A. Miller, *Old World Traits Transplanted* (New York: Harper, 1921). Because of the controversial circumstances involved in Thomas's dismissal from the University of Chicago, his manuscript was published under the authorship of Park and Miller. See Morris Janowitz, ed., *W. I. Thomas on Social Organization and Social Personality* (Chicago: University of Chicago Press, 1966), xvi.

20 Zorbaugh, *The Gold Coast and the Slums,* 134–5.

21 Park, "Community Organization and Juvenile Delinquency," 109–10.

22 Idem.

23 Robert E. Park, "Community Organization and the Romantic Temper," in Park and Burgess, eds., *The City,* 113–22.

24 Park, "The City," 7, 33–7.

25 William L. Riordan, *Plunkitt of Tammany Hall* (New York: Dutton, 1963), 3–6.

26 Ernest W. Burgess and Donald J. Bogue, "Research in Urban Society: A Long View," in Ernest W. Burgess and Donald J. Bogue, eds., *Urban Sociology* (Chicago: University of Chicago Press, 1967), 10.

27 Burgess, "The Growth of the City," 54.

28 Ibid., 61.

29 Roderick D. McKenzie, *The Neighborhood: A Study of Local Life in the City of Columbus, Ohio* (Chicago: University of Chicago Press, 1923), 797–9.

30 Burgess, "Can Neighborhood Work Have a Scientific Basis?" 142–5.

31 Park, "The City," 7

32 Robert E. Park, "Sociology, Community and Society," in Robert E. Park, ed., *Human Communities: The City and Human Ecology,* (Glencoe, Ill.: The Free Press, 1952), 196.

33 Faris, *Chicago Sociology,* 59.

34 Thomas and Znaniecki, *The Polish Peasant,* 1546.

35 Park, "Sociology, Community and Society," 196.

36 Louis Wirth, *The Ghetto* (Chicago: University of Chicago Press, 1928), 282–3.

37 Robert E. Park, "Foreword" to Wirth, *The Ghetto,* v–vi.

38 Zorbaugh, *The Gold Coast and the Slums,* 140–1.

39 Thomas and Znaniecki, *The Polish Peasant,* 1545.

40 Burgess, "The Growth of the City," 53–8.

41 Roderick D. McKenzie, "The Ecological Approach to the Study of the Human Community," in Park and Burgess, eds., *The City,* 63–79.

42 R. E. Park, "The Urban Community as a Spatial Pattern and a Moral Order," in Turner, ed., *Robert E. Park,* 60.

43 Paul F. Cressey, "Population Succession in Chicago," *American Journal of Sociology* 44 (1938–9): 61.

44 Clifford R. Shaw and Henry D. McKay, *Social Factors in Juvenile Delinquency: Report on the Causes of Crime,* vol. 2 (Washington, D.C.: National Commission on Law Observance and Enforcement, 1931), 60.

45 Clifford R. Shaw, *Delinquency Areas* (Chicago: University of Chicago Press, 1929), 198–203.

46 Mabel A. Elliot, *Correlations Between Rates of Delinquency and Racial Her-*

itage (Springfield, Ill., 1926), 25; Frederic M. Thrasher, *The Gang* (Chicago: University of Chicago Press, 1927), 22; Andrew W. Lind, "The Slum and the Ghetto," *Social Forces* 9 (1930): 208; Edwin H. Sutherland, "Is There Undue Crime Among Immigrants?" *Proceedings of the National Conference of Social Work* (1927): 578

47 Louis Wirth, "Culture Conflicts and Misconduct," *Social Forces* 9 (1931): 488–9.

48 Floyd Allport, "Culture Conflict Versus the Individual as Factors in Delinquency, *Social Forces* 9 (1931): 492–7.

49 Park, "The City," 28.

50 Shaw and McKay, *Social Factors in Juvenile Delinquency,* 109.

51 Shaw, *Delinquency Areas,* 10.

52 Harold Finestone, *Victims of Change: Juvenile Delinquents in American Society* (Westport, Conn.: Greenwood Press, 1976), 145–56.

53 William F. Whyte, *The Street Corner Society* (Chicago: University of Chicago Press, 1943), 98–104; 273–4.

54 Ibid., 36–7.

55 Herbert J. Gans, *The Urban Villagers* (New York: Macmillan, 1962), 264–5, 268–9; Marc Fried, *The World of the Urban Working Class* (Cambridge: Cambridge University Press, 1973).

56 Zorbaugh, *The Gold Coast and the Slum.*

57 E. Franklin Frazier, *The Negro Family in Chicago* (Chicago: University of Chicago Press, 1932), 91–116.

58 St. Clair Drake and Horace R. Cayton, *Black Metropolis: A Study of Negro Life in a Northern City* (New York: 1962).

59 Homer Hoyt, *One Hundred Years of Land Values in Chicago* (Chicago: University of Chicago Press, 1933).

60 Walter Firey, *Land Use in Central Boston* (Cambridge, Mass.: Harvard University Press, 1947).

61 Burgess and Bogue, "Urban Sociology," 179.

62 Persons, *Ethnic Studies at Chicago,* 45–59; Fred R. Wacker, *Ethnicity, Pluralism and Race: Race Relations Theory in America Before Myrdal* (Westport, Conn: Greenwood, 1983), 13–40.

63 Robert E. Park and Ernest W. Burgess, *An Introduction to the Science of Sociology,* 2d ed. (Chicago: University of Chicago Press, 1924), 504–784.

64 Robert E. Park, "Immigrant Heritages," *Proceedings of the National Conference of Social Work* (1921): 494–5.

65 Park and Burgess, *An Introduction to the Science of Sociology,* 737.

66 Park and Miller, *Old World Traits Transplanted,* 308.

67 Horace Kallen, *Culture and Democracy in the United States* (New York: Boni and Liveright, 1924).

68 Persons, *Ethnic Studies at Chicago,* 60–97; and Wacker, *Ethnicity, Pluralism and Race,* 41–59.

69 Robert E. Park, "Our Racial Frontier on the Pacific," *Survey Graphic* 9 (1926): 192–6.

70 Park and Burgess, *An Introduction to the Science of Sociology,* 735.

71 Robert E. Park, "The Concept of Social Distance," *Journal of Applied Soci-*

ology 8 (1924): 329–34; Emory Bogardus, *Immigration and Race Attitudes* (Boston: Heath, 1928), 10–11.

72 William Carlson Smith, *Americans in the Making: The Natural History of the Assimilation of Immigrants* (New York: Appleton-Century-Crofts, 1939), 114–19.

73 Emory Bogardus, "A Race Relations Cycle" *American Journal of Sociology* 35 (1930): 612–17; Emory Bogardus, "Scales in Social Research," *Sociology and Social Research* 24 (1940): 69–75

74 Robert E. Park, "The Race Relations Cycle in Hawaii," in Park, ed., *Race and Culture,* 191–4.

75 Caroline F. Ware, *Greenwich Village, 1920–1930* (Boston: Houghton Mifflin, 1935), 5–6, 131, 204–5.

76 W. Lloyd Warner and Leo Srole, *The Social Systems of American Ethnic Groups* (New Haven, Conn.: Yale University Press, 1945), 33–52.

77 Stephen Thernstrom, *Poverty and Progress: Social Mobility in a Nineteenth Century City* (Cambridge, Mass.: Harvard University Press, 1964), 225–39.

78 Carol Agocs, "Who's in on the American Dream? Ethnic Representation in Suburban Opportunity Structures in Metropolitan Detroit," *Ethnic Groups* 4 (1982); 239–54.

79 Judith Kramer and Seymour Leventman, *The Children of the Gilded Ghetto* (New Haven, Conn.: Yale University Press, 1961).

80 Nathan Kantrowitz, *Ethnic and Racial Segregation in the New York Metropolis: Residential Patterns Among White Ethnic Groups, Blacks and Puerto Ricans* (New York: Praeger, 1973); Nathan Kantrowitz, "Racial and Ethnic Residential Segregation in Boston, 1830–1970," *Annals of the American Academy of Political and Social Science* 441 (1979): 41–54.

81 Stanley Lieberson and Donna K. Carter, "Temporal Changes and Urban Differences in Residential Segregation: A Reconsideration," *American Journal of Sociology* 88 (1982): 296–310.

82 Noel J. Chrisman, "Ethnic Persistence in an Urban Setting," *Ethnicity* 8 (1981): 256–92.

83 Milton Gordon, *Assimilation in American Life: The Role of Race, Religion and National Origins* (New York: Oxford University Press, 1964).

84 Ruby Jo Reeves Kennedy, "Single or Triple Melting Pot: Intermarriage Trends in New Haven, 1870–1940," *American Journal of Sociology* 49 (1944): 331–9.

85 Will Herberg, *Protestant, Catholic, Jew* (Garden City, N.Y.: Doubleday, 1955).

86 Richard Bernard, *The Melting Pot and the Altar, Marital Assimilation in Early Twentieth Century Wisconsin* (Minneapolis: University of Minnesota Press, 1980), 3–41, 115–130; Ceri Peach, "Which Triple Melting Pot? A Reexamination of Ethnic Intermarriage in New Haven, 1900–1950," *Ethnic and Racial Studies* 3 (1980): 1–16.

87 Andrew Greeley, "Religious Musical Chairs," in Thomas Robbins and Dick Anthony, eds., *In Gods We Trust: New Patterns of Religious Pluralism in America* (New Brunswick, N.J.: Transaction Books, 1981), 101–26; Richard Alba, "Social Assimilation Among Catholic National Origin Groups," *American Sociological Review* 41 (1976): 1030–46.

88 Nathan Glazer, "Universalization of Ethnicity," *Encounter* 2 (1975): 16.
89 Herberg, *Protestant, Catholic, Jew,* 260.
90 Halle, *America's Working Man: Work, Home, and Politics Among Blue Collar Property Owners* (Chicago: University of Chicago Press, 1984), 271.
91 Herbert Gans, "Symbolic Ethnicity: The Future of Ethnic Groups and Cultures in America," in Herbert J. Gans, ed., *On the Making of America: Essays in Honor of David Reisman* (Philadelphia: University of Pennsylvania Press, 1979), 193–220.
92 Steinberg, *The Ethnic Myth;* Irving Howe, "The Limits of Ethnicity," *New Republic,* June 25, 1977, 19; Richard D. Alba, "The Twilight of Ethnicity Among Catholics of European Ancestry," *Annals of the American Academy of Political and Social Science* 454, (1981), 86–97.
93 Douglas S. Massey, "Social Class and Ethnic Segregation: A Reconsideration of Methods and Conclusions," *American Sociological Review* 46 (1981): 641–50; Ceri Peach, "Conflicting Interpretations of Segregation," in Peter Jackson and Susan J. Smith, eds., *Social Interaction and Ethnic Segregation* (London: Academic Press, 1981), 19–33.
94 Pierre Van Den Berghe, *The Ethnic Phenomenon* (New York: Elsevier–North Holland, 1981); Stephen Steinberg, *The Ethnic Myth: Race, Ethnicity, and Class in America* (New York: Atheneum, 1981).
95 Ira Katznelson, *City Trenches: Urban Politics and the Patterning of Class in the United States* (New York: Pantheon, 1981), 25–44.
96 Timothy L. Smith, "Religion and Ethnicity in America," *American Historical Review* 83 (1978): 1155–85.
97 Oscar Handlin, *The Newcomers: Negroes and Puerto Ricans in a Changing Metropolis* (Garden City, N.Y.: Doubleday Anchor, 1962); Nathan Glazer and Daniel P. Moynihan, *Beyond the Melting Pot: The Negroes, Puerto Ricans, Jews, Italians and Irish of New York City* (Cambridge, Mass.: MIT Press, 1963).
98 Oscar Lewis, "The Culture of Poverty," in Daniel P. Moynihan, ed., *On Understanding Poverty* (New York: Basic Books, 1968), 187–200.
99 Charles A. Valentine, *Culture and Poverty: Critique and Counter-Proposals* (Chicago: University of Chicago Press, 1968), 18–42; Nathan Glazer, "Slums and Ethnicity," in Thomas D. Sherrard, ed., *Social Welfare and Urban Problems* (New York: Columbia University Press, 1968), 84; Gerald D. Suttles, *The Social Order of the Slum: Ethnicity and Territory in the Inner City* (Chicago: University of Chicago Press, 1970).
100 W. L. Yancey, E. P. Ericksen, and R. N. Juliani, "Emergent Ethnicity: A Review and Synthesis," *American Sociological Review* 41 (1975): 391–403.

6. Ethnicity and industrialization

1 John Higham, "Immigration," in C. Vann Woodward, ed., *The Comparative Approach to American History* (New York: Basic Books, 1968), 91–103.
2 Oscar Handlin, *The Uprooted* (Boston: Little, Brown, 1951), 1–12.
3 Maldwyn A. Jones, "Oscar Handlin," in Marcus Cunliffe and Robin Winks,

eds., *Pastmasters: Some Essays on American Historians* (New York: Harper & Row, 1969), 239–77.

4 Frank Thistlethwaite, "Migration from Europe Overseas in the Nineteenth and Twentieth Centuries," *XIe Congrès Internationale des Sciences Historiques,* vol. 5 (Stockholm; Almquist and Wiksell, 1960), 32–60; Marcus L. Hansen, *The Atlantic Migration, 1607–1860* (Cambridge, Mass.: Harvard University Press, 1940).

5 John Higham, "Integrating America: The Problem of Assimilation in the Nineteenth Century," *Journal of American Ethnic History* 1 (1981): 7–25; Olivier Zunz, "American History and the Changing Meaning of Assimilation," *Journal of American Ethnic History* 4 (1985): 53–84.

6 Josef J. Barton, "Religion and Cultural Change in Czech Immigrant Communities, 1850–1920," in Randall M. Muller and Thomas D. Marzik, eds., *Immigrants and Religion in Urban America* (Philadelphia: Temple University Press, 1977), 3–24.

7 Oscar Handlin, *Boston's Immigrants, 1790–1865: A Study in Acculturation* (Cambridge, Mass.: Harvard University Press, 1939).

8 Oscar Handlin, "Immigration in American Life: A Reappraisal," in Henry S. Commager, ed., *Immigration and American History, Essays in Honor of Theodore C. Blegen* (Minneapolis: University of Minnesota Press, 1961), 8–25.

9 Robert Ernst, *Immigrant Life in New York City: 1825–1863* (New York: King's Crown Press of Columbia University, 1949), 46.

10 Ibid., 41.

11 Theodore Hershberg, Alan N. Burstein, Eugene P. Ericksen, et al., "Tale of Three Cities: Blacks and Immigrants in Philadelphia, 1850–1880, 1930 and 1970," *Annals of the American Academy of Political and Social Science* 441 (1979): 55–81.

12 Dennis Clark, *The Irish in Philadelphia: Ten Generations of Urban Experience* (Philadelphia: Temple University Press, 1973), 24–43; Jay P. Dolan, *The Immigrant Church: New York's Irish and German Catholics* (Baltimore: Johns Hopkins University Press, 1975), 87–98; James W. Sanders, *The Education of an Urban Minority: Catholics in Chicago, 1833–1965* (New York: Oxford University Press, 1977).

13 David Ward, "The Ethnic Ghetto in the United States: Past and Present," *Transactions of the Institute of British Geographers* 7 (1982): 257–75.

14 Kathleen N. Conzen, *Immigrant Milwaukee, 1836–1860: Accommodation and Community in a Frontier City* (Cambridge, Mass.: Harvard University Press, 1976); Christiane Harzig, "Chicago's German North Side, 1880–1900: The Structure of a Gilded Age Ethnic Neighborhood," in Hartmut Keil and John B. Jentz, eds., *German Workers in Industrial Chicago, 1850–1910: A Comparative Perspective* (DeKalb, Ill.: Northern Illinois University Press, 1983), 127–44.

15 Carol Groneman, "Working-Class Immigrant Women in Mid-Nineteenth Century New York: The Irish Women's Experience," *Journal of Urban History* 4 (1978): 255–71.

16 William F. Whyte, *Street Corner Society: The Social Structure of an Italian*

Slum, enlarged ed. (Chicago: University of Chicago Press, 1954), xix; William M. De Marco, *Ethnics and Enclaves: Boston's Italian North End* (Ann Arbor, Mich.: UMI Research Press, 1981), 15–29.

17 Rudolf J. Vecoli, "Contadini in Chicago: A Critique of *The Uprooted,*" *Journal of American History* 51 (1964): 404–17.

18 Dino Cinel, *From Italy to San Francisco: The Immigrant Experience* (Stanford, Calif.: Stanford University Press, 1982).

19 Joseph Barton, *Peasants and Strangers: Italians, Rumanians, and Slovaks in an American City, 1890–1950* (Cambridge, Mass.: Harvard University Press, 1975), 89.

20 Michael F. Funchion, "Irish Chicago: Church, Homeland, Politics and Class, The Shaping of an Ethnic Group, 1870–1900," in Melvin G. Holli and Peter d'A. Jones, eds., *The Ethnic Frontier: Group Survival in Chicago and the Midwest* (Grand Rapids, Mich.: Eerdman's, 1981), 8–39.

21 June G. Alexander, "Staying Together: Chain Migration of Slovak Settlement in Pittsburgh Prior to World War I," *Journal of American Ethnic History* 1 (1981): 56–83.

22 Howard P. Chudacoff, "A New Look at Ethnic Neighborhoods: Residential Dispersion and the Concept of Visibility in a Medium-Sized City," *Journal of American History* 60 (1973): 76–93; Kathleen N. Conzen, "Immigrants, Immigrant Neighborhoods, and Ethnic Identity: Historical Issues," *Journal of American History* 66 (1979): 603–15.

23 Thomas Kessner, *The Golden Door: Italian and Jewish Immigrant Mobility in New York City, 1880–1915* (New York: Oxford University Press, 1977), 145–7, 157–60; Jeffrey Gurock, *When Harlem Was Jewish, 1870–1930* (New York: Columbia University Press, 1979), 157–68.

24 Vecoli, "Contadini in Chicago," 404–17; Edwin Fenton, *Immigrants and Unions: A Case Study in Italian and American Labor, 1870–1920* (New York: Arno, 1975), 31–70.

25 Thomas L. Philpott, *The Slum and the Ghetto: Neighborhood Deterioration and Middle-Class Reform, Chicago, 1880–1930* (New York: Oxford University Press, 1979), 137–44.

26 Olivier Zunz, *The Changing Face of Inequality: Urbanization, Industrial Development, and Immigrants in Detroit, 1880–1920* (Chicago: University of Chicago Press, 1982), 78–9.

27 Ibid., 146–52.

28 Virginia Yans-McLaughlin, *Family and Community: Italian Immigrants in Buffalo, 1880–1930* (Ithaca, N.Y.: Cornell University Press, 1977); Tamara K. Hareven, *Family Time and Industrial Time: The Relationship Between the Family and Work in a New England Industrial Community* (Cambridge: Cambridge University Press, 1982); Donna R. Gabaccia, *From Italy to Elizabeth Street: Housing and Social Change Among Italian Immigrants, 1880–1930* (Albany: State University of New York Press, 1983), 53–66.

29 Karl E. Tauber and Alma F. Tauber, "The Negro as an Immigrant Group: Recent Trends in Racial and Ethnic Segregation in Chicago," *American Journal of Sociology* 69 (1964): 374–82.

30 Joseph Garoznik, "The Racial and Ethnic Make-up of Baltimore Neighbor-

hoods, 1850–1870," *Maryland Historical Magazine* 71 (1976): 396; Paul A. Groves and Edward K. Muller, "The Evolution of Black Residential Areas in the late Nineteenth Century," *Journal of Historical Geography* 1 (1975): 169–92; James Borchert, "Urban Neighborhood and Community Informal Group Life, 1850–1970," *Journal of Interdisciplinary History* 11 (1981): 607–31.

31 Gilbert Osofsky, *Harlem: The Making of a Ghetto, Negro New York, 1890–1930* (New York: Harper, 1966); Alan Spear, *Black Chicago: The Making of a Negro Ghetto, 1890–1920* (Chicago: University of Chicago Press, 1967); David M. Katzman, *Before the Ghetto: Black Detroit in the Nineteenth Century* (Urbana, Ill.: University of Illinois Press, 1973).

32 Lee Williams, "Concentrated Residences: The Case of Black Toledo," *Phylon* 43, no. 2 (1982): 167–76.

33 Timothy L. Smith, "Immigrant Social Aspirations and American Education, 1880–1930," *American Quarterly* 21 (1969): 523–43; Timothy L. Smith, "Native Blacks and Foreign Whites: Varying Responses to Educational Opportunity in America, 1880–1950," *Perspectives in American History* 6 (1972): 309–35.

34 August Meier, *Negro Thought in America, 1880–1915* (Ann Arbor, Mich.: University of Michigan Press, 1963), 121–38.

35 E. Franklin Frazier, *The Negro in the United States,* rev. ed. (New York: Macmillan, 1957), 3–21; Daniel P. Moynihan, *The Negro Family: The Case for National Action* (Washington, D.C.: Office of Planning and Research, Department of Labor, 1965).

36 Carl N. Degler, *Neither Black nor White: Slavery and Race Relations in Brazil and the United States* (New York: Macmillan, 1971), 170–6; Herbert G. Gutman, *The Invisible Fact: The Black Family in American History, 1850–1930* (New York: Pantheon, 1974); Elizabeth H. Pleck, *Black Migration and Poverty, Boston 1865–1900* (New York: Academic Press, 1979).

37 Linda Gordon, "Single Mothers and Child Neglect, 1880–1920," *American Quarterly* 37 (1985): 173–92.

38 David Montgomery, "To Study the People: The American Working Class," *Labor History* 21 (1980): 485–512; John J. Bukowczyk, "The Transformation of Working Class Ethnicity: Corporate Control, Americanization, and the Polish Immigrant Middle-Class in Bayonne, New Jersey, 1915–1925," *Labor History* 25 (1984): 53–82.

39 Charles Stephenson, "A Gathering of Strangers? Migration, Social Structure and Political Participation in the Foundation of Nineteenth Century American Working Class Culture," in Milton Kantor, ed., *American Working Class Culture* (Westport, Conn.: Greenwood Press, 1979), 31–69.

40 Charles Tilly and C. Harold Brown, "On Uprooting, Kinship and the Auspices of Migration," *International Journal of Comparative Sociology* 8 (1967): 139–64; A. Gordon Darroch, "Migrants in the Nineteenth Century: Fugitives or Families in Motion," *Journal of Family History* 6 (1981): 257–77; John Bodnar, *The Transplanted: A History of Immigration in Urban America* (Bloomington, Ind.: Indiana University Press, 1985), 1–84.

41 David Ward, *Cities and Immigrants: A Geography of Change in Nineteenth*

Century America (New York: Oxford University Press, 1971), 11–83; Philip Taylor, *A Distant Magnet: European Emigration to the USA* (New York: Harper & Row, 1971), 91–168.

42 Harry Jerome, *Migration and Business Cycles* (New York, National Bureau of Economic Research, 1926); Brinley Thomas, *Migration and Economic Growth: A Study of Great Britain and the Atlantic Economy* (Cambridge: Cambridge University Press, 1954).

43 Louis Hartz, *The Founding of New Societies* (New York: Harcourt, Brace & World, 1964).

44 Caroline Golab, *Immigrant Destinations* (Philadelphia: Temple University Press, 1977); Edna Bonacich and Lucie Cheng, "Introduction: A Theoretical Orientation to International Labor Migration," in Lucie Cheng and Edna Bonacich, eds., *Labor Immigration Under Capitalism* (Berkeley: University of California Press, 1984), 1–56; Dirk Hoerder, "An Introduction to Labor Migration in the Atlantic Economies, 1815–1914," in Dirk Hoerder, ed., *Labor Migration in the Atlantic Economies* (Westport, Conn.: Greenwood Press, 1985), 3–31.

45 Michael Merrill, "Cash Is Good to Eat: Self-Sufficiency and Exchange in the Rural Economy of the United States," *Radical History Review* 3 (1976): 42–71; Harriet Friedmann, "World Market, State, and Family Farm: Social Bases of Household Production in the Era of Wage Labor," *Comparative Studies in Society and History* 20 (1978): 545–86; Kevin D. Kelly, "The Independent Mode of Production," *Review of Radical Political Economics* 11 (1979): 38–48; Christopher Clark, "Household Economy, Market Exchange, and the Rise of Capitalism in the Connecticut Valley, 1800–1860," *Journal of Social History* 13 (1979): 169–89.

46 Ewa Morawska, *"For Bread and Butter": Life-Worlds of East Central Europeans in Johnstown Pennsylvania, 1890–1940* (Cambridge: Cambridge University Press, 1985); John Bodnar, *Worker's World: Kinship, Community, and Protest in an Industrial Society* (Baltimore: Johns Hopkins University Press, 1982), 171; Robert L. Bach and Lisa A. Schramal, "Migration, Crisis and Theoretical Conflict," *International Migration Review* 16 (1982): 320–41.

47 Oliver MacDonagh, "The Irish Emigration to the United States," *Perspectives in American History* 10 (1976): 421–46; Kerby A. Miller, *Emigrants and Exiles: Ireland and the Irish Exodus to North America* (New York: Oxford University Press, 1985), 293–98.

48 Joseph Lee, *The Modernization of Irish Society, 1848–1918* (Dublin: Gill and Macmillan, 1973).

49 Cormac O'Grada, "Irish Emigration to the United States in the Nineteenth Century," in David N. Doyle and Owen P. Edwards, eds., *America and Ireland, 1776–1976: The American Identity and the Irish Connection* (Westport, Conn.: Greenwood, 1980), 93–104.

50 Joseph Lee, "Commentary," in Michael Fogarty, Liam Ryan, and Joseph Lee, eds., *Irish Values and Attitudes* (Dublin: Dominican Publications, 1984), 113.

51 Mack Walker, *Germany and the Emigration, 1816–1885* (Cambridge, Mass.:

Harvard University Press, 1964); Ingrid Semmingsen, "Emigration from Scandinavia," *Scandinavian Economic History Review* 20 (1972); Robert P. Swierenga and H. S. Stout, "Social and Economic Patterns of Migration from the Netherlands in the Nineteenth Century," in Paul Uselding, ed., *Research in Economic History* 1 (1976).

52 Philip Taylor, *A Distant Magnet,* 91–168.

53 Leo Schelbert, "Emigration from Imperial Germany Overseas, 1871–1914: Contours, Contexts, Experiences," in Volker Durr, Kathy Harms, and Peter Hayes, eds., *Imperial Germany* (Madison, University of Wisconsin Press, 1985), 112–33.

54 Simon Kuznets, "Immigration of Russian Jews to the United States: Background and Structure," *Perspectives in American History* 9 (1975): 35–124.

55 J. D. Gould, "European Inter-continental Emigration. The Road Home: Return Emigration from the USA," *Journal of European Economic History* 9 (1980); M. Palairet, "The New Immigration and the Newest: Slavic Emigration from the Balkans to America and Industrial Europe Since the Late Nineteenth Century," in T. C. Smout, ed., *The Search for Wealth and Stability: Essays in Economic and Social History Presented to M. W. Flinn* (London: Macmillan, 1979), 43–65.

56 Robert F. Foerster, *The Italian Immigrant of Our Times* (Cambridge, Mass.: Harvard University Press, 1919); J. S. MacDonald, "Some Socio-Economic Emigration Differentials in Rural Italy, 1902–1913," *Economic Development and Cultural Change* 7 (1958); John Bodnar, *The Transplanted: A History of Immigrants in Urban America* (Bloomington: Indiana University Press, 1985), 23–56.

57 Josef Barton, *Peasants and Strangers: Italians, Rumanians, and Slovaks in an American City, 1890–1950* (Cambridge, Mass.: Harvard University Press, 1975), 27–47; John W. Briggs, *An Italian Passage: Immigrants to Three American Cities, 1890–1930* (New Haven, Conn.: Yale University Press, 1978); Dino Cinel, *From Italy to San Francisco: The Immigrant Experience* (Stanford, Calif.: Stanford University Press, 1982).

58 Taylor, *A Distant Magnet,* 48–65.

59 Florette Henri, *Black Migration, Movement North, 1900–1920* (Garden City, N.Y.: Anchor, 1976).

60 Roger Daniels, "American Historians and East Asian Immigrants," *Pacific Historical Review* 43 (1974): 449–72; Stanford Lyman, *The Asian in North America* (Santa Barbara, Calif.: ABC-Clio, 1977); Lawrence Cardosa, *Mexican Emigration to the United States, 1897–1931* (Tucson: University of Arizona Press, 1980); Arthur F. Corwin, ed., *Immigrants – and Immigrants: Perspectives on Mexican Labor Migration to the United States* (Westport, Conn.: Greenwood, 1978).

61 Stephen Thernstrom, *The Other Bostonians, Poverty and Progress in the American Metropolis, 1880–1970* (Cambridge, Mass.: Harvard University Press, 1973), 220–61.

62 Isaac A. Hourwich, *Immigration and Labor: The Economic Aspects of European Immigration to the United States* (New York: Huebsch, 1922), 148–76.

63 Herman Feldman, *Racial Factors in American Industry* (New York: Harper, 1931), 137.

64 Ibid.

65 W. Lloyd Warner and Leo Srole, *The Social Systems of American Ethnic Groups* (New Haven, Conn.: Yale University Press, 1945), 63–5.

66 Robert E. Park, "Succession: An Ecological Concept," *American Sociological Review* 1 (1936), 171–9.

67 Thernstrom, *The Other Bostonians*, 160–75.

68 Michael Hechter, "Ethnicity and Industrialization: On the Proliferation of the Cultural Division of Labor," *Ethnicity* 3 (1976), 214–24; Michael J. Piore, *Birds of Passage: Migrant Labor and Industrial Societies* (Cambridge: Cambridge University Press, 1979), 141–66.

69 Hubert M. Blalock, Jr., *Toward a Theory of Minority Group Relations* (New York: Wiley, 1967); Ivan Light, *Ethnic Enterprise in America: Business and Welfare Among Chinese, Japanese and Blacks* (Berkeley: University of California Press, 1972); Edna Bonacich, "A Theory of Middlemen Minorities," *American Sociological Review* 38 (1973): 583–94.

70 Edna Bonacich, "A Theory of Ethnic Antagonism: The Split-Labor Market," *American Sociological Review* 37 (1972): 547–59; Michael T. Hannen, "The Dynamics of Ethnic Boundaries in Modern States," in John W. Meyer and Michael T. Hannen, eds., *National Development and the World System* (Chicago: University of Chicago Press, 1979), 253

71 Clyde Griffin, "The Old Immigration and Industrialization: A Case Study," in Richard L. Ehrlich, ed., *Immigrants in Industrial America, 1850–1920* (Charlottesville: University of Virginia Press, 1977), 176–210; Burton W. Folsom, *Urban Capitalists: Entrepreneurs and City Growth in the Lackawanna and Lehigh Regions, 1800–1920* (Baltimore: Johns Hopkins University Press, 1981); Tamara Hareven and Randolph Langenbach, *Amoskeag: Life and Work in an American Factory City* (New York: Pantheon, 1978).

72 John T. Cumbler, *Working-Class Community in Industrial America: Work, Leisure, and Struggle in Two Industrial Cities, 1880–1930* (Westport, Conn.: Greenwood Press, 1979); Alan Dawley, *Class and Community: The Industrial Revolution in Lynn* (Cambridge, Mass.: Harvard University Press, 1976); Susan E. Hirsch, *Roots of the American Working Class: The Industrialization of Crafts in Newark, 1800–1860* (Philadelphia: University of Pennsylvania Press, 1978); Paul G. Faler, *Mechanics and Manufacturers in the Early Industrial Revolution: Lynn, Massachusetts, 1780–1860* (Albany: State University of New York Press, 1981).

73 Christine Stansell, "The Origins of the Sweatshop: Women and Early Industrialization in New York City," in Michael H. Frisch and Daniel J. Walkowitz, eds.; *Working Class America* (Urbana: University of Illinois Press, 1983), 78–103.

74 Carol Groneman, "Working-Class Immigrant Women in Mid-Nineteenth Century New York: The Irish Experience," *Journal of Urban History* 4 (1978): 255–73.

75 Hasia R. Diner, *Erin's Daughters in America: Irish Immigrant Women in*

the Nineteenth Century (Baltimore: Johns Hopkins University Press, 1983), 70–105.

76 Douglas Shaw, *The Making of an Immigrant City* (New York: Arno Press, 1976); Hirsch, *Roots of the American Working Class;* Robert Ernst, *Immigrant Life in New York City: 1825–1863* (New York: King's Crown Press of Columbia University, 1949).

77 Albon P. Mann, Jr., "Labor Competition and the New York Draft Riots of 1863," *Journal of Negro History* 36 (1951): 375–405; Leonard P. Curry, *The Free Black in Urban America, 1880–1850* (Chicago: University of Chicago Press, 1981), 1–36.

78 Ernst, *Immigrant Life in New York City;* Amy Bridges, *A City in the Republic: Antebellum New York and the Origins of Machine Politics* (Cambridge: Cambridge University Press, 1984), 45–58.

79 Theodore Hershberg, Michael Katz, Stuart Blumin, Lawrence Glasco, and Clyde Griffen, "Occupation and Ethnicity in Five Nineteenth Century Cities," *Historical Methods Newsletter* 7 (1974): 174–216; Thernstrom, *The Other Bostonians.*

80 Kathleen N. Conzen, *Immigrant Milwaukee, 1836–1860: Accommodation and Community in a Frontier City* (Cambridge, Mass.: Harvard University Press, 1976), 19–36; Nora Faires, "Occupational Patterns of German-Americans in Nineteenth Century Cities," in Hartmut Keil and John B. Jentz, eds., *German Workers in Industrial America, 1850–1910: A Comparative Perspective* (DeKalb, Ill.: Northern Illinois University Press, 1983), 37–51.

81 Jo Ellen Vineyard, *The Irish on the Urban Frontier, Detroit, 1850–1880* (New York: Arno, 1976); Dennis Clark, *Hibernia America: The Irish and Regional Cultures* (Westport, Conn.: Greenwood, 1986), 117–38.

82 Moses Rischin, "Immigrants, Migrants and Minorities in California," *Pacific Historical Review* 41 (1972): 71–90; R. A. Burchell, *The San Francisco Irish, 1846–1880* (Berkeley: University of California Press, 1980); James P. Walsh, "The Irish in the New America: 'Way Out West," in David N. Doyle and Owen P. Edwards, eds., *America and Ireland, 1776–1976: The American Identity and the Irish Connection* (Westport, Conn.: Greenwood, 1980), 165–76.

83 Richard Edwards, *Contested Terrain: The Transformation of the Workplace in the Twentieth Century* (New York: Basic Books, 1979); Daniel Nelson, *Managers and Workers: Origins of the New Factory System in the United States, 1880–1920* (Madison: University of Wisconsin Press, 1975); David Montgomery, *Workers' Control in America: Studies in the History of Work, Technology, and Labor Struggles* (Cambridge: Cambridge University Press, 1979); David Brody, *Steelworkers in America: The Nonunion Era* (Cambridge, Mass.: Harvard University Press, 1960).

84 Hourwich, *Immigration and Labor,* 168–9.

85 David N. Doyle, *Irish Americans, Native Rights, and National Empires, 1890–1901* (New York: Arno, 1976), 38–90; David Montgomery, "The Irish and the American Labor Movement," in David N. Doyle and Owen P. Edwards, eds., *America and Ireland, 1776–1976: The American Identity and the Irish Connection* (Westport, Conn.: Greenwood Press, 1980), 205–18.

86 David Brundage, "Irish Land and American Workers: Class and Ethnicity in Denver, Colorado," in Dirk Hoerder, ed., *Struggle a Hard Battle: Essays on Working-Class Immigrants* (DeKalb, Ill.: Northern Illinois University Press, 1986), 46–67.

87 John Jentz, "Skilled Workers and Industrialization: Chicago's German Cabinetmakers and Machinists, 1880–1900," in Keil and Jentz, eds., *German Workers in Industrial Chicago, 1850–1910*, 73–85; Bruce Laurie, Theodore Hershberg, and George Alter, "Immigrants and Industry: The Philadelphia Experience, 1850–1880," in Theodore Hershberg, ed., *Philadelphia: Work, Space, Family, and Group Experience in the Nineteenth Century* (New York: Oxford University Press, 1981), 93–119; Hartmut Keil, "German Working-Class Radicalism in the United States from the 1870's to World War I," in Hoerder, ed., *Struggle a Hard Battle*, 71–94.

88 Olivier Zunz, *The Changing Face of Inequality: Urbanization, Industrial Development, and Immigrants in Detroit, 1880–1920* (Chicago: University of Chicago Press, 1982); Hartmut Keil, "Chicago's Working Class in 1900," in Keil and Jentz, eds., *German Workers in Industrial Chicago, 1850–1910*, 19–36.

89 James Henretta, "The Study of Social Mobility: Ideological Assumptions and Conceptual Bias," *Labor History* 18 (1977): 165–78.

90 Olivier Zunz, *The Changing Face of Inequality;* John Bodnar, *The Transplanted*, 117–43.

91 Andrew M. Greeley, "The American Achievement: A Report from Great Ireland," in Doyle and Edwards, eds., *America and Ireland, 1776–1976*, 231–46.

92 Niles Carpenter, "Nationality, Color and Economic Opportunity in the City of Buffalo," *University of Buffalo Studies* 5 (1927): 95–194.

93 Peter Roberts, *The New Immigration: A Study of the Industrial and Social Life of Southeast Europeans in America* (New York: Macmillan, 1913); Isaac A. Hourwich, *Immigration and Labor*, 159–69; Henry B. Leonard, "Ethnic Cleavage and Industrial Conflict in Late Nineteenth Century America: The Cleveland Rolling Mill Company Strikes of 1882 and 1885," *Labor History* 20 (1979), 524–48; James R. Barrett, "Unity and Fragmentation: Class, Race and Ethnicity on Chicago's South Side, 1900–1922," *Journal of Social History* 18 (1984): 37–55; Montgomery, *Worker's Control in America*, 117–22.

94 Nelson, *Managers and Workers*; John F. Bodnar, *Immigration and Industrialization: Ethnicity in an American Hill Town* (Pittsburgh: University of Pittsburgh Press, 1977).

95 John T. Cumbler, *Working Class Community in Industrial America: Work, Leisure and Struggle in Two Industrial Cities, 1880–1930* (Westport, Conn.: Greenwood, 1979).

96 Golab, *Immigrant Destinations;* Michael Hechter, "The Position of Eastern European Immigrants to the United States in the Cultural Division of Labor: Some Trends and Prospects," in Walter L. Goldfrank, ed., *The World-System of Capitalism: Past and Present* (Beverly Hills, Calif.: Sage, 1979), 111–29; Stanley Lieberson, *A Piece of the Pie: Blacks and White Immigrants Since 1880* (Berkeley: University of California Press, 1980).

97 Donna Gabaccia, "Neither Padrone Slaves nor Primitive Rebels: Sicilians on Two Continents," in Hoerder, ed., *Struggle a Hard Battle,* 95-117.

98 Moses Rischin, *The Promised City: New York's Jews, 1870–1914* (New York: Harper, 1962); Thomas Kessner, *The Golden Door, Italian and Jewish Immigrant Mobility in New York City, 1880–1915* (New York: Oxford University Press, 1977); Harry H. L. Kitano, "Japanese Americans: The Development of a Middleman Minority," *Pacific Historical Review* 43 (1974): 500–19; Edna Bonacich and John Modell, *The Economic Basis of Ethnic Solidarity: Small Business in the Japanese-American Community* (Berkeley: University of California Press, 1980).

99 Herman D. Bloch, *The Circle of Discrimination: An Economic and Social Study of the Black Man in New York* (New York: New York University Press, 1969), 31–46; Robert Higgs, *Competition and Coercion: Blacks in the American Economy, 1865–1914* (Cambridge: Cambridge University Press, 1977), 37–94, 118–146.

100 Thomas Sowell, *Race and Economics* (New York: Longman, 1982), 59-156.

101 W.E.B. Du Bois, *The Philadelphia Negro* (Philadelphia: University of Pennsylvania Press, 1899), 36–46.

102 Theodore Hershberg, et al., "A Tale of Three Cities: Blacks and Immigrants in Philadelphia, 1850–1880, 1930, and 1970," *Annals of the American Academy of Political and Social Science* 441 (1979): 55–81.

103 John Daniels, "Industrial Conditions Among Negro Men in Boston," *Charities and Commons* 15 (1905–6): 33–4; Fannie B. Williams, "Social Bonds in the Black Belt of Chicago," *Charities and Commons* 15 (1905–6): 35.

104 Peter Gottlieb, *Making Their Own Way: Southern Blacks' Migration to Pittsburgh, 1916-1930* (Urbana: University of Illinois Press, 1987), 63–116; Dennis C. Dickerson, *Out of the Crucible: Black Steelworkers in Western Pennsylvania, 1875–1980* (Albany: State University of New York Press, 1986), 27–54; John F. Bodnar, "The Impact of the New Immigration on the Black Worker: Steelton, Pennsylvania, 1880–1920," *Labor History* 17 (1976): 214–29; John C. Leggett, *Class, Race and Labor, Working Class Consciousness in Detroit* (New York: Oxford University Press, 1968), 3–42; Lieberson, *A Piece of the Pie.*

105 St. Clair Drake and Horace R. Cayton, *Black Metropolis: A Study of Negro Life in a Northern City,* rev. and enl. ed., vol. 1 (New York: Harper, 1962), 214–340.

106 David Ward, "Social Structure and Social Geography in Large Cities of the U.S. Urban-Industrial Heartland," *Historical Geography Research Series* 12 (1983): 1–31.

107 Alan R. Pred, "Manufacturing in the American Mercantile City: 1800–1840," *Annals of the Association of American Geographers* 56 (1966): 307–38; Alan N. Burstein, "Immigrants and Residential Mobility: The Irish and Germans in Philadelphia, 1850–1880," in Theodore Hershberg, ed., *Philadelphia: Work, Space, Family and Group Experience in the Nineteenth Century* (New York: Oxford University Press, 1981); Stephanie W. Greenberg, "Industrial Location and Ethnic Residential Patterns in an Industrializing City: Philadelphia, 1880," in Hershberg, ed., *Philadelphia,* 204–32.

108 David Ward, "Some Locational Implications of the Ethnic Division of Labor in Mid-Nineteenth Century American Cities," in Ralph Ehrenberg, ed., *Pattern and Process: Research in Historical Geography* (Washington, D.C.: Howard University Press for the National Archives and Records Service, 1975), 258–70.

109 David M. Gordon, "Capitalist Development and the History of American Cities," in William K. Tabb and Larry Sawers, eds., *Marxism and the Metropolis* (New York: Oxford University Press, 1978), 25–63; Roger Friedland, *Power and Crisis in the City: Corporations, Unions and Urban Policy* (New York: Schocken, 1983); Stephen Meyer, "Adapting the Immigrant to the Line: Americanization in the Ford Factory, 1914–21," *Journal of Social History* 14 (1980): 67–82.

110 Zunz, *The Changing Face of Inequality.*

111 William I. Thomas and Florian Znaniecki, *The Polish Peasant in Europe and America* (New York: Dover, 1958), 1545.

112 A. J. Scott, "Industrialization and Urbanization: A Geographical Agenda," *Annals of the Association of American Geographers* 76 (1986): 25–37.

113 John D. Kasarda, "Urban Change and Minority Opportunities," in Paul E. Peterson, ed., *The New Urban Reality* (Washington, D.C.: The Brookings Institution, 1985).

114 Raymond Breton, "Institutional Completeness of Ethnic Communities and the Personal Relations of Immigrants," *American Journal of Sociology* 70 (1964): 193–205; Lance Roberts and Edward Boldt, "Institutional Completeness and Ethnic Assimilation," *Journal of Ethnic Studies* 7 (1979): 103–8.

115 Timothy L. Smith, "Religion and Ethnicity in America," *American Historical Review* 83 (1978): 1155–85; Martin E. Marty, *A Nation of Behavers* (Chicago: University of Chicago Press, 1976; John M. Cuddihy, *No Offense: Civil Religion and Protestant Taste* (New York: Seabury Press, 1978).

116 Ivan Light, *Ethnic Enterprise in America* (Berkeley and Los Angeles: University of California Press, 1972), 170–90.

117 David Ley, *The Black Inner City as Frontier Outpost* (Washington, DC.: Association of American Geographers, 1974), 241–66.

118 Charles Murray, *Losing Ground: American Social Policy: 1950–1980* (New York, Basic Books, 1984); Lawrence M. Mead, *Beyond Entitlement: The Social Obligations of Citizenship* (New York: The Free Press, 1986).

119 Chris Hamnett, "Area-based Explanations: A Critical Appraisal," in David T. Herbert and David M. Smith, eds., *Social Problems and the City* (Oxford: Oxford University Press, 1979), 244–60.

120 Sam B. Warner, Jr., and Colin Burke, "Cultural Change and the Ghetto," *Journal of Contemporary History* 4 (1969): 173–87.

121 William Julius Wilson, *The Truly Disadvantaged: The Inner City, the Underclass and Public Policy* (Chicago: University of Chicago Press, 1987); William Julius Wilson, *The Declining Significance of Race: Blacks and Changing American Institutions,* 2d ed. (Chicago: University of Chicago Press, 1980).

Index